The Pit Bull Placebo

The Media, Myths and Politics of Canine Aggression

by

Karen Delise

Anubis Publishing

The Pit Bull Placebo
The Media, Myths and Politics of Canine Aggression
Copyright © 2007 Karen Delise

Published by Anubis Publishing

For further information, please contact:
Kaynine3@aol.com
or go to the National Canine Research Council at
www.nationalcanineresearchcouncil.com

Cover photo credit: Jon T. Miller

Book design by
Arbor Books, Inc.
19 Spear Road, Suite 301
Ramsey, NJ 07446
www.arborbooks.com

Printed in the United States

The Pit Bull Placebo
The Media, Myths and Politics of Canine Aggression
Karen Delise
1. The Pit Bull Placebo: The Media, Myths and Politics of Canine
Aggression   2. Karen Delise   3. Pets/Pit Bulls/Human-animal communication

Library of Congress Control Number: 2006910964

ISBN 10: 0-9721914-1-0
ISBN 13: 978-0-9721914-1-8

Dedication

To my wonderful father, Mario Delise,
who taught me about love and respect for all life

and

To Bianca, again and always—
a dog whose courage, loyalty, and devotion
is a testament to the timeless spirit of the dog.

Table of Contents

Acknowledgements

I wish to express my deep gratitude and thanks to Michael Denneny, whose advice and insight were invaluable in the creation of this book. It has been my great fortune and pleasure to have you as my editor.

To Jane Berkey, I am truly indebted for your contribution and support. Your relentless pursuit of perfection, your passion, energy and determination are a great source of inspiration.

To all those at the Animal Farm Foundation, especially Kate Fraser and Don Cleary, thank you for your assistance, ideas, and suggestions.

Much gratitude to Marcy Setter, Sonya Dias, and Ledy VanKavage, for their assistance in searching out the truth and for fighting to overcome the hysteria and myths surrounding dog attacks.

Thanks to Jim Crosby for extraordinary field work and investigations into recent cases of fatal dog attacks.

I wish to express my respect and thanks to Diane Jessup, who is a great source of knowledge about Pit bulls, dog breeds and canine behavior.

Special thanks to my good friend Jennifer Shryock for valuable insight on canine behavior, and for providing education about dog bite prevention and safety.

I am thankful for my two wonderful brothers, Tom and Gary, whose support and dependability are a constant comfort to me.

To my dearest friend, Jane Moreau—thank you the laughs, long talks and entertainment which gave me much needed breaks during this past year. It is rare to find such a true friend and you are much appreciated. (Also thanks for the great idea of the "Pit Bull Paparazzi.")

To my canine family: Presto, Sandy, Brooks, Hamlet, Pransa, Bianca, Darwin, Java, Inda, Bailey, Skye, Nikko, Tanq, and their canine cousins, Roscoe, Preakness and Blue—you have all taught me invaluable lessons about canine behavior and the giving and forgiving nature of dogs.

Eternal love and special thanks to Tanq, my constant and devoted canine companion, who never left my side during the long days and nights writing this book.

◆ ◆ ◆

We—the silent, the abused, the forgotten, the exiled, and the forsaken—wish there was a way to express our gratitude to our stalwart defender, Jane Berkey. After decades of abuse at the hands of those we love most, few have come forth to recognize our continued devotion to "mankind." Few have stood up and given voice to our suffering—few have fought so passionately in our defense.

To our crusader, Jane Berkey, we, the Pit bulls, thank you.

Introduction

Memorial at Gettysburg: Sallie, Bulldog mascot to the 11th Pennsylvania Infantry.

Soldiers dressed in blue marched true and tall under a cloudy sky. Off to one side, a lanky man stood watching when his gaze momentarily focused on the lead marcher. His eyes showed a hint of amusement and respect, and a faint smile appeared on his gaunt face. It was then that President Abraham Lincoln is reported to have doffed his stove-pipe hat at the 11th Pennsylvania Volunteer Infantry in tribute to the soldiers and to their regimental mascot, the Bulldog Sallie, proudly prancing at the front of her regiment.

Placing Sallie at the head of their parade when marching in review past the Commander-in-Chief was this regiment's testimony to the honor and respect they had for the little Bulldog who had proved herself a loyal and devoted member of the 11th Pennsylvania Volunteer Infantry during the Civil War. And the respect and honor this dog earned is still visible today on the battlefield at Gettysburg, in the cast bronze replica of Sallie that rests at the base of the monument to the 11th Pennsylvania Infantry, a lasting tribute to Sallie's contribution to our nation during one of our most difficult times.

This heroic dog has alternately been described as a Staffordshire Terrier, a Bull Terrier, a Bulldog and a Bulldog mixed breed. The story of this brave "Bulldog-type dog" allows for some unsettling comparisons with her ubiquitous "Bulldog" cousins that fill our shelters, homes, streets and yards a century and a half later. Sallie, a recognized canine hero, would today be classified as simply another Pit bull-type dog and, as such, the possibility that she would be euthanized in a shelter because of her breed or banned from residing in many cities and towns across our nation because of her appearance is a shocking reality at the beginning of the 21st century.

In 2006 a Texas couple, Stan and Amy, acquired a malnourished, neglected puppy. Not really planning on getting a dog, they could not ignore this small, needy pup. They named the seven-week-old, 4 lb. dog Sugar and decided the dog would become their traveling companion while they drove across the country for their hauling business. On a cold day in March, Stan and Amy arrived outside Denver to pick up a load, but due to a snow delay, they had to check into a motel for the night. Early the next morning Amy was walking Sugar outside the motel when an Animal Control officer from the city of Denver stopped them. He claimed she was breaking the law and that she needed to hand the small pup over to him. Incredulous, Amy summoned her husband who was also informed of their alleged "illegal" activity. The Animal Control officer stated that if they turned the puppy over to him immediately, he would see to it that she would be killed right away and the couple could avoid the criminal charges and animal control costs that went along with owning an illegal Pit bull in the city of Denver. The couple pleaded with the officer, stating they lived in and operated their business out of Texas and were only in Denver on business, but to no avail. The tiny pup was taken from the couple and delivered to the Denver Municipal Animal Services. Scared and confused, Stan and Amy drove their rig to the animal shelter in hopes of getting their puppy back. Only through good fortune were they able to locate someone who assisted in the difficult process of having the puppy released back to them.

In the past two decades, hundreds of cities and communities have enacted bans or restrictions against certain breeds or types of dogs. Forty-five years ago American novelist John Steinbeck was able to put his dog in the car and travel across the country chronicling his adventure in *Travels with Charley: In Search of America.* Today, if Steinbeck owned a dog that resembled a Pit bull, he could probably not drive a few hundred miles before he came upon a town that refused him and his dog entry. He would spend much of his time trying to avoid towns, cities and counties that have banned or restricted Pit bull-type dogs within their borders.

Yet in 1903 a Bulldog named Bud accompanied Horatio Nelson Jackson on America's first transcontinental automobile trip. Shortly after leaving California with his co-driver and mechanic Sewall Crocker, Jackson added a light-colored Bulldog to the expedition. After his new masters fitted the Bulldog with goggles to protect his eyes from the road dust and debris, the threesome became a national sensation as they journeyed across America. Jackson would later brag that the Bulldog was "an enthusiast for motoring" and was "the one member of [our] trio who used no profanity on the entire trip."

How have Bulldog-type dogs, in only a few decades, been transformed from nationally celebrated heroes to "persona non grata" in hundreds of cities across America? How has the

BUD.
PHOTO CREDIT: MARY LOUISE BLANCHARD

Bud: Bulldog companion on the first transcontinental automobile trip. Photo Credit: Mary Louise Blanchard, 1903

landscape of America and the mindset of Americans changed so dramatically in only a few decades?

Is it canine behavior that has changed so drastically? Or have we, with our growing ignorance of dogs, become so unreasonable that any flaw found in an individual dog is taken as ample justification for vilifying all their innocent brethren? Have we, in morbid fascination, concentrated so intensely on emphasizing the bad that some dogs do that we can no longer recognize the myriad of good and positive things that most dogs contribute to our lives?

Or, as some lawmakers and the media would have us believe, are some dog breeds inherently more dangerous and aggressive than others? Are Pit bull-type dogs becoming increasingly more dangerous than they were a century ago? Are most such dogs wonderfully tolerant and manageable or are these dogs unpredictable and untrustworthy, waiting to explode in a fury of aggression against everyone and anyone?

Within the last decade or two, a new phenomenon has not only drastically influenced the public's perception of certain breeds of dogs, but contributed greatly to a generalized ignorance of canine behavior. Technology, vis-à-vis the Internet, has allowed for instant accessibility to highly publicized media accounts of individual cases of dog attacks. Editorial columns about the vicious nature of certain breeds, dog-bite attorneys' websites filled with photos and statistics about dog attacks, quotes from politicians and outraged citizens about the nature and behaviors of certain dogs, and sensationalized headlines of dog attacks all seemingly offer instant and ample "proof" of the vicious nature of certain dogs. To many people these Internet sources are perceived as a reliable and accurate source of information on what they believe to be a recent epidemic of canine aggression.

But does this plethora of information present the public with a balanced, reasonable or accurate portrayal of the frequency of dog attacks, or of the type of dogs involved in such attacks, or of the forces directly responsible for such extreme canine aggression?

Fortunately, the Internet has also provided a more obscure but vital source of information that can provide a much needed perspective on the incidence, severity, and ultimately the causes of dog attacks.

Recently, many newspapers from the 1800s have been scanned in their entirety and placed on the Internet. Although the vast majority of available nineteenth century archived material is comprised primarily of local and major newspapers in the northeast quadrant of the United States, they are nevertheless a valuable source of data for examining individual cases of dog attacks. This resource provides a unique opportunity to view both the style of media reporting and the prevailing attitudes towards dogs in 19th Century America.

An examination of the last 150 years of severe dog attacks as reported in these newspapers reveals a dramatic shift in the style of reporting and the type of information found describing a dog attack. For those interested in understanding canine behavior and the forces which contribute to severe attacks, modern-day media sources are sorely lacking in vital information surrounding these events. For this reason, in more modern cases, I have, whenever possible, consulted and interviewed law enforcement investigators, animal control personnel and coroners in an effort to obtain for each incident as much relevant information as possible, about the dog, the victim and the owner. Photographs of the dogs involved and autopsy and bite reports are additional important sources of information I have used to present and discuss the cases which have occurred in recent decades.

Seeking out alternate sources of information due to the scarcity of details in modern-day media sources has demonstrated that the very absence of these details has led to a general hysteria about certain breeds, along with wildly inaccurate conclusions about the reasons and causes for canine aggression. Critical events leading some dogs to extreme aggression— from two dogs suffering the agony of ingesting rat poison to dogs near death from malnutrition and dehydration—are shockingly absent in modern media accounts of severe or fatal dog attacks.

Only about half a dozen studies have been conducted on fatal dog attacks in the United States, and these were all conducted in a 25-year period (1977–2001). Unfortunately, most of these studies focused on only two or three aspects surrounding fatal attacks, with the breed of dog being the single most studied aspect. Besides the small database (less than 240 cases), despite the limited time period (a single era when certain breeds were exceedingly popular), despite the use of media reports for identification of breeds, and despite the failure to address the relevant human and canine behaviors which preceded an attack, these studies have often been put forth as the "science of fatal dog attacks." But the severe limitations and scope of these studies do not allow for their use in any rational or practical approach to the understanding of dog attacks. The "scientific method" cannot be applied to the study of dog bites, as severe and fatal dog attacks on humans occur in the most uncontrolled and unscientific settings and involve dozens of variables and circumstances which cannot be measured accurately.

The best that can be done is to study dog attacks empirically, through practical observation of every possible aspect surrounding these events. In furtherance of these goals the author has researched and conducted investigations on the largest number of dog attacks, over the greatest period of time, along with every available detail relevant to these incidents. This has resulted in a database of over 750 cases of fatal dog attacks and over 1000 cases of severe attacks in the United States, from 1850 to the present.

Empirical analysis of this large amount of data has revealed a pattern of circumstance and behavior seen consistently over the last century which offers tremendous insight into the reasons and causes of dog attacks. The recent failure, by both experts and laymen, to take this type of comprehensive and practical approach to the problem of dog attacks has allowed for meaningless statistics and pseudoscience to replace rational thought and basic, common-sense knowledge of the canine and human behaviors which have long been recognized to contribute to dog attacks.

Whether our goal is community safety, understanding canine behavior, furtherance of humane treatment towards dogs, or the advancement of the human-dog bond, it is critical that we examine *all* the details available about dog attacks. However, perhaps as important is that we recognize that often times the information disseminated about dog attacks is presented by individuals or organizations whose agenda is the furtherance of goals unrelated to the human-dog bond.

This examination of actual cases of severe dog attacks during the last 150 years—the circumstances, the individual dogs involved, the victims and our interpretations of these events—is presented in an attempt to address these concerns and offer a balanced perspective on the behavior of dogs and the critical role humans play in the management and treatment of our canine companions.

Only by stepping back from the swirl of present-day hysteria surrounding isolated cases of severe canine aggression and examining the problem from a broader and more objective perspective can we hope to understand how some humans come to be victims of a dog attack.

CHAPTER 1

The Function of Dogs
in 19th Century America

"Henry Carey, ten years old, who resided at Gloucester, N.J., was attacked by a bloodhound, about a fortnight ago, and was so terribly injured that he died soon after. Accompanying the boy was a small dog, which attacked the savage animal and fought him desperately in defense of the child, but was terribly torn himself..."

Trenton Gazette, December 1864

This historic case of a fatal dog attack in New Jersey is significant because it can help to create a frame of reference by which we can begin to study the causes for dog attacks. Additionally, this 19th century newspaper article can begin an examination into society's changing attitude towards dogs and how certain forces have come to shape and influence the public's perceptions of canine aggression over the past 150 years.

From small local newspapers, such as the *Appleton Post-Crescent,* to major publications like the *New York Times,* severe dog attacks on humans have always been reported in the news as they seem to be of both interest and dismay to many people. Maladies, diseases and accidents unrelated to animals cause thousands of deaths daily, many of which go unreported in the newspapers. However, fatal attacks by dogs have always gotten attention in the media, despite—or perhaps because of—their rarity.

Historically and in the present day, dog attacks cause on average only one to two dozen human deaths per year in the United States. Yet millions of people live in close proximity to dogs and have daily interactions with our canine companions. These interactions run the gamut from the most positive and rewarding relationships to cases of abuse and neglect. Yet the number of incidents a year involving a human fatality generates a shock and disbelief which has never been proportionate to the number of dogs, the frequency of exposure to them or the myriad situations in which dogs interact with humans.

While the study and examination of individual cases of fatal dog attacks on humans can provide insight into canine behavior, equally revealing is the examination of human reactions and interpretations of canine behavior after an attack. One remarkable aspect of the human/dog bond is the extreme and often emotional public reaction towards an episode of fatal canine aggression. Another relevant and significant factor is the style of media reporting of these incidents. How the media presents these cases shapes and influences future public reactions and emotions in subsequent cases of canine aggression. As seen in the case cited above, besides reporting an individual attack, the author of this article also gave recognition to the uniqueness of the human/dog bond. Implied in this account was the understanding that the small dog had a familiar bond with the young boy and hence would exhibit behavior vastly different than the Bloodhound, which was unfamiliar to the boy. This has long been the essence of the human/dog bond: that dogs will exhibit or inhibit natural canine behaviors in service or defense of those with whom they have formed attachments.

In fact, the dog is the only animal in the world which can be expected to attack another being in defense of the humans with whom they have formed a bond. This behavior is one of the cornerstones on which thousands of years of dog ownership and maintenance have been based. And implied in this relationship is the expectation and acceptance of canine aggression in certain circumstances. The Greek philosopher Plato acknowledged this basic principle of canine behavior over two thousand years ago when he wrote:

"The disposition of noble dogs is to be gentle with people they know and the opposite with those they don't know."

The Republic, Ch. 2

From ancient Greek culture to newspaper accounts from the 19th century, humans have historically demonstrated a keen understanding of the essence of the familiar bond between dogs and their masters. Only recently have both the media and the public failed to acknowledge or recognize this basic principle of canine behavior and the significance of this bond in the display of canine aggression. For this reason, dog attacks, human perceptions of canine aggression and the role of the media in reporting these events need to be examined, beginning from a historical context.

◆ ◆ ◆

Throughout recorded history, dogs have been owned and maintained, not for their ability to befriend all, but for their ability and willingness to forge alliances. The appeal of dogs was the natural bonding of dogs with their owners to the exclusion of others. In a time and world fraught with dangers, dogs were often relied on to be a front line of defense against threats by other beings. Dogs readily accepted this role and for centuries have served as guardians and protectors of their master and his possessions. Alliances between men and dogs were often invaluable as travelers huddled by lonely campfires in the wilderness or walked desolate roads and trails. Herdsmen slept more soundly knowing their faithful dogs were protecting their livestock and livelihood from thieves, wolves, bears and mountain lions. History is replete with accounts of dogs saving their masters and mistresses from all types of predatory animals, of both the two-legged and four-legged variety.

All breeds of dogs have the ability to perform the basic natural canine behaviors: hunting, tracking, chasing, fighting, herding, guarding and protecting. But over the centuries humans have manipulated dogs through artificial selection to exhibit specialized natural canine behaviors. Historically, dogs with specialized abilities were grouped or classified by function. Groupings typically included scent hounds, hunting dogs, war or fighting dogs, shepherd or guarding dogs, toy or companion dogs, and mongrels.

Some breeds we know today as a specific phenotype (appearance) previously encompassed a number of different-looking dogs that performed a similar task. The Bloodhound is an example of a type of dog that today is an individual and unique-looking breed, but in the 1800s "Bloodhound" often described a type of dog that was used for scent tracking and did not necessarily denote a particular appearance. While breeding for a specific look began to gain widespread popularity in the late 1800s, for many centuries function was more important than appearance.

The wonder of dogs is that they can be manipulated to excel at performing a particular function and they will then perform this function in service to those with whom they have formed attachments. In service to their masters, dogs track, fight, protect, chase, herd, guard, and hunt everything from large game or predatory animals to small vermin. Dogs often forsake their own kind on command or in defense of their owners. But of all the functions that dogs are required to perform, perhaps the most controversial, and often the most disastrous for dogs and humans alike, is the task of protecting man from his fellow man.

Guard/Protection Dogs

Protection or guarding has been one of the primary functions of dogs throughout their alliance with humans. This function was an important element in the acquisition and maintenance of dogs in the 1800s and early 1900s. To serve in this capacity came quite naturally for dogs. As pack animals with a social hierarchy, dogs seem to easily embrace the concept of friend versus foe or known versus unknown. Dogs were also understood to be territorial and this served well in the guarding of homes and businesses.

As predators, dogs are physically able to serve in defense of their masters, and different breeds were developed to enhance this ability. Just as one would not brandish a sapling to ward off an attacker, small dogs were not routinely maintained as protection or guard dogs. Large, powerful breeds, such as the Mastiff, Newfoundland, Bulldog, and Bloodhound, as well as huge mongrel dogs, were used as guard dogs in the latter part of the 19th century as their size enabled them to excel in the task of guarding and protection.

Less than ideal conditions, and many times seriously abusive conditions, frequently accompanied the ownership of guard dogs in the late 19th century. Newspaper accounts of dog attacks were often brutally honest in their description of the attack and of the treatment and care the dogs received at the hands of their owner and/or victim. It was not uncommon for accounts of dog attacks to state that the dog was beaten or abused by either his owner or the victim prior to the attack. In a much less litigious society there was less apprehension in revealing unflattering details about individuals and their behaviors than is now permitted in the recounting of events that contributed to a fatal dog attack. Fortunately, this aspect of late 19th century and early 20th century society allows us to have enormous insight into the factors that precipitated and contributed to severe canine aggression.

While accounts of such attacks were always sympathetic and mournful of the injuries to the victim, this did not interfere with the observation of the events that may have contributed to the attack, and so, in many cases, we have a vivid account of the circumstances and/or trigger that set some of these dogs off into a frenzied and unrelenting attack.

Many of the guard dogs in the latter part of the 19th century were kept chained for long periods of time in cellars or sheds until they were needed to patrol factories, slaughterhouses, livery stables, stone yards, warehouses or shops.

In December of 1882, a bookkeeper boiling a kettle of water at a packing house in New Haven, Connecticut, was savagely attacked by a large Bloodhound kept on the premises as a watchdog. The dog lacerated the man's throat, severed an artery in his arm and bit him more than twenty times. While the animal's behavior was not excused (the dog was referred to as "savage" and a "brute"), the attack was not viewed as inexplicable. The article goes on to recount that the dog had previously been punished by the night watchman with a kettle of scalding water. By using the kettle, the unsuspecting bookkeeper triggered the Bloodhound's "recollection of the brutal treatment by the watchman," causing the dog to attack.[1]

In February of 1888, a butcher in St. Louis, Missouri, owned a 2-year-old Newfoundland dog that was trained to guard his shop at night. The dog was kept chained during the day and was known and encouraged to be vicious. The butcher entered the yard one evening to release the dog and when the man "claimed the right to rule there and enforced his claim with a kick," the dog responded by furiously attacking him. Four members of the butcher's family rushed to his aid, but the man's chest, neck and arms were so severely lacerated that although not dead at the time of the report, he was not expected to survive his injuries.[2]

While not directly physically abusive, the owner in the next account placed the dog in circumstances which clearly were abusive and stressful. This 1893 report offers the important details that contributed to the aggressiveness of the dog involved. It describes how a baker found a cur dog on the streets of New York City and chained the dog in his bakery cellar where the temperature reached over 100 degrees much of the time. This newly acquired, chained, heat-stressed dog not surprisingly attacked the baker when he entered the cellar to light the ovens.[3]

While it was not unusual for guard dogs to rebel violently against their abusive owners, the majority of their victims were usually unsuspecting children or unfortunate adults who happened quite innocently to encounter these fierce animals. A common thread seen in many of the attacks by guard dogs on innocent victims can be found in the account of an attack in the summer of 1874 on a small girl in Brooklyn, New York. A large Newfoundland dog had been recently obtained by a hair-dealer to guard his shop at night. In the morning before being taken to the basement to be chained for the day, the dog was taken to the backyard of the store to be fed. In the midst of eating, a 3-year-old girl approached the dog. The dog lunged at the child, seizing her by the shoulder. The child's cries brought her father rushing to her aid. After "some determined effort" he got the dog to release the child, but in the process had one of his fingers bitten off. It was determined the child's wounds were "serious and may prove fatal."[4]

The hypocrisy of keeping guard dogs is that when the dog is called upon to fulfill the task of protection by attacking an intruder, the dog is almost always viewed as vicious. Most victims of guard/protection dogs were not burglars, but children or respectable adults who entered the property to visit or conduct business. The inherent problem with guard dogs is that they are expected to assess the legitimacy of the intruder to justify an attack. Of course, this is impossible. Whether a person entering a property has legitimate reasons to be there or whether they are intent on evil-doing is not within the comprehension of dogs. The dog views the intruder as either an unknown or known being, and as either a threatening or non-threatening situation.

Clearly, any attack on a child, even if the child was an intruder or provoked the guard dog in any sense, was unforgivable, dooming the dog to immediate destruction. The fate of guard dogs that attacked an adult allowed for only the slightest chance of redemption, but only if the intruder was clearly intent on criminal activity or if the intruder was considered a social outcast or an unsympathetic figure.

Mentioned frequently in the keeping of guard dogs during the 19th century was the task of chasing away "tramps." There seemed to be a measurable level of aggression allowed guard dogs in chasing off these social outcasts. In June 1879, it was reported that a woman living three miles out of town (Fort Wayne, Ind.) owned a Newfoundland dog that was a "terror to tramps." The recounting of the attack on a tramp entering into the woman's yard is one of the few reports that did not describe the attacking dog as savage or a brute. After describing the owner beating the dog to release his victim, it was noted that the tramp got away "without a second warning."[5]

A Newfoundland protecting his mistress on the outskirts of town seemed to fall into the classification of acceptable canine aggression. The fact that the woman fought furiously to free the tramp from the dog's grip, along with the fact that the victim was viewed as unsympathetic, made this attack more palatable.

A fatal dog attack near Findlay, New Jersey, in 1889 clearly demonstrates that some canine and human behaviors, even against tramps, were not permitted. A brief article noted that authorities were investigating a case where a farmer was reported to have "looked on" as his savage dog killed a tramp. The unfortunate victim was then buried in a field.[6]

A common thread seen in the recounting of dog attacks, both historically and in more modern day cases is the transference of cruel human traits onto dogs. There were no unkind superlatives assigned to the farmer who stood by and looked on as his dog killed a hapless tramp, yet his dog was described as savage. Time and again, dogs encouraged by their owners to act aggressively and allowed to be dangerous are assigned vicious or treacherous traits, while the owners responsible for the behavior found in their guard dogs appear to escape without noticeable public criticism.

This is not to say that owners in the late 19th century and early 20th century were not at times held responsible for the actions of their dogs. There were cases when owners were arrested, fined or sued civilly for the injuries their dogs inflicted. But public condemnation of guard dog owners usually resulted only when there was extreme negligence or when owners incited or actively encouraged a dog during an attack.

A notable exception to this was a disturbing incident that occurred in the spring of 1884 in Rockaway, New York. The article detailing the events leading up to the attack takes a rather indirect route before finally implicating the owner as the responsible party for the grievous injuries inflicted on the victim. The case involved a woman inspecting the grounds of a hotel on Long Island before taking possession of the property for the season. It was noted that no one informed her of the large Bloodhound kept on the premises to guard the unoccupied hotel. Upon entering the grounds, the woman was almost immediately set on by the dog. A watchman who heard her screams ran to her aid and only with great difficulty succeeded in getting the dog to release the woman from its grasp. The woman was gravely injured and after the amputation of one badly mangled arm, it was pronounced that she was not expected to recover. Early in the newspaper account it was insinuated that, prior to her arrival, this unfortunate woman should have been warned by the owners of the property about the dog. The article concludes in a much more direct fashion, stating:

> "The Bloodhound has been the terror of the neighborhood for some time, and the
> fact that so dangerous an animal was permitted to roam about the hotel grounds
> has drawn forth the severest condemnation."
>
> *Decatur Daily Republican,* April 12, 1884

The position guard dogs found themselves in during the late 1800s and early 1900s was far from enviable. The line between a justified attack and an attack that would cost the dog its life was thin indeed. Guard dogs had no way of distinguishing a burglar from a visiting neighbor, or a tramp from a peddler. Yet this distinction was critical in determining the legal and moral accountability of owners for injuries caused by their dogs. This distinction was also critical in determining the nature and ultimately the fate of the dog. A dog that attacked a tramp was justifiably protecting its owner; a dog that attacked a peddler was ferocious.

The interesting aspect of reporting severe/fatal attacks in the late 1800s was the recognition and admission by owners of the potential danger of the guard dog prior to an attack. The owners and persons managing these dogs knew the threat they could pose, as this was ultimately the true function of the dog—to be dangerous and ward off intruders. The problem was, of course, that with no direction or training by their owners, the dog decided who was an intruder based on its own perceptions.

In 1879, an account is given which perfectly describes all the behaviors, circumstances and events which culminated in one near-fatal attack by a guard dog:

> "Judge Fain, living about four miles from this city, has a very large and savage dog which he keeps as a watchdog upon his premises. He had only had the animal about two months and during that time his niece, Miss Mary Hamilton, was the only member of the household who could with some degree of safety, go within reach of the animal, which was kept chained all day and turned loose at night.
>
> "Miss Hamilton fed the animal, and by kind words and gentle treatment managed to control it. On Friday evening, when she went to unfasten the dog, she was accompanied by Miss Fannie. As soon as the animal was given its liberty it at once jumped upon Miss Fannie and after throwing her to the ground began to tear away at her…"

The article goes on to describe the behaviors seen regularly in severe and fatal attacks—an intense focus on and refusal to release one victim, despite the attempts of rescuers. It is then reported that a gun was finally procured and that the first shot into the side of the dog "instead of killing the animal it only seemed to make him more vicious." The second shot fired into the dog is described even more graphically: "The muzzle of the gun was placed so close to the dog that the flame scorched its shaggy coat." This was successful in making the dog release the woman, but the article goes on to describe the final act of this enraged animal:

> "The second load seemed to stagger the brute, and as he fell Miss Fannie jumped up and ran in the direction of the house. The dog, rallying from the shot, pursued her a distance of twelve steps and then fell dead in his tracks."
>
> *Decatur Daily Review,* September 3, 1879

Like most cases of canine aggression, this attack was the culmination of circumstances, events, and human and canine behaviors which provided both the means and opportunity for this dog to engage in an episode of extreme aggression. The events begin with the acquisition of a dog for an intended function as a guard dog and escalate from there:

- Newly acquired dog
- Dog known to be vicious and encouraged to be aggressive
- Dog chained for long periods of time with little human interaction, with the exception of the owner's niece

- Familiar bond beginning to be established between dog and niece (This excluded her from being the object of the dog's aggression, but the bond was not yet strong enough for her to maintain control over the dog.)
- Dog released from chain (Many dogs explode out of kennels, doorways, or off of chains in a rush of excitement. This release could also have been interpreted by the dog as the silent consent of the niece to drive off the intruder.)
- Dog's perception of the unfamiliar woman as intruder
- Dog's intense, focused and unrelenting attack on the intruder

This incident demonstrates that canine behaviors follow the intent of the owner, who in this case had bought a "savage" dog to protect his family from intruders. The fact that the behavior of the dog escalated into completely unacceptable levels of aggression was the result of the original function of the dog, coupled with mismanagement, failure to control the dog and the failure to anticipate the results of allowing the dog to be potentially dangerous.

On the rarest of occasions, a guard dog attack fell within all the parameters of acceptability. A case where three dogs accomplished their protection duties with stunning precision occurred in Indiana in 1902. A wealthy farmer was riding home with three large dogs in the back of his wagon when a highwayman stepped out, grabbed the horse's reins and drew a revolver. Before the highwayman could react the farmer turned the dogs loose on the would-be robber. The dogs attacked the man, knocking him to the ground, biting him and tearing off his clothes. The farmer called the dogs off and rode home. He returned later with a search party and found that the unidentified man had died from his injuries.[7] The key to this attack being deemed acceptable was that the dogs were acting under the control of their owner, and were directed by human perceptions of what was a valid threat. The owner assessed the situation, perceived it to be a real threat and then permitted his dogs to behave aggressively. The decision to attack came from the owner's interpretation of the situation, not the dogs'.

The problem with guard dogs is that when the owner is not present, the dogs operate solely from a canine perspective as to what constitutes threatening behavior. The child approaching perilously close to the dog's food bowl is a potential robbery, the woman entering a chained dog's space is a home invasion, and a boy retrieving a ball into a fenced yard is a trespasser. The dogs may be taking appropriate actions from a canine point of view but are making serious and often unforgivable errors in judgment from a human perspective.

One century ago, owners of guard dogs knew them to be dangerous, and encouraged this ferocity. Despite the understanding and expectation of guarding behaviors from dogs, these behaviors were rarely excused after the fact (i.e., attack). However, every once in a while a clear mind put aside the emotional aspect of a dog attack and showed a reasonable and genuine understanding of canine behaviors. An incident in 1891 demonstrates that, despite being attacked by his guard dog, one gentleman not only understood the situation from the dog's perspective, but also allowed for the dog's error in judgment as he, the owner, should have anticipated it:

> "A farmer in Salem, New Jersey, purchased a Mastiff dog to guard his residence. A few days after acquiring the dog the farmer entered the yard late in the evening. The dog sprang on the man, knocking him to the ground and biting him on the arms and legs. The farmer stated he had forgotten the dog was in the yard and 'he blames himself for letting the animal loose before it knew the members of the household.'"
>
> *New York Times,* August 8, 1891

Tracking or Scent Dogs

While guard dogs were owned by a significant percentage of 19th century Americans, dogs used for tracking and/or law enforcement were not nearly as numerous. Yet the function of these dogs at times required them to have aggressive traits similar to those of the guard/protection dogs.

Ideally, the primary function of tracking/scent hounds was to pursue and locate a quarry. This usually involved following the scent of either a lost child (or adult), a suspected criminal fleeing from authorities or an individual who had escaped confinement. There were extremely varied levels of aggression required or encouraged, depending on the specific tracking requirements. The mildest type of aggression was found in the true scent hounds. The function of these dogs required them to track down a quarry and alert its handler to the location and/or to hold the quarry at bay. Naturally, a scent hound assigned the task of locating a lost child was not encouraged, nor permitted, to display any type of aggression towards the object of pursuit. In this purest form of tracking, no aggression was required or tolerated. Unfortunately, this was not the main function of scent hounds during the 1800s and early 1900s.

The most extreme type of aggression in scent hounds and dogs used in law enforcement was found in the huge Bloodhound-type dogs used to track down fleeing criminals, escaped convicts or runaway slaves. Often these dogs were encouraged to display an increased level of aggression towards humans in the performance of these tasks. While professional and respectable law enforcement agencies trained their scent dogs to limit their aggression to tracking and holding their victim, there was certainly no shortage of cruel or barbaric dog handlers in the 19th century.

There is ample documentation that large Bloodhound-type dogs were used by some individuals and certain authorities to chase down, harass, worry, and inflict wounds on the target of their pursuits. Two popular images that come to mind in association with scent dogs pursuing fleeing humans are runaway slaves being chased down by baying Bloodhounds or escaped convicts desperately running from a pack of hounds on their trail. Undoubtedly, there were cases in which these images were a reality. But how much of these images was fiction and how much was based on truth was a highly contentious topic even in the era in which these incidents were reportedly taking place.

There was little dispute that reportedly fierce Cuban Bloodhounds were obtained during the Second Seminole War (1835–1842) by the U.S. Army to pursue and worry the Seminole Indians who sought refuge in the swamps of Florida. And as late as 1892, the *Washington Post* reported that Bloodhounds were being used to hunt down Apache Indians in the Southwest:

> "The Arizona legislature at its last session passed a bill for the especial benefit of
> Cochise county, authorizing the equipment of a company of rangers to relieve
> that section from the depredations of the renegade Apaches. As a preliminary step
> four bloodhounds have been imported from Mexico and will be used for trailing
> the murderous savages to their mountain lair."[8]

It is known that Bloodhound-type dogs were used by both the Union and Confederate armies to hunt down enemy soldiers, as well as in prison camps. And there is little dispute about the fact that Bloodhounds were used to hunt down fleeing suspects. The real dispute at the time was the level of aggression attributed to these dogs. For every media account of a scent dog attacking and inflicting harm on its human quarry, there were long editorials submitted to the newspapers by Bloodhound aficionados explaining the noble and gentle characteristics to be found in this breed. The obvious point that seemed to escape notice was the fact that dogs did indeed perform in both of these fashions, i.e., savagely attacking their quarry at times and at times showing tremendous restraint and gentleness upon reaching their quarry. As the debate swirled about the true nature and behavior of the Bloodhound, the evidence that owners/handlers determined behavior was seldom discussed.

Yet the evidence did present itself, time and again, that dogs mirrored the aggression of their owners/handlers. Perhaps one of the most notable cases of canine abuse by authorities occurred during the Civil War and involved the infamous Confederate prison, Camp Sumter. This prisoner of war camp was widely known as Andersonville Prison and became notable for the abuse and cruel conditions the Union soldiers had to endure under the command of Captain Henry Wirz. The conditions at Camp Sumter were appalling, and Union war prisoners were constantly seeking to escape. The prison was reported to have maintained a pack of "40 part bloodhounds and two monstrous Cuban bloodhounds" used to recapture escapees. These dogs had an additional function: to attack and injure prisoners at the direction of the guards or the Commanding Officers.

After the Civil War, Captain Henry Wirz, Commandant of Andersonville Prison, was arrested for war crimes, and after his court martial was sentenced to death by hanging. In addition to the deaths caused directly by his own hand, Captain Wirz was also found guilty of murder by inciting the camp dogs to kill Federal soldiers. In his court martial, the findings of the court charge, under Specification #11, that:

> "Henry Wirz, an officer in the military service of the so-called Confederate States of America, at Andersonville, in the state of Georgia, on or about the 1st day of July, A.D., 1864, then and there being commandant of a prison there located, by the authority of the said so-called Confederate States, for the confinement of prisoners of war, taken and held as such from the armies of the United States of America, while acting as said commandant, feloniously, and of his malice aforethought, did cause, incite, and urge certain ferocious and bloodthirsty animals, called bloodhounds, to pursue, attack, wound, and tear in pieces a soldier belonging to the Army of the United States, in his, the said Henry Wirz's custody as a prisoner of war, whose name is unknown; and in consequence thereof the said bloodhounds did then and there, with the knowledge, encourage-merit [sic], and instigation of him, the said Wirz, maliciously and murderously given by him, attack and mortally wound the said soldier, in consequence which said mortal wound he, the said prisoner, soon thereafter, to wit, on the 6th day of July, A.D. 1864, died."[9]

This is the most extreme example of the sanctioned use of canine aggression by an authority. Tracking dogs were handled by every conceivable type of owner, from the most inhumane and morally corrupt to humane and serious professionals. Law enforcement departments considered the addition of a Bloodhound a major advancement in their crime fighting abilities. Some departments proudly announced the purchase of what they considered to be quality scent hounds, used exclusively to pursue and locate fleeing suspects. Other law enforcement agencies obtained dogs they considered to be more aggressive and seemed either unconcerned about the negative reputation of the type of Bloodhound they acquired or purposely sought out this particular type of dog because of their reputation.

In February 1903, the city of Perry, Iowa announced the upcoming acquisition of two Bloodhounds, making particular note that these were Southern or Cuban Bloodhounds, known as the "most reliable man-hunting dog on earth…"[10] This variety of Bloodhound was widely believed in the 1800s to be a pugnacious and fierce type of tracking dog. Other towns or cities, when acquiring Bloodhounds for their law enforcement agencies, made special note to declare the dogs they were acquiring were of the "Texas" variety, described as the true descendants of the British Bloodhounds, known for their superb tracking abilities coupled with a noble and gentle character.

So while the functions of all types of scent dogs were based on their natural and specialized ability to excel in tracking quarry, their aggression towards their quarry was often determined by their handlers. Handlers who sought out the allegedly fiercer varieties of Bloodhounds certainly would either directly or indirectly encourage this behavior. Handlers specifically seeking out gentler, more tractable varieties would almost certainly encourage their dogs to be less aggressive. While certain behavior may be influenced by breed, the function or purpose for which a handler/owner obtained a dog is the controlling factor in any future behavior displayed by the dog.

In addition to the use of tracking dogs by authorities, individuals also at times fancied themselves as "professional" handlers of scent dogs, and anyone with a type of Bloodhound and a scent to follow could consider themselves a tracker. And as is often the case with dog ownership, a lack of humanity and/or intelligence did not prevent the acquisition, training or keeping of dogs. An 1894 article, sarcastically titled "A Lovely Father," describes how a man recently purchased a Bloodhound and decided to test the tracking abilities of the dog on his fourteen-year-old son. The boy was given a 15-minute head start before the father released the dog to pursue the fleeing lad. Not surprisingly, the dog did indeed catch up with his quarry, and upon reaching the unfortunate boy inflicted numerous wounds before the father could club the dog off his son.[11]

Fatal dog attacks on humans, while not unheard of or terribly surprising, were considered aberrations in the 1800s and early 1900s. Dogs rarely attack and kill humans, even when incited or encouraged to view humans as prey. There certainly may be undocumented cases in which tracking dogs attacked and killed fleeing individuals (Indians, enemy soldiers, criminals). But, 19th century American society did not condone the killing of persons by dogs, even persons deemed undesirable. So the combination of this being viewed as unacceptable and potentially illegal, along with the fact that dogs rarely exhibit this behavior, explains the few recorded examples of fatal attacks by tracking/scent dogs in the United States.

One of the rare documented cases in which tracking dogs did indeed kill a fleeing suspect was reported in Illinois in 1910. A residence in the town of Carrier Mills was discovered to have been burglarized and tracking dogs were brought to the scene. The article "Bloodhounds Kill a Man" describes the pursuit as follows:

"The trail was taken up immediately and so eager were the hounds to land their quarry they broke loose from the keeper and chased the man they were pursuing to an old barn. There he was pounced upon by the animals and so badly mangled that recognition was impossible…Roberts, the owner of the dogs, was exonerated."

The Washington Post, December 31, 1910

An interesting observation in the description of this attack is that, unlike most accounts in the 1800s and early 1900s, in which the dogs involved were described as savage or vicious, the dogs in this account were called "eager." The description and attitude towards these dogs are vastly different from the adjectives used to describe most other fatal attacks.

Hunting Dogs

Unlike guard dogs or tracking dogs, there was no seemingly useful purpose in encouraging or allowing hunting or retrieving dogs to behave aggressively towards humans. The function of hunting dogs was to assist their masters in the pursuit, capture or retrieval of game, so, not surprisingly; there are few documented cases of severe or fatal attacks by dogs used for hunting. While many other types of dogs were expected to perform dual functions as pet and protector, hunting dogs were not usually obtained or encouraged to double as protection dogs. While all dogs will provide some level of protection and guarding, the value or primary function of hunting dogs did not include the encouragement of aggression towards humans.

Aggression was more clearly directed or channeled in the hunting dogs and so there was less confusion as to what was and was not acceptable behavior (at least towards humans) as compared to dogs used for guarding/protection. But hunting or retriever dogs will behave aggressively in the same types of situations seen with all breeds. Hunting dogs are found lashing out in pain, attacking from apparent territorial issues (chained dogs), exhibiting extreme aggression operating as a pack, and resource guarding (possessive aggression), as well as attacking for seemingly no apparent reason.

Exact breed identification was not considered of paramount importance in 19th century accounts describing the events that contributed to severe dog attacks, and so the dogs involved were described in broad terms as "hound," "retriever," "bird dog," "coonhound," "spaniel" or simply "hunting dog." While the breed identifications given by the 19th century newspapers were often vague, the circumstances believed to be driving behaviors in dogs were often recorded with precision.

In 1888, a child in Lockport, N.Y., was "fearfully disfigured" by a large hunting dog. The article reports that "there are some hopes for the boy's recovery." It is explained that the 5-year-old was attacked after he "approached the brute while he was gnawing a bone and the dog thinking he was going to take it away jumped at this throat."[12]

A case of pack aggression in an extremely large group of hounds is found in a 1903 account. The unfortunate victim was a 15-year-old boy approaching a kennel in which 25 hunting dogs were kept. The dogs managed to break loose of the kennel and rushed to attack the youth. The boy was quickly overcome and not even the interference of the dogs' owner could stop the attack by such a large number of dogs. In desperation the owner mounted a horse in the hopes of trampling some of the dogs to save the boy. The frenzied hounds attacked and severely injured both horse and rider. The owner survived, the youth did not.[13]

Even the best of dogs with strong attachments to their owners are capable of lashing out with extreme aggression when in pain. In 1904, a report of a bird dog attacking his owner was published:

"Amos Miller had his face horribly mangled by his bird dog yesterday. It got its foot fast in the wire fence and he attempted to loose it, the dog sprung like a tiger upon him, bit through his right cheek and tore it beyond recognition. It required a desperate effort before the firmly-set jaws of the dog could be removed. His right hand was also badly bitten."

The Newark Daily Advocate, December 10, 1904

A case of a Water spaniel attack found in 1896 offers no possible explanation for the extremely aggressive behavior found in this dog:

"At Winchester, Ohio, the 3-year-old child of Mrs. Marie Cotty, was attacked by a large Water-spaniel dog belonging to E.A. Cutter, the well-known horseman, and before assistance could be had, was literally chewed to pieces, one hand being almost bitten off..."

The Daily Herald, July 15, 1896

Despite the fact that the function of hunting and retrieving dogs rarely encouraged or permitted aggression towards humans, all dogs regardless of breed or function are capable of displaying aggression towards humans under certain circumstances.

Farm Dogs

One can hardly imagine an idyllic early American farm scene without envisioning a dog somewhere in the landscape. Dogs were an integral part of farm living in America, and for good reason. Besides the basic services all dogs provide (protection and companionship), farm dogs contributed additional and often vital services to their owners.

Raising and managing livestock was costly, arduous, and often times dangerous work. Farm dogs contributed greatly to both the economic and physical welfare of their owners for a miniscule financial investment (cost of feeding). During the course of a long day, dogs worked tirelessly alongside their owners, helping to herd and control sheep, cattle and swine. Long after the day ended, dogs were still working to protect their owners' livestock from nightly predators.

Besides the everyday tasks of farm living that dogs assisted with, they frequently performed a more dramatic service of protecting or saving their owners from charging bulls or aggressive hogs. Cattle caused a significant number of deaths in the late 1800s and early 1900s. There are scores of accounts of farmers being gored, trampled and killed by bulls. In addition to farmers, children, women and elderly persons were also killed when they had the misfortune to encounter an aggressive bull. In one twenty year span, from 1880 to 1899, there were over 150 recorded newspaper accounts of people being attacked and killed by cattle. Clearly, cattle presented a real and constant danger.

An attack by an enraged bull was a predicament few people were able to survive. Aside from the deadly horns and their sheer size, many weighing over 1500 lbs., bulls were often relentless in their attack, goring and trampling their victims unmercifully. In many cases, the arrival of a brave and loyal farm dog was undeniably a live-saving turn of events. All types of farm dogs, from Collies and Shepherds to mongrels and small dogs, could be found attacking massive bulls and hogs in defense of their owners.

In February 1926, *The Washington Post* reported that an old Collie dog saved the life of his 45-year-old owner. A prominent dairy farmer from Glenmont, Maryland, was being gored by an infuriated bull and was only saved from death when the old Collie rushed to his aid, biting the bull in the throat and allowing his master to escape.

On November 11, 1916, the *Lima Times Democrat* reported that a Collie dog in Ohio saved the life of his mistress after she was knocked down and butted by an enraged cow in a corn field.

On September 15, 1928, the *Appleton Post Crescent* reported the life-saving actions of a Shepherd dog in Menominee, Michigan. A widowed farm woman was trying to drive a bull out of the barn when it turned and attacked her. Three times she was battered to the ground by the bull before Flossie, her Shepherd dog, came rushing to her aid. The dog began biting the hind legs of the bull, allowing her mistress to drag herself to a platform, where she collapsed.

On July 30, 1910, the *Coshocton Daily Tribune* tells of an equally heroic Shepherd dog who rescued his master from a vicious bull on a farm near Tiverton, Ohio. The bull had recently gored another man and this farmer was about to experience a similar fate. A number of the man's ribs were broken by the impact of the bull, but the arrival and attack on the bull by the Shepherd dog most assuredly saved his life.

There are also numerous accounts of unidentified breeds or mongrels performing similarly heroic rescues from deadly attacks by cattle. But while Collies, Shepherd dogs, and mongrels are found frequently rushing to the aid of their owners, Bulldogs seemed particularly quick to engage an infuriated bull or vicious hog in defense of their master or mistress. Clearly, these dogs saved more than a few lives and their acts of bravery were frequently recognized and reported in both the local and national newspapers in the late 1800s and early 1900s.

In 1883, a hired hand on a farm in Pennsylvania owed his life to his Bulldog. The man had been attacked and tossed three times by a bull and only managed to escape when his Bulldog attacked the bull. The dog was also thrown by the bull, but was reported to have finally "conquered the bull" and both he and his master survived (*The Messenger,* October 17, 1883).

A father in Illinois reported that his Bulldog saved the life of his daughter after she entered a pasture in which a bull resided. The bull charged the young girl and she made a desperate run to a nearby tree. The family Bulldog jumped the pasture fence, attacking and driving the bull away from the terrified girl (*Decatur Review,* September 13, 1929).

A Bulldog in Moultrie, Georgia, gave his life to prevent a bull from goring his young master. The boy was driving the bull from a field when the bull turned and charged him. The boy's faithful Bulldog rushed in between his master and the charging animal, gripping the bull by the nose. The dog clung to the bull until the boy had reached the safety of a nearby fence, at which point the bull shook the dog loose and gored it to death (*The Havre Daily News,* December 13, 1930).

While bulls frequently killed people, an attack by a hog could also prove fatal. An incident that occurred in Indiana shows that the arrival of a Bulldog could quickly turn a helpless situation into a chance of escape and survival. Two women, the wives of prominent farmers, were attacked by "six maddened brood sows." Their screams brought the resident Bulldog scrambling to their rescue. With one woman knocked to the ground by the sows and the other woman fighting in vain to save her companion, the "arrival of the Bulldog ended the combat, but not without a battle, in which one of the hogs lost part of an ear" (*The Indianapolis Sunday Star,* November 13, 1921).

Not only are Bulldogs found defending their masters and mistresses from cattle and hogs, but in 1884, we find a Bulldog saving a man from being killed by a horse:

"Thomas Scott, of the vicinity of Sandusky, was being mangled by a stallion, known as the man-eater, when a Bulldog caught the horse by the nose and forced it to release its hold on the man. The dog saved the man's life and several persons will contribute for a collar to present to the dog."

The Ohio Democrat, November 6, 1884

While these accounts all portray fearless dogs, sometimes the true measure of bravery is for a dog (or human) to take on danger while fear is cautioning against action.

An amusingly honest account of a dog, not necessarily fearless but certainly committed and loyal to his mistress, was told in 1907. Near Johnstown, Pennsylvania, a young woman, accompanied by her large, faithful dog, had gone out to the barn to milk the cows. Before reaching the barn she encountered a "maddened" bull. The bull charged her and she desperately tried to protect herself with a milking stool. The bull quickly knocked her down and was attempting to gore her, when her dog began snapping at the bull's hind legs. The article describes how the dog became increasingly bolder, the snaps turning into bites and the bites then beginning to penetrate the flesh. Finally the bull turned his fury on this new enemy and, with a snort of rage, charged the dog. The dog took flight and thus began a wild chase, with the bull pursuing the dog through the farm and into nearby fields. The article reports that the dog returned home unharmed and the young woman survived with only a broken arm and some bruising, thanks to her faithful but not completely fearless dog.[14]

There are countless accounts of farmers being killed by livestock and numerous accounts of more fortunate individuals whose dogs saved them from fatal injuries, but there are exceedingly few accounts of working farm dogs attacking farmers or causing a human fatality. In a few of the rare cases of fatal aggression by farm dogs, the dogs were in or near henhouses, or inside barns, at the time of the attack.

In 1875, a young girl was visiting a farm in Courtland, New York, with her parents. The visiting girl and the farmer's young daughter decided to go out to the chicken coop. On the way they were joined by the large mongrel dog belonging to the farmer. As the girls reached the henhouse, the visiting girl opened the door and upon entering was immediately attacked by the dog. The other girl became so frightened she shut the henhouse door, trapping the poor child inside with the attacking dog. The child died later that night from her injuries.[15]

In 1885, an elderly farmer was removing a dead chicken from a henhouse when his dog attacked him. The attack was so relentless that the dog had to be killed before it would release the farmer from its grasp.[16]

In 1887, a dog chasing a hen under the henhouse turned and fatally bit his owner in the throat when the man crawled under the building and attempted to interfere.[17]

Other than these cases, there are few accounts of working farm dogs involved in severe/fatal attacks on humans. Unlike guard dogs, most working farm dogs were maintained in environments far more conducive to producing a balanced and therefore less aggressive dog. Farm dogs were afforded more opportunities to interact with humans and other animals in positive situations and as a rule were not encouraged or allowed to behave aggressively. Working farm dogs were maintained in an environment which provided healthy exercise and mental stimulation. Additionally, territorial issues would be far less intense with farm dogs than with chained dogs or guard dogs confined in strictly defined areas. In general, the function of farm dogs produced a more social and balanced dog, allowing for more normal and appropriate behaviors towards humans.

Stray or Wild Dogs

Both historically and in the present day, most dogs involved in fatal attacks had identifiable owners. Yet the abandonment of dogs has always been regularly practiced by persons who view dogs as disposable and easily replaced. The sad fate of abandoned dogs is obvious. Dogs cannot survive long or well without human assistance. Besides the difficulties of surviving off the land, the humans that dogs often need to save them from a hard and short life in the wild more often than not became their executioners.

A century ago (and even today), dogs without owners were usually viewed as high liability animals. At best, stray dogs were considered nuisances, at worst they were considered a direct threat to human welfare. Either way, these dogs were usually shot on sight in rural areas, or rounded up and executed in more urban environments. Despite this, stray and abandoned dogs were numerous and could be found around towns and roaming city streets.

As is usually the case with dogs, despite abandonment and starvation, untold millions of stray dogs were not involved in any type of aggressive encounter with humans. While there are numerous cases of abandoned or ownerless dogs attacking or killing livestock, incidents of wild or stray dogs attacking and severely injuring or killing a human were extremely rare.

The fact is, humans often do cruel and dangerous things to dogs and usually escape without injury. However, some acts are so reckless that an attack is almost guaranteed. In 1897, an instance of this occurred near Columbus, Ohio:

> "Johnny Ballinger lies at his home suffering intense agony from injuries inflicted by a pack of savage dogs. While passing the dump on the river bank where refuse from the slaughterhouse is thrown, he saw the dogs gnawing a bone. With a stick he struck the nearest dog which leaped upon him followed by a dozen others. He was rescued by some workmen. His legs, arms and head were lacerated in 26 different places and his scalp was torn in a horrible manner."
>
> *Fort Wayne News,* July 3, 1897

Whether the dogs in this case had owners who permitted them to wander and be naturally drawn to such a richly stimulating environment, or whether these were truly abandoned dogs that survived off the refuse from the slaughterhouse, will never be known.

Most cases found of a dog pack attacking a human suggest the dogs had owners. Only in the rarest of cases are dogs found to be truly abandoned and functioning independently of humans as a pack. One very notable and rather bizarre case in which there can be no doubt that the dogs were very wild was during the bitter cold winter of 1892. The owners that these dogs may once have had were certainly long forgotten as these dogs struggled to survive in the wilderness. The case involved a bold and particularly desperate attack by a pack of starving wild dogs in Sherman County, Kansas, which caused the death of a father and daughter. This was certainly a newsworthy event and as such the incident was reported by national newspapers *(The New York Times* and *The Washington Post)* as well as the local papers.[18]

Prior to this incident, rumors had occasionally emerged out of the harsh landscape of Colorado of wild dogs attacking and killing livestock and humans. At times, travelers reached their destination with tales of being chased through the woods by packs of wild dogs. But these were fireside tales and no one could prove or disprove such exciting yet frightful stories. All that changed in February 1892 when it was reported that a pack of wild dogs entered into the Northwest corner of Kansas from Colorado. There had been a particularly heavy snow that February, and this accounted for the boldness and ferocity of the attack. While there were no witnesses, the scenario that rescuers came upon left no doubt as to the events that took place. A stockman named John Pratt and his daughter had left Leonard, Kansas, on a Saturday evening to return to their house a number of miles away. When they did not arrive home, a search the next morning found their mangled remains about a mile from their destination. The wagon they had been riding in was overturned and the horses dead and partially devoured. The carcasses of several dogs were also found on the scene, as Mr. Pratt shot a number of them in a fierce battle to save himself and his daughter.

Nineteenth century America had rather rigid expectations of dogs in the performance of their respective functions. Guard dogs were usually disposed of if they attacked the "wrong" person. Likewise, hunting dogs that could not effectively perform their function were discarded or destroyed. There was little tolerance for a farm dog that harassed livestock or had any negative impact on the production of farm goods. Stray or abandoned dogs were considered a nuisance or liability and destroyed in staggering numbers.

But, as seen in the aforementioned examples, the function which provided the greatest potential for error for dogs was their use as protection or guard dogs. Unlike tracking or hunting dogs, more often than not performing their functions in the *presence* of an owner, guard dogs' functions were rooted in the premise that the dog would act appropriately in the *absence* of their owner.

The unreasonable expectation that dogs could independently assess the intent of intruders by human standards and morals doomed many dogs to failure and resulted in serious injury to innocent people who encountered these dogs.

CHAPTER 2

Imagery and the Media in 19th Century America: The Bloodhound

As it relates to dog breeds, form often defines function. A Jack Russell Terrier could easily be trained to be an attack dog, as a Newfoundland dog could easily be trained to be a guide dog for the blind. Both breeds have the innate canine intelligence and behaviors that would allow them to be trained for these functions. But for obvious reasons, the Jack Russell Terrier would not be taken as seriously, nor could perform the task as efficiently, as some of the larger breeds. The Newfoundland might perform his assigned function with reasonable satisfaction, yet his large size might make some tasks cumbersome, and the long coat might make this breed overheated in situations another breed may tolerate better. This realization—that certain physical traits (form) will assist in certain tasks (function)—has resulted in the creation and maintenance of "breeds" of dogs.

Humans have artificially manipulated dogs to be excessively small or excessively large, to be long-haired or short-haired, as well as a host of other physical traits that are either useful for a particular function or simply because we find them aesthetically appealing. Besides manipulating a particular appearance in a breed to assist in a specialized function, humans have also artificially selected to enhance or subdue some natural canine behaviors to assist in performing a particular function. We have created hundreds of different dog breeds, a fascinating mixture of sizes, colors, shapes, and specialized skills.

While the physical characteristics of a particular breed of dog cannot be changed once it is born, behavioral characteristics can still very much be influenced by humans. In other words, once the Newfoundland puppy is born, little can be done to change the pre-determined breed appearance, but its behavioral traits are still subject to influence, control and the manipulation of humans. So while a dog may come with a set of "breed blueprints" to excel at a particular function, humans are in essence architects, and can either use those blueprints to build on those behaviors or ignore the blueprints and build/train the dog for a different function.

Indeed, dogs rarely perform or are expected to excel at the function for which their individual breed was originally created. Not even in the 1800s and early 1900s, when dogs were used much more as working animals, were most dogs expected to perform the function associated with their breed. Many people owned Bloodhounds in the late 1800s, and most of these dogs were never used to track a scent. The Newfoundland, a breed developed to aid fishermen and rescue drowning victims, also became very popular in the late 1800s, yet many of these dogs never saw a fisherman or entered a body of water.

Besides not performing the function the breed was developed for, some dogs may excel at a function associated with a completely different breed. In 1907 there was a case of a Newfoundland saving his master from a raging bull, and in 1906, a case of a Bulldog saving a young boy from drowning. Clearly, dogs can and were obtained and used for purposes other than the original breed design. Part of the wonder of dog breeds is this potential to perform specialized tasks along with the ability to function outside of a breed-designed behavior.

◆ ◆ ◆

During the second half of the 19th century, Bloodhounds were frequently reported as the breed most responsible for severe and fatal attacks on humans. In only a ten-state area, there were at least 38 severe or fatal attacks by Bloodhounds reported in the news media from 1855–1910.

The fact that Bloodhounds figure predominantly in cases of extreme canine aggression in the later part of the 19th century, and the fact that fatalities associated with this breed are virtually non-existent in the 20th century, offers a unique opportunity to examine the critical issues that suggest breed-based aggression. While this presents a unique opportunity to study the factors within a breed that may contribute to canine aggression, it also presents the same type of inherent problems seen in more modern times when attempting to label aggressive behavior as a breed-specific trait.

The first obstacle encountered when trying to determine breed involvement in cases of aggression is in ascertaining the correct breed identification. While this may not seem so difficult a task: in reality, it is hugely problematic and presents a host of possibilities for misidentification and erroneous conclusions. The case of Bloodhounds' involvement in attacks on humans in the 19th century demonstrates that before any conclusions about breed-specific behavior can be drawn, there needs to be an examination of the reliability of breed identification and an understanding of the complexities involved in the relationship between owners and dogs.

In the 1800s, the term "Bloodhound" was applied loosely. Newspaper accounts from the period are found describing dogs involved in severe or fatal attacks as: Cuban Bloodhound, Spanish Bloodhound, Florida Bloodhound, Southern Bloodhound, Negro Bloodhound, Texas Bloodhound, Russian Bloodhound, Siberian Bloodhound, British Bloodhound, St. Hubert's Bloodhound, Bloodhound Mix, True Bloodhound, Valuable Bloodhound, and, simply, Bloodhound. It quickly becomes apparent that all these references to Bloodhounds cannot possibly be describing a single or uniform breed of dog.

For most people today the term Bloodhound easily conjures up an image of a huge, lumbering dog with long ears, a sad countenance, and black and tan markings. This dog is the breed known as the British or St. Hubert's Bloodhound. The first St. Hubert's Blood-hound was registered in 1885, in the newly formed American Kennel Club. Undoubtedly, the dog we view as a Bloodhound today was also the standard for the breed description a century ago. This type was also referred to as the "true" Bloodhound and the admirers and breeders of these dogs were constantly found defending their breed against a barrage of imposters, myths and bad press.

In the 1800s, "Bloodhound" was still a description more of function than of breed and a number of very dissimilar dogs were all grouped together in this broad category.

The Cuban Bloodhound

The Cuban Bloodhound is also known as the Southern, Spanish, Negro or Florida Blood-hound.

To the true Bloodhound aficionado, no insult to their breed was more objectionable than to attribute the behaviors of a Cuban Bloodhound to those of the "true" or St. Hubert's Blood-hound. And their objections were not without merit, for the breed known as the Cuban Bloodhound was considered a particularly fierce and aggressive animal and the function of these dogs usually involved cruelty and subjugation.

The true origins and parentage of the Cuban Bloodhound was speculative even at the time they existed. An 1888 article in the *Denton Journal* attempted to explain to readers the difference between the types of Bloodhounds, taking great pains to disavow any rela-tionship between the British (St. Hubert's) Bloodhound and the other varieties. The author claimed the Cuban Bloodhound to be a combination of "the Deer Hound, the ferocious Mas-tiff and Russian (Siberian) Greyhound."[1]

Another article in 1891 claimed the Cuban Bloodhound to be "produced by a cross between a Mastiff and a Pointer..."[2]

The 1913 edition of *Webster's Dictionary* defines Bloodhound as:

"A breed of large and powerful dogs, with long, smooth, and pendulous ears, and remarkable for acuteness of smell. It is employed to recover game or prey which has escaped wounded from a hunter, and for tracking criminals. Formerly it was used for pursuing runaway slaves. Other varieties of dog are often used for the same purpose and go by the same name. The Cuban Bloodhound is said to be a variety of the Mastiff."

The 1945 edition of *The Observer's Book of Dogs* describes the Cuban Bloodhound as a "large and ferocious Dogue de Bordeaux/Bloodhound cross, bred for hunting fugitive slaves in Cuba and Florida."

A modern-day, well-researched description lists the Cuban Bloodhound to be a combination of: "English Mastiffs, Deutsche Doges, French Mastiffs, St. Hubert Bloodhounds, English Greyhounds and a variety of the old British bulldogges."[3]

But while there was much dispute about the origins of this breed, there was little dispute about the function of these dogs: They were used not only to track, but also to harass and injure their human quarry. The reputation and origins of aggressive behavior in these animals resulted from their use by the Spanish conquistadors to subjugate and decimate the native populations in the New World. An account from Bartolome de Las Casas (1474–1566), a Spanish missionary and historian,[4] described some of the atrocities practiced by the Spaniards against the natives in the Caribbean and Central America during early colonial times:

> "They entered into towns and villages, sparing neither children nor old men and women. They ripped their bellies and cut them to pieces…They tried to flee from these men. Men who were empty of all pity, behaving like savages.The evil men had even taught their hounds, fierce dogs, to tear natives to pieces at first sight…"[5]

It is interesting to note that five centuries ago, Bartolome de Las Casas recognized that the dogs were "taught" to behave so ferociously. He understood that the savagery shown by these dogs towards the natives was an extension of the savagery of their masters.

In the United States, the purchase and use of Cuban-bred Bloodhounds by the Van Buren administration to assist in the removal of the Seminole Indians from their tribal lands drew bitter criticism from the public and from rival politicians. The war against the Seminoles who refused to be expelled from Florida was becoming longer and more costly with each passing year (1835–1842) and when authorization was given in 1840 to purchase 33 Cuban Bloodhounds, there was a public outcry. Though the government insisted the dogs were to be used only to ferret out the Indians, this was hardly believable, given the reputation and history of cruelty associated with this breed.

The Cuban Bloodhound is also the breed associated with the hunting down of fugitive slaves in the years before the Civil War, and during the Civil War there are references made to both Confederate and Union regiments using Cuban Bloodhounds to hunt down enemy soldiers.

So while there can be debate over which breeds of dog contributed to the genetic makeup of the Cuban Bloodhound, it is really of little significance. The behaviors of these animals had little to do with breed genetics and everything to do with the depravity of their masters.

There is also little doubt that the ferocity and aggressiveness of these dogs was a direct result of human manipulation; many of these dogs were not merely encouraged to behave ferociously but were cruelly forced to behave this way. While the Spanish conquistadors were known to brutalize their dogs in order to force them to attack and devour Indians, this was not a phenomenon exclusive to that era. American history is replete with examples of brutal treatment towards dogs and humans. In a speech given in Taunton, England,

on September 1, 1846, Frederick Douglass, the famed 19th century African-American abolitionist, orator and author, described a process used to train Bloodhounds to pursue Negro slaves:

> "Slaves frequently escape from bondage, and live in the woods. Sometimes they
> are absent eight or nine months without being discovered. They are hunted with
> dogs, kept for the purpose, and regularly trained. Enmity is instilled into the
> blood-hounds by these means: A master causes a slave to tie up the dog and beat
> it unmercifully. He then sends the slave away and bids him climb a tree; after
> which he unties the dog, puts him upon the track of the man and encourages him
> to pursue it until he discovers the slave. Sometimes, in hunting negroes, if the
> owners are not present to call off the dogs, the slaves are torn in pieces…"[6]

Clearly the owners of these dogs understood how this abusive training would foster
agression.

As is often the nature of man, cruelty begets cruelty, as the case of a freed Negro slave
beating a Bloodhound demonstrates. Also demonstrated is that consumption of copious
amounts of alcohol can inspire some to behave with reckless cruelty towards dogs:

> "Moses Spratt, a negro, owns and works a small farm at Fairview. Before the war,
> Spratt was a slave in Virginia. He came North after emancipation bringing with
> him a pair of Southern bloodhounds of the kind that were formerly used in hunting
> fugitive slaves. With these he went into the business of breeding bloodhounds. He
> always had a large stock of the animals on hand which he keeps chained to kennels
> in the yard. Wednesday night Spratt had a party of friends at the house and liquor
> was passed around so liberally that they all got drunk. About midnight Spratt went
> out to the yard and the dogs began to growl. He spoke to them, but his voice being
> husky with liquor they failed to recognize it and growled the more. In his drunken
> recklessness Spratt picked up a stick and struck Pomp, one of the most ferocious of
> the animals. The dog sprang at him and the chain snapping, the infuriated beast
> fastened his teeth in Spratt's throat. In the desperate struggle that ensued he was
> thrown to the ground, falling near the kennel of another dog. That dog also attacked
> him. Spratt's cries brought his companions to his assistance, but before they could
> rescue him he was almost torn to pieces."
>
> *New York Times,* June 12, 1880

This case may also be the closest to an authenticated case of a fatality related to a true Cuban
Bloodhound, as the breed, function and origin of these dogs are described.

It is unquestioned that the Cuban Bloodhound bore little resemblance to the British variety
of Bloodhound, but this dog was considered a Bloodhound nonetheless since it fit the functional
description of Bloodhound (i.e., a dog used to track a quarry by scent, or a "hunter of blood").

"He is not naturally such a ferocious animal as his name might imply, but he is deservedly dreaded by those, who are unacquainted with him." (Francis Butler, 1860)

St. Hubert's/British Bloodhound or "True" Bloodhounds

This breed was viewed as the "true" Bloodhound in the latter 1800s and is the standard that we recognize today. The history of the breed can be traced back centuries, beginning in Europe and then becoming associated almost exclusively as a British import. This breed is known, first and foremost, for its ability to follow a scent and was used to track everything from stags and boar to sheep rustlers and criminals. The handlers and breeders of these dogs took great pride in declaring their breed to be a gentle and noble dog and were constantly defending the reputation of the Bloodhound from the widely held belief that they were a fierce and savage animal.

No dog involved in a fatality was ever specifically identified as a British or St. Hubert's Bloodhound. Occasionally, there were reports of a "valuable" Bloodhound belonging to a wealthy or prominent individual involved in a serious attack. This is as close as we can come to identifying an attack by a St. Hubert's Bloodhound. Though Bloodhounds were reported to be very popular in the late 1800s, there is little doubt that most of these dogs were not true Bloodhounds, as a St. Hubert's or British Bloodhound was clearly a valuable and expensive animal and not within the financial grasp of most people.

The case previously discussed of the Bloodhounds killing a burglary suspect they were tracking may be a case of "true Bloodhounds" since these dogs were owned by professionals, worked exclusively as tracking dogs, and were identified by the authorities as Bloodhounds. There is no indication that these dogs were trained to perform any task other than tracking, as it was specifically noted that the dogs were not released to attack the suspect, but had broken free from their handler. Though it may be speculated that the dogs involved in this fatality were indeed St. Hubert's Bloodhounds, it is far from a factual conclusion. And so we find, despite the numerous reports of Bloodhound related attacks and fatalities, there is no documented case where a St. Hubert's/British or "true" Bloodhound was ever positively identified.

Siberian or Russian Bloodhound

The Siberian or Russian Bloodhound bore little to no resemblance to the St. Hubert's or British variety. The Siberian Bloodhound was reported to be a massive animal and, like the Cuban Bloodhound, along with being a scent hound, these dogs were created, manipulated and encouraged by humans to behave aggressively towards other humans.

It is impossible to expect dogs to behave reasonably when human nature is such that we behave so wantonly, recklessly and cruelly, as the following 1880 account demonstrates. In the winter of 1880, a brutal exhibition was staged in St. Louis, where a professional prize-fighter was matched against a Siberian Bloodhound. In attendance at an old stable where the fight took place were an ex-police chief, an ex-judge, a physician, and three members of the House of Delegates. Though the newspapers that covered this appalling display condemned the event, they nevertheless used a lot of ink in describing it "blow by blow." The fight is finally described as ending when the prize-fighter, Patsy Brennan, "caught the dog by the neck and kicked the life out of him."[7]

The few accounts where we find Siberian Bloodhounds attacking individuals in the United States seem relatively mild and restrained compared to the ferocity that was encouraged and the brutal treatment many of these dogs received. Here again, we find a breed used extensively as guard dogs attacking the "wrong" people because dogs often fail to differentiate between legitimate persons and trespassers.

The following lose-lose situation for a Siberian Bloodhound took place in 1882 in New York City. The son of a policeman was walking a huge Siberian Bloodhound on a "cord" when approached by the owner of a varnishing company. The merchant wished to purchase the dog to guard his factory. The dog was sold for $5 and promptly put to use. Shortly thereafter, an employee showed up one Sunday night to set up the ovens for the next day. The Bloodhound attacked the man and the dog was shot the next morning for his troubles.[8]

While there was a spate of reported attacks by Siberian Bloodhounds in the 1880s, it is highly doubtful if these dogs were indeed purebred Siberian Bloodhounds. The fact that in the previous account the dog was sold for $5 indicates that this was probably not a valuable (purebred) dog. In comparison, there was a reported attack by a Bloodhound on a man riding a bicycle in Babylon, New York. The dog was described as a "five-hundred-dollar prize Bloodhound, belonging to Malcolm W. Ford."[9]

There are no documented cases of a genuine Russian or Siberian Bloodhound involved in a fatal attack in the United States. However, in 1906, on the Northwest Russian border with Europe, there came the report of a peasant killed by Bloodhounds near the border crossing. The border guards kept four large hounds as watchdogs and one night in mid-November the dogs tore away from the guards and ran into the neighboring forest. Minutes later, screams were heard and the guards rushed to find the dogs had killed a man and chased his 13-year-old son into a tree. The boy had been severely bitten also, but explained to the guards that he and his father were not smugglers or attempting to leave the country but were trying to avoid paying tax at the customs by going through the woods and around the border station.[10]

Here again, we have dogs that, although prized for aggression towards humans, still functioned as tracking or scent dogs, which makes the designation "Bloodhound" technically correct.

Bloodhound

How is it that the Bloodhound came to have such a fierce and negative public image in the late 1800s and early 1900s? A number of factors coincided to create a public image or perception about the behavior of Bloodhounds that was to last more than half a century. And the perception still lingers a hundred years later, as one today can easily imagine a pack of baying hounds pursuing a frightened and desperate fugitive. The danger implied in this imagery is not foremost from the humans in pursuit, but in being overrun and attacked by the dogs.

How accurate this scenario was hardly mattered. What percentage of Bloodhounds in the 19th century attacked their quarry also mattered little. An image was created in the collective consciousness of the public that would not easily be shaken loose. The factors that combined to create this image are:

Illustration of a Great Siberian Bloodhound, (*Breeding, Training, Diseases of Dogs,* Francis Butler, 1860).

1. A broad-based grouping of dogs listed as one breed/type
2. Breed/type dog used in functions associated with aggression
3. Media portrayal of breed as aggressive
4. Increased popularity of breed and consequent increase in number of substandard owners

The first two factors have been discussed—there was a wide variety of breed/types of dogs that were all grouped under the breed "Bloodhound" and the functions of these dogs often required them to be protection dogs, attack dogs or tracking dogs. Bloodhound-type dogs were also popular at the time but as we shall see, popularity is often spawned by a *negative* media image and so these dogs became even more sought after when their dangerous image increased.

Fatal animal attack stories have a type of macabre appeal and it was not uncommon for newspapers in the mid-19th century to report dog attacks in graphic detail. Dogs involved in attacks were described by breed and temperament and other circumstances considered relevant or of interest were noted. Dogs were very commonly reported as "a savage Bloodhound" or a "fierce Mastiff" or a "valuable Bulldog." At times, the injuries these dogs inflicted on their victims was reported in shockingly descriptive terms.

All these circumstances and details were included to add substance and interest to a story. A headline reading, "Child attacked by fierce Siberian Bloodhound" sounds much more menacing and interesting than the headline "Child bitten by dog." Bloodhounds in the latter part of the 1800s were considered menacing animals, so it is not surprising to find them identified (correctly or incorrectly) in newspaper accounts of dog attacks.

But the overwhelming perception of Bloodhounds as fierce came not from actual reports of attacks, but rather from a fictional visual impression. In 1851, Harriet Beecher Stowe's novel *Uncle Tom's Cabin* began the first of 40 installments published in the abolitionist periodical, the *National Era.* On March 20, 1852, *Uncle Tom's Cabin* was released in book form and was enormously successful, selling over 300,000 copies the first year, becoming the best selling American novel of the 19th century. Before the turn of the century, it is estimated that over 2 million people read this dramatic portrayal of American slavery. Though the references to Bloodhounds in Stowe's novel were scant and may have contributed only nominally to the negative image of this breed, it was the stage productions or "Tom shows" which most negatively influenced the reputation of the Bloodhound.

Stage dramatizations of fictional works were not properly regulated by copyright laws at the time, and within a year of the publication of *Uncle Tom's Cabin,* a number of stage productions based on the novel were already in progress. The success of these productions cannot be overstated; it is estimated that over 3 million people viewed some form of stage production based on the novel.[11] In American theaters, one version or another of *Uncle Tom's Cabin* was being staged continuously for nearly 79 years (1852–1930).

Some of these plays remained faithful to Stowe's plot, but many of these productions were little more than minstrel shows, loosely based on the novel but with grossly exaggerated caricatures of African-Americans and full of melodrama. Producers of these shows quickly noticed an intense and emotional reaction from the audience to one scene in particular, that of the escaped slave Eliza, baby in arms, fleeing barefoot across the frozen Ohio River from a pack of pursuing Bloodhounds. The dramatic impact this scene had on the audience was not lost on producers, and they quickly capitalized on this imagery. The "Bloodhound pursuit" of Eliza became the dramatic highpoint of many of the "Tom Shows."

By 1880 it was noted that no production of *Uncle Tom's Cabin* was complete without a pack of Bloodhounds and even the poorest of wandering troupes kept a pack of dogs to play out this dramatic scene. In addition to the on-stage attention given to this scene, many playbills and posters promoting the stage productions began featuring the "Bloodhound pursuit" with, of course, all the dogs looking suitably menacing and vicious. Many of these playbills touted their dogs to be "fierce Siberian Bloodhounds." The probability of all the troupes touring the country in the 1890s having purebred Russian/Siberian Bloodhounds or any purebred Bloodhound is practically nil. While it is certainly possible that some of these traveling shows may have had true Siberian Bloodhounds, as there were breeding facilities that supplied some of the larger productions with purebred dogs, all evidence indicates that purebred Bloodhounds (of any variety) would have been the exception and not the rule.

Playbill for a stage production of *Uncle Tom's Cabin*: Bloodhounds chasing the escaped slave Eliza and her baby across the river.
Photo Credit: Special Collections, University of Virginia Library.

But this ploy was successful in promoting and selling the show, as born out by the reviews and editorials written by newspaper staff and the viewing public. One viewer wrote, "How the barking of these dogs behind the scenes used to make us catch our breath! That alone was worth the price of admission…"

Producers, always looking to expand on a commodity, began to use Bloodhounds as sidewalk props in front of opera houses and theaters to promote and draw attention to the upcoming performance. A review of the Nevada Theater describes the atmosphere that surrounded many of these events:

"As soon as the doors were thrown open the body of the house was soon filled up and at 8 o'clock many went away on account of not being able to hardly find standing room…The street exhibition of the bloodhounds worked people up to the highest pitch, and if some of the people had been compelled to sell some of their already scant wardrobe they would have done so just to see the bloodhounds perform…"

Nevada State Journal, Saturday, April 22, 1882

In addition to sidewalk exhibitions, elaborate parades were often staged on the afternoon of the show. The parades were a popular attraction and included a brass band, actors marching in dress costume and, of course, a pack of Bloodhounds.

The following review of a performance of *Uncle Tom's Cabin* at the Ming Opera House in Helena, Montana, provides us with an invaluable example of how mood, imagery and drama can create an enduring perception or belief that will often become fixed in the public's mind:

"Perhaps the most interesting scene in the whole piece—or at least the most stirring—is the one in which the bloodhounds (four in number—big and terrible) are in pursuit of Eliza and her child. And where they are seen following the fugitives across the drifting cake ice on the Ohio river and close upon them, the interest becomes intense. Indeed, so far as the brutes are concerned, there is no acting, for true to their own ferocious instincts their thirst for blood is evidenced by their savage baying and eagerness to get at the prey. Sometimes, too, the beasts have been known, in their eagerness, to break loose from the restraining leash and to leap upon the fleeing ones with savage fury. This, however, seldom happens, for great care is exercised to guard against such accidents, for the consequences might be terrible. But, however risky the introduction of bloodhounds on the stage may be to the people in the play, they cannot be dispensed with, for in these days *Uncle Tom's Cabin* without them would not satisfy the public."

Daily Helena Independent, August 8, 1882

This review is enlightening on a number of levels. It describes not only the immediate entertainment, but also the formation of lasting impressions. The reviewer describes the use and staging of Bloodhounds to create an image (to sell tickets and dramatize a play). It also shows how the audience and reviewers alike bought rather easily and fervently into an obvious and deliberately manipulated portrayal of Bloodhounds. For a drama to be entertaining it needs villains, monsters or frightening obstacles to overcome. Being chased by a pack of baying, fierce Bloodhounds tapped into a primal fear humans have of predators and was therefore great entertainment.

One can't help but point out that, despite the insistence of the reviewer that Bloodhounds have a "ferocious instinct" and that it was "risky" for the actors to have these dogs on the set, many times the show managers would solicit the young boys of the town to serve as dog walkers at the parade before the show. These boys would then be given free tickets to the show for helping to lead these "ferocious" Bloodhounds in the parade. But reasoning often needs to be suspended for entertainment, and Tom Shows were great entertainment. By 1879, approximately 50 Tom Shows were on the road and by the 1890s there were between four and five hundred Tom Shows touring the country.[12]

There can be no doubt that this type of media hype had a tremendous influence on the public's perception as to the nature and disposition of the Bloodhound. And as is often the case with the perverse nature of humans, for every person who feared a Bloodhound, there seemed to be a person who sought this type of dog out for precisely that reason. An inescapable part of human nature is the need for some people to increase their sense of power or influence by obtaining things that serve to intimidate, frighten, or impress others. And there is no question that dogs can empower their owners by intimidating others.

When the media portrays a particular breed as vicious, there is an immediate increase in the number of substandard owners of that breed. There was a direct correlation between the popularization of Bloodhounds as fierce and an increase in their population among substandard owners, and therefore an increase in Bloodhound attacks in the later part of the 1800s.

Remember, by 1880, it was declared that no Tom Show was complete without a pack of menacing Bloodhounds. No small coincidence that the highest number of severe and fatal attacks by Bloodhounds occurred during the decade to follow (1880–1889), with 18 severe/fatal attacks in this decade in only a ten-state area (See Appendix A).

Three factors are at work here: the media's attention and diligence in reporting and identifying specific breed attacks, the fictional use of Bloodhounds as fierce, and the subsequent effect this had on increasing the popularity of this breed with poor quality or abusive owners.

Evidence of an increase in poor quality owners is found in an increase in the number of reports of cruel acts associated with this breed. Cruelty against animals has never been considered particularly unusual or newsworthy, so to see reports of these incidents in the newspapers during this decade (1880–1889) indicates a change in the degree or amount of cruelty. A few examples of deliberate acts of cruelty with and against Bloodhounds in this decade include:

1880—Two men are arrested for unchaining a large Bloodhound and inciting the dog to attack a homeless youth. The boy was severely bitten and taken to New York Hospital.

1880—Owner matches Siberian Bloodhound against prize-fighter for entertainment in St. Louis. After a long battle the dog is finally kicked to death by prize-fighter.

1880—Man breeding Bloodhounds in New Jersey is gravely injured by the dogs when in a drunken stupor he starts to beat the chained dogs with a piece of wood.

1888—Man arrested for cruelty when walking his Bloodhound in New York City; he allows the dog to attack and terribly injure a small black and tan dog named Gip. Bail was set at $100 for cruelty to animals, as he made no attempt to stop his dog from mauling the small dog.

1889—Man arrested in Milford, Connecticut, for ordering his Bloodhound to attack and kill another man trespassing on this property.

These incidents were newsworthy because they were not the run-of-the-mill type of abuse and violence regularly seen with animals.

Bloodhound attacks became so frequent and so frequently expected that even some in the media could not help but comment on the "art becomes reality" aspect of Bloodhound attacks in the late 1800s. In 1898, a *New York Times* article called a Bloodhound attack on a woman in New York City an "Impromptu Open-Air Uncle Tom's Cabin Performance."[13]

While the *New York Times* article was a deliberate mixing of fact and fiction, this was almost certainly the exception, as most people and other media sources had a much more difficult time separating fact from fiction when it came to Bloodhounds. Clearly the media hype influenced the reputation of the Bloodhound among the general public. A few fanciers of the breed understood the dynamics and made attempts to educate the public about the true nature of the Bloodhound.

Perhaps the most insightful summary of the Bloodhound dilemma was given in 1892, when the following editorial was printed:

"I have heard it said that Mrs. Stowe, in her *Uncle Tom's Cabin,* did much toward bringing upon the bloodhound his disrepute. To see if this were so I read over Mrs. Stowe's book recently and was surprised to find that she only once alluded to bloodhounds in all her highly colored narrative, and never a single time brought them on the scene. She had other objects in view without going out of her way to malign a family of dogs. But those who dramatized Mrs. Stowe's story used the bloodhound with great realistic effect, and none of the wandering troupes which have played this drama has been so poor that it has not had a pack of dogs. But I have never known a troupe to have a pack of real bloodhounds. Instead they have mongrels of various kinds, but always mongrels that looked savage and bloodthirsty. The bloodhound is not only not savage, but does not look so. On the contrary, he is amiable in disposition and has a singularly dignified and benevolent expression."

The Daily News, April 8, 1892

But any reasoning or insight fell on deaf ears, as the public was interested in being entertained, not educated. And these dogs did entertain; so much so that we may venture to say the dogs out-acted all other "Tom Show" performers. The canine "actors" gave such credible performances that a half-century of viewers were thoroughly convinced that Bloodhounds were a fierce and savage breed of dog.

The recognition of any Bloodhound characteristics in a mixed breed dog was usually all the identification needed to label the dog a Bloodhound or "part Bloodhound." The term Bloodhound was used for dogs that were clearly not purebred, but may have shown any traits that could be attributed to this breed. Once the dog could be recognized as having any Bloodhound characteristic, this appeared to be sufficient identification and there was no further attempt to determine what other breed(s) contributed to the genetic make-up of the dog.

We find an example of this with the previously discussed case of Camp Sumter and the court martial transcript of Commandant Henry Wirz. The United States Government's (War Department) findings of the court in Specification #11 list the dogs used by the Confederate army at Andersonville Prison as "ferocious and bloodthirsty animals, called bloodhounds…" There is no evidence to indicate that these dogs were the "true" or St. Hubert's Bloodhound or the breed we now recognize as a Bloodhound. By all accounts the dogs at Andersonville prison were a mixed lot; perhaps part Bloodhound and part unknown. Here also we find that the term Bloodhound was not used so much to identify breed but to identify function (i.e., tracking or hunting down of escaped Union soldiers).

In additional to all the different types or varieties of Bloodhounds, and mixes thereof, there were also outright imposters. An 1855 report of court proceedings in New York City lists the complaints made by two separate individuals for the injuries they received after being attacked by dogs. Along with a recounting of the injuries inflicted on the victims, the following report was given:

"Mr. O'Connor made complaint yesterday before Justice Pearcey, of having been attacked in his yard by a large yellow dog belonging to a baker named

Schaffer…German bakers and rum-sellers are almost without exception, provided with ferocious brutes resembling bloodhounds." [14]

It is obvious that any attempt to sort out which dogs were true Bloodhounds (by either breed or function) or to attempt to classify the behavior of any of these dogs by breed would be an exercise in futility. Not only is it impossible to determine individual breeds, but it is also irrelevant. The behavior of these Bloodhound-type dogs was either the direct result of human encouragement for aggressiveness or the direct result of humans failing to control or use reasonable care with these animals.

Unfortunately, none of the true aficionados of the Bloodhound, who so ardently defended their reputation in the 1800s, lived to witness the vindication of the breed they so admired. During the height of the breed's popularity, the voices of the true admirers of the Blood-hound were lost in a clamor of rumors and hysteria. The public could not or cared not to see beyond the media hyped image of the breed and recognize that the extreme behaviors of a small number of dogs were the direct result of the cruel use and mismanagement of these dogs by violent and abusive owners.

However, those who defended the "true" Bloodhound so fervently were guilty of the same stereotyping of which they complained so loudly. Their claim was that the behaviors of the Cuban Bloodhounds and other Bloodhound imposters had tarnished the reputation and prejudiced the public against their breed. Their defense of the Bloodhound often became 'it is not our British hounds that behave so ferociously, it is the fierce Cuban Bloodhound, mistaken for our dogs, that has brought disrepute to the breed.'

After thirty-three Cuban Bloodhounds were shipped to Florida in 1840 to aid in the capture of the Seminole Indians, eleven of them were taken by the Army to Garey's Ferry on Black Creek, located about thirty miles southwest of Jacksonville. The dogs were being trained to hunt their new quarry (Seminole Indians) and were being worked in field trials.

The arrival of these dogs from Cuba and their subsequent use by the Army was a politically charged and newsworthy event. As such, a correspondent from the *Savannah Georgian* visited Garey's Ferry in March 1840 to report on the use of the Bloodhounds by the Army and dryly observed:

"Eleven of these Florida bloodhounds, alias Cuba curs, are now at this post, feasting upon their six pounds of fresh beef per day…

"As to their ferocity, it is all humbug—a child may fondle with them. They have been more grossly misrepresented than any set of animals in the world, the army not excepted."[15]

Cuban Bloodhound, Siberian Bloodhound, British Bloodhound—it matters little, for when these breeds left the hands of those looking for a vicious tracking, attack, or guard dog, severe and fatal attacks by these breeds virtually disappeared from newspaper reports.

As owners looking for a new intimidation dog turned their attentions in the early 20th century towards the Bulldog and German Shepherd, the Bloodhound population stabilized and Bloodhound ownership largely returned to the true admirers of the breed. This scenario would repeat itself over the next century; as certain breeds became increasingly popular in negative functions, and subsequently more popular with substandard owners, incidents of aggression within the breed would increase. When breed popularity decreases with substandard owners and returns into the hands of more serious enthusiasts, incidents of aggression decrease.

CHAPTER 3

Creating Dangerous Dogs: The Newfoundland and the Northern Breeds

The Newfoundland

Like the Bloodhound, the Newfoundland is another breed of dog that figured predominantly in fatal and severe attacks in the latter part of the 19th century, yet has ceased to be an issue in fatalities in the 20th century. The Newfoundland dog was commonly found in episodes of canine aggression from the late 1800s into the early 1900s. In just one city, Chicago, there were two fatal attacks by a Newfoundland dog during this time period. However, after the second decade of the 20th century, the Newfoundland dog all but disappears from reported cases of attacks.

As with Bloodhounds, the question becomes, how is it that this breed was over-represented in aggressive encounters with humans during one era and vastly under-represented during another time period?

Most people today have an image of the Newfoundland dog as a large, black, shaggy dog that has been known to be used by fishermen and to aid drowning victims. While this perception is unchanged from the uses and image that 19th century America had of the New-foundland, it appears this breed of dog played another important role in the 1800s that accounts for its appearance in severe and fatal attacks on humans. Newspaper accounts indicate that Newfoundlands were used frequently as guard and protection dogs during the late 1800s. This may seem strange to many, as the Newfoundland breed is usually associated with humane service towards man. However, the basis for using the Newfoundland as guard dogs in the 19th century is supported by the description of the breed in the 1911 *Encyclopedia Britannica:* "They are easily taught to retrieve on land or water, and their strength, intelligence and fidelity make them specially suitable as watchdogs or guardians." Additionally, the Newfoundland is a working breed, originally bred by the early settlers of Newfoundland Island in Canada to pull sleds, hunt and guard.

The Newfoundland dog seems to have been exceedingly popular in the latter part of the 19th century, and like the Bloodhound was one of the first breeds registered by the newly formed American Kennel Club in 1886. Newspapers of the day were filled with tales of everyday life with Newfoundland dogs. Along with the more mundane events of owners and their dogs there were also numerous reports of Newfoundlands being alternately heroic or vicious. The newspapers at the time seemed to relish a good "dog rescues boy" story as much as a "dog attacks boy" story, and the Newfoundland dog seemed to provide much fodder for both these human-interest stories.

The popularity of the breed, their use as guard dogs, and incidents of physical abuse ensures that a number of Newfoundland dogs would be found in cases of aggression against humans.

Most dogs suffer abuse and provocation without retaliation and this often leads to reckless behavior by some individuals. The forgiving nature of dogs allows most humans to escape unscathed from negligent and cruel acts towards our canine companions, but not always. An 1890 article entitled "A Dog's Revenge" describes the events preceding a fatal mauling of an infant by a Newfoundland dog. And here again, 19th century accounts were brutally honest in detailing harsh treatment dogs received at the hands of humans and how this was believed to have contributed to an attack by the dog. The Newfoundland in this incident was recently obtained by a family and the mother "had occasion to punish the dog." How severely or what form of punishment was used on the dog was not described. The rest of the report goes on to tell how the woman then left the dog and infant on the front porch of the cabin and went down to the creek. When she returned she found the dog had killed the child.[1]

Human behavior is often even more inexplicable than canine behavior. In 1893, a 14-year-old boy for unknown reasons decided to kick a large Newfoundland dog he encountered on the streets of Cincinnati. It was reported in the newspapers that the dog "resented" the kick and responded by attacking the boy so savagely that he died from his injuries.[2]

Another case of a boy teasing a dog and the animal attacking an innocent girl occurred in Ohio in 1891. It was reported as follows:

"Yesterday evening, as the little daughter of James Walker was walking along a street, on the West Side, a boy jerked a bone from a Newfoundland dog with which he was playing, and threw it, the bone falling on the pavement near the little girl's feet. The dog made a rush for it, knocking the girl down. She fell upon the bone, hiding it from view, when the dog planted its teeth in her cheek. He bit her several times, and her face and neck were terribly mangled before the dog could be driven away."

Weekly News, Mansfield, Ohio, June 4, 1891

Although the history of the Newfoundland was based in guarding, hunting and sledding, it was with the increased use of the breed in the late 19th century as guard dogs and the physical abuse directed towards many of these dogs that explains their appearance in incidents of aggression towards humans.

Rabies (Hydrophobia)

Interestingly there seemed to be a disproportionate number of reported "mad" or "rabid" Newfoundland dogs attacking people. While some of these dogs were described with obvious signs of the disease, it appears that others were suspected of being rabid because the behavior (attack, bite) was not within the expected temperament of the breed.

It is not possible to know whether the scores of reports of "mad" Newfoundland dogs were an aberration, whether the breed was so popular that there would understandably be increased cases of rabies within the breed, or whether the aggressiveness in these dogs seemed so out of character that rabies seemed the only reasonable explanation for attacks on humans. Though there exists a remote possibility of rabies involvement in any of the severe/fatal attacks during the 19th century, undoubtedly most severe dog attacks were due to non-rabies related aggression.

While rabies was greatly, and to some degree legitimately, feared, deaths from the virus were not nearly as common as people believed. More than a few persons of some authority were quoted in the late 1800s and early 1900s as stating that the number of deaths and confirmed cases of rabies did not support the hysteria surrounding the disease. There is little question that the fear of rabies was much greater than the probability of contracting the disease.

While the incidence of rabies may have been limited, the fear of the disease was very real. Reports of individuals committing suicide after being bitten by a suspected rabid dog illustrate the hysteria that could so easily be roused by even the suggestion of a rabid animal. Any abnormal behaviors in a dog could easily be a death sentence for that animal when a wave of rabies hysteria overcame a community. For these reasons it was vitally important for the people in the late 1800s and early 1900s to have been observant of normal versus abnormal canine behaviors. This could be one explanation for the insightful accounts of dog attacks reported in the news. Understanding triggers or provocation that contributed to normal canine aggression would alleviate the fear that the dog was behaving erratically or unpredictably (a sign of rabies). Many dog bite articles paid special attention to differentiating between a "maddened" dog and a "mad" dog. It was common to find the dogs involved in attacks described as "an ill tempered brute, but not mad" or "an enraged, but not mad dog."

The rabies virus is fascinating in that in order for the disease to transmit from host to host, the virus requires a change in the infected animal's behavior to cause it to bite another victim. The virus accomplishes this by increasing the aggression in some animals, causing them to bite indiscriminately. This behavior change usually does not occur until the end stages of the disease, when other symptoms of the disease are also visible. Once the virus is transmitted through the saliva of an infected animal, the incubation or latent period of the disease normally lasts 3–12 weeks. During this time the infected animal usually appears healthy and its behavior is not noticeably affected. But once the virus has migrated to the

A dog with late stage rabies: CDC's Public Health
Image Library, ID#2626

central nervous system (spinal cord and brain), symptoms begin to appear and the disease spreads rapidly. The first phase of symptoms of rabies tends to be subtle, lasting only two to three days. In the second phase, also known as the "furious" phase, signs of the disease become much more obvious, with dogs displaying erratic behaviors, including episodes of aggression, ingesting inedible objects, disorientation and other abnormal behavior. The third and final stage of symptoms is unmistakable and lasts approximately 2–4 days. Here the animal may appear to be choking; there is a dropping of the lower jaw, and the inability to swallow—leading to the drooling and foaming of saliva ("foaming at the mouth"). Paralysis then occurs and the animal rapidly enters into a coma and dies.

Dogs in the final stages of rabies were seemingly not difficult to diagnose. However, it was the first stage of symptoms when signs were more subtle, where errors would be most often found as to what was driving an attack (i.e., rabies versus normal canine aggression).

An 1889 dog attack in Hoboken, N.J., appears to be a legitimate case of rabies infection. Although no mention is made of physical signs of rabies, the behavior of this dog is clearly not the behavior seen in normal types of canine aggression. The byline to the article, "Men and animals bitten by a dog attacking all in its way," is a common description of the behavior in reported cases of rabid dogs. The account of this attack begins with a dog running into a stable near the railroad station and biting a man working there. The dog is then reported as running out into the street and attacking a young boy at a fruit stand. On its way down the street, the dog attacks another dog, before running towards the docks. There the dog darts into a group of six men, biting one of them. Before the police catch up with the dog, it had also attacked and bitten a draught horse.[3]

This type of indiscriminate snapping and random biting appears typical of rabid dogs.

Non-rabid dogs involved in severe/fatal aggression are typically very focused during an attack, choosing one victim and attempting to return to that victim even after being pulled or beaten off.

Rabid dogs were often reported biting multiple types of animals in rapid succession or, as the previous article stated, "attacking all in its way," whether it be cows, horses, cats, other dogs or humans. This type of attack was greatly distressing, as people feared not necessarily the physical damage done by the dog during an attack, but the transmission of rabies and ultimate death from the disease process of the virus.

An exceedingly rare event was the death of a person due to an apparently rabid dog attacking with such forceful aggression as to cause traumatic wounds resulting in the immediate death of the victim (i.e., loss of blood, shock).

A few cases were found where dogs attacked with such ferocity that it must have seemed to the persons of the time that rabies could be the only explanation. Reviewing some of these suspected cases of rabies reveals dogs exhibiting the same behaviors found in most cases of severe/fatal aggression found in non-rabid dogs—that is, attacking one victim with unrelenting intensity and then not attacking others attempting to interfere. In deference to the subjective beliefs of the witnesses at the time these cases were not included in the listing of attacks.

However, a fatal attack could be found in 1894 which appears to be a legitimate case of a rabid dog. The attack occurred in Dallas, Texas, and involved a St. Bernard reported to be "mad." The dog had bitten seven people, killed two cats and attacked another dog. One of the seven people attacked was "Albert Adams, a negro boy, who was bitten so badly that he died from his wounds."[4]

Obviously, since accurate laboratory testing was not available at the time, rabies could only be determined by observation of behavior and by physical signs of the disease, certainly far from a foolproof system. However, since many a person's life depended on observations of whether the aggression was due to rabies, and the people of the time showed a rather acute understanding of what constituted normal canine aggression, it is within reason to concede to their conclusions as to whether a dog attack was due to rabies infection. If anything, fear, bordering on hysteria, may have made the incidence of rabies over-reported in severe or fatal attacks by dogs.

There was no hope for a cure until the 1880s, when Louis Pasteur, the famed chemist and bacteriologist, began studying the disease. Pasteur was able to isolate the virus and in May 1884 produced the first rabies vaccine for dogs. In July 1885 Pasteur successfully tested the vaccine on a human. In 1887, two years after Pasteur's treatment for rabies was developed, a rather interesting observation was made:

"It is noticeable that notwithstanding the numerous cases of bites by vicious dogs which have been recorded this summer, hardly a suggestion has been made of hydrophobia. Is it because Pasteur has robbed the disease of its terrors, or is it simply because the good sense of the people is improving?"[5]

This makes sense. Once a cure for an ailment becomes available, the terror associated with the disease decreases.

While rabies was a continuous worry during the 19th century in the United States, the disease was not as feared, and was noted to be less of an issue, in the Northern regions of Canada. However, other issues dealing with "normal" canine aggression could be found in the cold and harsh Northern landscape where dogs performed a function exclusive to these snowbound regions.

The Northern Breeds

Not surprisingly, most of the severe and fatal attacks by the Northern breeds occurred in Alaska, Canada, and the Northern Territories.

If it seemed that separating the Bloodhound breed/types was a difficult task, attempting to make correct breed identifications with the Northern breeds involved in attacks would require supernatural powers. The only information available about the breed or type of dog involved in fatalities in Alaska, Canada and the Northern Territories was that the dogs may have been one of the following breed/types: Husky, Siberian husky, Alaskan husky, Malamute, Alaskan malamute, Eskimo dog, Labrador dog, Newfoundland dog, Arctic sled dog, sled dog, sleigh dog, sledge dog, wolf dog, wolf hybrid and any dog that might have been a mixture of these types/breeds. Many times the victim was described as being killed by a dog team or in a dog lot. Once again, breed identification in cases of aggression is not only impossible to document accurately, but it will be seen that the identification of individual dog breeds is of no relevance in the understanding or recognition of the circumstances which directly contributed to the development of severe aggression in these dogs.

Fatal attacks by the Northern breeds in the late 1800s and early 1900s were not considered terribly unusual or unexpected. The dogs kept in these frigid environs were considered only once removed from their direct ancestor, the wolf. Today, we accept the fact that people will die in automobile crashes as a necessary evil of being able to travel and move goods from place to place. One hundred years ago, sled dogs provided the only means of communication, human transport and exchange of goods during the long winter months in Alaska, Northern Canada and the Northern Territories. Sled dogs were often risky business and the human deaths associated with keeping these dogs, though repugnant, were considered the cost of doing business.

There is no denying the danger posed by some of these animals. A century ago, most sled dogs were semi-wild, poorly socialized, poorly fed, maintained as a pack, and treated harshly. Needless to say, this is the formula to use if one wishes to create a dangerous dog. How many Eskimos or native people were killed by these dogs will never be known. Even when the victims of these dogs were white settlers, there are only scant references to the incident. Most times, cases of fatal dog attacks by sled dogs are only mentioned in stories or reports on related matters. An important factor in the lack of documented cases of fatal attacks was the remoteness of the areas, poor communication and obvious lack of news-papers and community facilities (clerks, courts, police, medical examiners, etc.).

The following case of a fatal dog attack in Canada demonstrates the remoteness and difficulty in getting both information and persons out of these areas. A letter was received on April 28, 1925, at the Royal Canadian Mounted Police post in Regina, Saskatchewan, Canada, announcing the death of a woman at Chesterfield Inlet, in the northwestern extremity of Keewatin, on Hudson Bay near the Arctic. The letter gave news of the circumstances that caused the death of Mrs. S.G. Clay. On Sept. 19, 1924, Mrs. Clay, the wife of a Royal Canadian Mounted Police Sergeant, was walking alone near the police camp when a sled dog attacked her. Immediately every other dog in the pack joined in the attack. She had been severely mauled before help from the mounted police camp arrived. Her leg had been so terribly lacerated that amputation was deemed necessary. The nearest surgeon was 1,000 miles away in Manitoba, so the local missionary and a member of the Mounted Police decided to take on the task. The unfortunate woman died two days later.[6]

The fact that this attack occurred in September of 1924 and news of it was not received until April of 1925 demonstrates the difficulty in getting information out of these desolate areas. No doubt, a special effort was made to relay this news because of the familiar aspect; it was news being sent about one mounted police wife to the wife of another mounted police officer, who, like the victim, was once stationed at this remote Hudson Bay post. It is no small irony that the news of Mrs. Clay's death was sent from Hudson Bay to Saskatchewan by dog team.

Occasionally, an article or report on the viciousness of the Northern breeds would list recent human fatalities caused by the sled dogs of the region. An article entitled "Devil Dogs of Labrador," published in 1908, talks of the sled dogs on the desolate coast of Labrador. This coastal area was reported to be "peopled by 4,000 whites, 1,500 Eskimos, and frequented every summer by 30,000 Newfoundland fisher folk in the quest of cod."[7] The only means of transportation in this area was by boat in summer and by dog team in winter. The author talks of the violent nature and behavior of the sled dogs in this region and lists the attacks that had occurred recently on the Labrador coast by sled dogs:

"Some years ago, during the summer, at Hebron, dogs killed an Eskimo boy of 13, who was dragging a seal from his father's boat to their tent…At Hopedale an Eskimo boy and girl were killed and devoured…At Nain, dogs dragged a missionary's baby out of its cradle and reduced it to bone before the distracted mother found out…At Dommo, dogs devoured a middle-aged woman before help could arrive…At Bardana, dogs killed a fifteen-year-old girl going to a well for water."

A few years earlier, in 1903, another article about the dogs of Labrador recounted two fatalities that occurred the year before:

"In Cartwright, a child wandered from home and when the distracted mother flew to where a pack of angry dogs were ravening, she found nothing but the bones of her offspring…A little girl was so badly mangled by them at Punchbowl last year that she never recovered."[8]

Obviously, none of these attacks are verifiable. But there is more than a ring of truth to these accounts, as locations, victim's ages and small details of the attack are given. Also lending credibility is the fact that these victims fit the profile of most dogs attack (i.e., infants, children wandering away from parents, and/or vulnerable persons walking alone). The accuracy of these individual attacks is not of paramount importance because there is little doubt that some of these dogs posed a significant danger to humans. Knowing exactly which humans they attacked is not critical in the examination of the forces involved in sled dog aggression.

There was little disagreement that the sled dogs used in the late 1800s and early 1900s were a fierce lot. There is also little disagreement about the fact that these dogs were treated very harshly. An additional, but necessary, danger was the maintaining of sled dogs as an active functioning pack.

While acts of extreme cruelty towards animals are still very prevalent today, it certainly is not the norm. One century ago, extreme cruelty towards sled dogs *was* the norm.

"They may be beaten into submission, but that will not prevent them still snarling their hatred. They may be starved into apparent docility and then die suddenly, with teeth fast locked in a brother's throat."
> "The Wolf-Dog of the North," *The New York Times,* July 8, 1900
> —From *Harper's Weekly*

"They are the fiercest of any brutes trained to be of service to mankind; they will attack anything they believe weaker than themselves, and they are only kept in subjection by the unceasing use of the lash."
> "The Dogs of Labrador," *The Chronicle,* January 29, 1903

Besides the "unceasing use of the lash" and being "beaten into submission," sled dogs were often in a state of near starvation. Although fed well in the winter months when their energy was needed to pull heavy loads over long distances, in the summer months it was common to let the dogs forage for themselves. Many an attack on a person was recognized to be the result of this hungry pack condition. Unlike most descriptions of dog attacks where the victim was torn, lacerated or bitten by the dog(s), many of the victims of sled dogs were reportedly "devoured." After reviewing the circumstances and conditions of sled dogs in the early 20th century it is fair to say that this term was meant literally and was not used for dramatization.

In direct contrast to the elaborate recounting of Bloodhound attacks in the big city newspapers in the U.S., details of dog attacks in the remote areas of the North usually contained only a fleeting reference to a death by dogs. There was little sensationalism in these accounts and it is doubtful that the term "devoured" was used to embellish the story, as there was really no story attached to these attacks.

Most dogs found on the mainland United States did not operate and work together in large packs, as did the sled dogs of the North. Dogs in more densely populated and moderate climates, even if not fed, were able to scrounge for food near garbage dumps, homes or farms and usually had a variety of wild or domesticated animals on which to prey. The desolate and harsh Northern regions had much less to offer dogs that needed to fend for themselves. All resources available to sled dogs were limited and so their options for survival were also severely limited. Additionally, these dogs were not only poorly socialized with humans, but often the socialization they did have was decidedly negative. In extreme environments or in conditions with limited choices, extreme behaviors are more apt to occur.

The conditions we find with these dogs are: physically powerful dogs, very poorly socialized with humans, often starving with severely limited food resources, either tethered together as a pack or allowed to roam loose as a pack. Given these circumstances, predation does not seem unreasonable or exaggerated.

Another reason to take the term "devoured" seriously is that throughout the vast expanse of the Northern regions this description is used consistently over three decades (1900–1930). While an argument could be made that most accounts of fatalities and predation by sled dogs a century ago cannot be substantiated, there is a fully documented recent case which duplicates most of the conditions and pack dynamics reported in fatal attacks by sled dogs a century ago.

In August 1998, a family of four, consisting of a husband, wife and two male children, aged 8 and 10, arrived on Zacharias Island, off the Labrador coast. The island was inhabited by a team of eight Labrador/Husky sled dogs. The dogs had been left on the uninhabited island to roam during the summer months. The family was picking berries on the island when the wife became separated from her husband and two children. After hearing his wife scream, the husband found her being attacked by the dogs. Throwing rocks at the dogs managed to disperse them from the woman, but she was already dead. The older child ran back to the boat to get matches, so a fire could be built to keep the dogs away from the woman's body until help could arrive. The dogs left the area where the woman's body lay, and circled the shoreline. When the father and younger son arrived at the boat they found the dogs feeding on the body of the older son. Again they threw rocks at the dogs, but this time the dogs did not disperse and they turned on the father and remaining son. Only by running into the water were they able to escape.[9]

This case involved predation and both victims were partially consumed. Although these dogs were not found to be starved, the attack is consistent with behaviors seen in situations where sled dogs function as a pack. The dynamics of group hunting and feeding, dogs operating as a social unit without owner direction, poor socialization with humans, and territorial aggression all contribute to the likelihood of dogs operating under these conditions having an increased probability of aggressive encounters with humans.

If we subtract a century from the 1998 attack, add in some wolf strain, and consider a hungrier pack of dogs, the accounts of fatalities and predation in the earlier 1900s seem almost understated.

In 1903 the following statement describes the sled dogs and the atmosphere surrounding the settlements:

"The coast folk find them indispensable, yet live in fear of them. No man
ventures abroad without his whip, every woman carries a stout club; it is death to
a child to get among them."[10]

In more modern times (1961), the Royal Canadian Mounted Police decided to replace the native Huskies with a breed from Siberia after a series of attacks and fatalities by sled dogs. The RCMP commented:

"Natives usually let their dogs run wild in the summer, and the semi-starved
animals with a vicious wolf strain not deeply buried often attack humans,
especially children. Last year two persons were killed by sled dogs. These native
dogs are a menace by instinct. If you happen to fall, they'll be on you—just for
something to eat."

The Valley Independent, December 12, 1961

Time and again, much of the aggressiveness found in the Northern breeds is blamed on their affinity to the wolf. Breeding the native dogs with wolves was commonly practiced and, considering the condition and treatment these animals received, it is little wonder they would be a danger.

While it is of no significance whether sled dogs were part Husky, Malamute, or any other breed, the crossing of these breeds with wolves is relevant. Although dogs are the direct descendent of the wolf, dogs are nevertheless domesticated, meaning that over the centuries, dogs have developed behaviors that allow for bonding with humans.

Wolves are still very much wild animals. Adding wolf genes to a domesticated dog reduces the ability to bond with humans or the sociability of these animals. One century ago, sled dogs were poorly socialized with humans, treated harshly, and a pack mentality was a major factor in both their social behaviors and in their function as sled dogs. Add wolf genes into this already dangerously diminished bond with people and it is not difficult to see how aggression towards humans developed.

◆ ◆ ◆

For thousands of years, dogs have been inexorably interwoven into the lives of humans. However, it is extremely rare to find a person who has intimate knowledge or personal dealings with the two most extreme, yet diametrically different, types of canine behaviors, namely fatal aggression against humans versus dogs sacrificing their lives in the service of mankind.

Miss Emily Morgan was a Red Cross nurse serving in Alaska during the 1920s. For 18 months, Miss Morgan braved the fierce cold and blizzards in the Aleutian Islands to provide medical care to the native people. While living there she also worked as a matron at the Methodist Women's Missionary Society for Destitute Waifs. Here she helped nurse back to health a small Aleutian orphan child named Alice Devlin. The child had been brought to the mission after her mother was killed by starving Huskies. Although it is mentioned that the child arrived "with a scar on her sunken cheeks made by the dogs," it was not explained how the child came to survive this attack by the pack of sled dogs which killed her mother.

After serving in the Aleutian Islands, Miss Morgan went to Nome, Alaska. In 1925, Nome was in the midst of a diphtheria epidemic and Miss Morgan was reported to be the only Red Cross nurse in town to minister to those suffering from diphtheria. Her patients came to be the recipients of the serum which was delivered by the famous sled dog relay from Nenana to icebound Nome, a distance of 674 miles which took 20 men and over 200 dogs. More than one sled dog died during this frantic run to deliver life-saving serum. The dogs which perished during this tremendously arduous journey had literally run themselves to death in service to their masters and mankind.

Perhaps Miss Morgan never gave any conscious thought to the fact that she was a first-person witness to the absolute worst canine behaviors towards a human and also the absolute best behaviors that most dogs contribute so freely and frequently towards mankind.

Sled-dog: "*They are accustomed to hard work, scanty fare and ill-usage; yet they never desert their post or forsake their master*" (Francis Butler, 1860).

CHAPTER 4

How Popularity and Function Influence Aggression

From 1850 until 1899, there were dozens of different descriptions of dogs involved in severe and fatal attacks on humans. Some dogs were identified as a specific breed, others were described by their grouping (i.e., hound or spaniel), others by their function (i.e., sled dog or sheepdog), still others by their size (i.e., large dog) and some, simply by temperament (i.e., vicious dog).

Nearly half of the fatal attacks reported from 1850–1899 did not identify breed at all, describing the dog(s) primarily by temperament. The most popular descriptions were either a "savage" or "vicious" dog. Other times dogs were described simply by their physical condition ("large brown mongrel" or "starving dogs"). In 1888, a dog involved in a fatal attack on a 2-year-old boy in Zanesville, Ohio was identified as a "coal-mine dog." On the rarest of occasions a dog was very precisely identified, as in a case in 1893 when a woman was attacked and killed by a "black English Mastiff" in Kentucky.

Though the media in the 19th century was more attuned to presenting the triggers or causes for dog attacks, descriptions by breed or temperament were included to add interest or substance to a story. The case where a specific breed was identified in a news report was frequently accompanied by a description of the dog's immediate function. "Pet Collie," "Mastiff guard dog" and even "tramp Newfoundland" (presumably meaning an abandoned or stray dog) are found as additional clues to the behaviors of the specific dogs. Both the public and the media understood that these were relevant factors in attempting to understand cases of aggression and attacks.

The Mastiff

The Mastiff-type dog is an ancient breed, long used in human warfare, animal fighting, and guarding. The Mastiff-type dog is the progenitor of other giant breeds. Many of the fighting breeds and some of the scent hounds are also descended from the ancient Mastiff-type dogs.

In the Middle Ages, the primary function of the Mastiff became that of guardians of large estates. They were used to ward off intruders, poachers and undesirables from the lands of nobles and even less entitled landholders. Some of these dogs were known as Bandogs, being tied during the day and released in the evening to patrol and protect the homes of the wealthy. The function of the Mastiff in 19th century America was strikingly similar, except they were kept in much smaller confines, such as warehouses, factories, shops or livery stables. The manner of their keep was little changed, the dogs being chained during the day and then released at night.

It is no surprise that animals kept and prized for their protection and guarding abilities would be found in severe/fatal attacks on humans who trespassed and encountered these animals.

Here also, breed identifications are questionable, as one story of an attack on a little boy was reported to be a Mastiff in one newspaper and the same boy was reported to have been attacked by a Newfoundland in another newspaper covering the same incident. Dogs involved in attacks during the late 1800s are described as Mastiffs, English Mastiffs, or thoroughbred Mastiffs.

In 1891, it was reported that a "monster thoroughbred English Mastiff, kept by the Clark Thread Company as a watchdog" attacked two young boys. One boy was severely injured after the dog, "borne him to the ground and tore his scalp terribly."[1]

In 1893, a boy managed to survive an attack by a Mastiff due to his age and ability to crawl away from the chained animal. The 12-year-old was playing with a friend in a deserted coach and carriage shop in New York City. The owner kept a huge Mastiff dog chained at the shop. For some reason the boy came within reach of the dog and the animal grabbed him, savagely attacking him. The boy survived because "he contrived to crawl beyond the limits of the dog's tether."[2]

In 1878, in Bayonne, New Jersey, a large Mastiff dog escaped from his owner's yard and attacked a young girl on the street and, before anyone could intervene, killed her.

During the late 1800s there were a fair number of Mastiffs, chained in cellars or in deserted buildings, found in severe and fatal attacks. There is little doubt the harsh and isolated conditions in which they were kept were the forces behind the aggression in these dogs.

The Mastiff was overrepresented in reported attacks during the late 19th century because they were frequently used as guard dogs. When their popularity as guard dogs waned in the early 20th century and they were replaced by other protection breeds, severe and fatal attacks associated with this breed virtually disappeared.

◆ ◆ ◆

As Bloodhound, Newfoundland, and Mastiff attacks decreased dramatically beginning in the first decade of the 20th century, other breeds of dogs began emerging in reports of attacks as these new breeds caught the fancy of the American public and became popular.

Beginning in the 1900s, temperament descriptions are largely replaced with breed or function descriptions (i.e., Collie dog or police dog). The first half of the 20th century finds new and different breeds involved in fatal/severe attacks. Collies, Boston Terriers, St. Bernards, Airedale Terriers, Great Danes, Chow chows, German police dogs (German Shepherds),

Doberman Pinschers, and Huskies were only some of the new breeds seen in aggressive encounters with humans.

Collies

The Collie was technically a hold-over favorite from the 19th century, but the breed was not to reach the height of its popularity until the 20th century.

The Collie dog was well established in the United States during the 1800s. By the early 1900s this breed was already recognized as a hard-working, loyal farm dog and valuable companion animal. Like the Bloodhound and Newfoundland, the Collie was one of the earliest breeds recognized by the American Kennel Club, with the first dog registered in 1885. And like so many other breeds, there were different types of Collies and different names to describe the breed. Collie, Scotch Collie, Farm Collie, Smooth Collie, Rough Collie, Sheepdog, Shepherd dog and police dog all described a type of Collie dog.

In the first few decades of the 20th century there were numerous accounts of severe attacks by Collies reported in the newspapers of the day. And true to the reporting of the 19th century, early 20th century papers continued to reveal details believed to have contributed to the attack.

In 1915, a report is found of a "Collie Run Amuck." A large Collie was responsible for attacking two children on a street in Indianapolis. The dog's owner was not known, so the dog was captured and taken to a veterinary surgeon who declared the dog was not suffering from rabies. The article concludes with the explanation for the dog's aggressiveness: "It is believed the dog got lost and became frantic."[3]

A 10-year-old boy was attacked by a Scotch Collie in 1910. The "flesh and muscles of the boy's chest and both arms were torn by the teeth of the dog." This story is interesting because it reveals what would later (in modern-day attacks) become a familiar and common event—that is, persons being less than truthful about their involvement or actions towards a dog prior to an attack. Here the victim claims he was only shouting to his friend and the dog rushed out of the yard and attacked him. However, the constable investigating the incident wrote in his report that witnesses claimed this was not a true account of what transpired and that the dog was on the porch "and the boys were playing around the house and began to annoy the dog with sticks, and that the dog then attacked young Smith who was the leader among his tormenters."[4]

In 1913, a boy was bitten over 30 times by a Collie before being rescued. The dog was chained near an apartment in Tarrytown, N.Y., and attacked the boy when he attempted to pet it.[5]

In 1916, another account of an attack by a Collie on a young boy provides information which describes the classic triggers and circumstances found in dog attacks. The article reports that a 3-year-old boy was severely bitten in the head and face when he attempted to pet an old Collie on the head. The article goes on to state that "the dog, which was believed to be harmless, evidently mistook the boy's intentions in his semi-blindness."[6]

Fatal attacks on humans in which Collies were involved are found during the early to middle part of the 20th century, making Collies another example of a breed involved in increased severe/fatal attacks during a few decades and then becoming a non-issue in the decades to follow.

In 1922, a 7-year-old girl was killed by a Collie while playing in a friend's yard in New Bedford, Massachusetts. It was speculated at the time that the child was in possession of a doll which the Collie "wanted to recover." Apparently the child refused to relinquish the doll and the dog knocked her to the ground and then began attacking her. She died an hour later from dog bites to the head and face.

In Illinois, in 1930, another young girl was gravely injured by "six pedigreed Collie dogs" that escaped from a nearby kennel.

In November 1945, a young boy was killed by two Collies at the farm he was visiting with his parents in Roscoe, Texas.

There were also scattered cases of Collie mixes or Collies packed up with other dogs which resulted in fatalities during the first half of the 20th century. But Collies have never been considered a vicious breed of dog, not even at the time when there was a noticeable increase in severe and fatal attacks, and the reasons for this are not terribly surprising.

The Collie breed appeared to have much credit in the bank of public opinion by the time severe/fatal attacks by Collies began to be reported in the papers (around 1910). Collies had proven to be valuable and loyal working dogs and pets during the previous decades. Additionally, almost all functions associated with the Collie breed were positive (guarding sheep, herding, all-purpose farm dog, police dog and companion animal). Another bonus to the breed was the pages and pages of good press given to these dogs when they performed a service to their masters. As discussed in the chapter on farm dogs, Collies saved many a person from raging bulls and other dangers, and they often received the recognition they deserved for these acts of bravery and loyalty.

No small contribution to the positive image and popularity of the Collie was the 1919 publication of *Lad: A Dog,* a book which introduced the Collie on a much larger scale to the American public. The tales of Lad include rescuing an invalid child from a venomous snake, fighting off burglars, winning ribbons as a show dog and performing other heroic deeds. Eric Knight's novel *Lassie Come Home,* released first as a short story in 1938 and then in book form in 1940, would further endear the Collie breed in the heart and mind of the public.

The Collie breed had built a strong foundation as one of the "good breeds." This foundation would be permanently cemented with the release of the 1943 movie *Lassie Come Home* and later with the long-running *Lassie* television series (1954–1974).

It is clear how the Collie image was able to weather a decade or two of increased attacks and an occasional bit of bad press. The breed had so much credit to draw on and was so overwhelmingly portrayed in the media as a "good" breed that a handful of errant dogs could not tarnish the image of the breed.

Even through times of immense popularity and indiscriminate breeding, the Collie remained a steady and reliable breed. While some may rightly attribute this to overall breed temperament, a vital additional factor is that the Collie was bred, maintained and obtained almost exclusively for humane and positive functions. A person looking for an aggressive watchdog or an attack dog was not about to seek out a Collie. The huge media events surrounding the Collie did increase their popularity with the average American family, but did not substantially increase their popularity amongst substandard or aggressive owners.

St. Bernard

Like the Collie, the St. Bernard's popularity overlapped from the late 1800s into the early part of the 1900s. The St. Bernard presents a rather unique case of very sporadic episodes of severe/fatal aggression, seemingly unrelated to function. Attacks are found around the turn of the century, then the breed disappears from severe/fatal attack episodes, only reappearing in the 1970s, in which a spate of fatal attacks are found.

In the later part of the 1800s and early 1900s, the St. Bernard was fairly popular and an easily recognizable breed in the United States. Unlike the other breeds seen in fatalities during this time, the St. Bernard's popularity did not seem based on their use as guard dogs. Not only were the St. Bernard dogs involved in such attacks not defined as guard dogs, but the attacks did not occur in locations usually associated with guard dogs (i.e., factories, stables and business establishments).

An 1894 attack by a St. Bernard demonstrates again the unrelenting nature of some attacks, with the dog intently focused on returning to the primary target of his rage. Here again, we find a frenzied situation where rescuers swing objects madly at the dog and in the process injure other persons.

Mangled by a St. Bernard

"A full grown St. Bernard dog attacked and nearly killed 6-year-old George Barrett. The enraged animal had thrown the child down and was viciously biting it when the child's father, attracted by the screams of his son, came to the rescue. With a baseball bat he drove the dog away, but when Mrs. Barrett attempted to carry the child into the house the dog returned and again attacked the boy. There ensued a terrible battle between the man and the dog, during which Mr. Barrett in attempting to hit the animal, struck his wife, who was trying to protect the child, knocking her insensible. Finally an officer killed the savage beast. The child is in a precarious condition."

The News, Frederick, Maryland, July 25, 1894

In 1901, a 10-year-old boy was playing with his friends on a street in Paterson, N.J., when a large St. Bernard dog came rushing at him. The other boys scattered, but the dog seemed intent on this one particular boy, knocking him down and attacking him so savagely he died within minutes.

The breed does not appear again in fatal attacks until 70 years later in 1972, when a St. Bernard killed a young girl playing with him in California. The breed went on to be involved in an increased number of fatalities during the next decade and then only in a few sporadic cases found every decade or so following.

During this seven-decade-long void of reported fatal attacks in the U.S. (although some non-fatal attacks were reported), a few fatalities due to St. Bernard dogs could be found in other parts of the world.

This is interesting on many levels. The St. Bernard has never been associated with negative functions; if anything, the only functions assigned to the breed are extremely positive, namely, companion animal and rescue dog. The St. Bernard has never been considered a vicious breed, however, the St. Bernard demonstrates better than any other breed how sometimes there are no answers or reasonable explanations for some canine behavior and that the behavior of one—or even one hundred dogs—cannot be used to define the temperament of an entire breed.

One case in particular demonstrates the unexplained nature of some attacks, along with how quickly the aberrant behavior of a single dog resulted in the condemnation and demand for the destruction of the entire pack by the outraged father of a victim.

In May of 1937, a French doctor accompanied by his three daughters were on a skiing trip in Switzerland when they decided to visit the famous Monks of the Mount St. Bernard Monastery, the ancestral home of the St. Bernard breed. Since the 12th century the St. Bernard dogs kept by the monks would rush out en mass to greet visitors to the monastery. This day, the pack approached the visitors and one of the dogs lunged at the man's 10-year-old daughter, killing her almost instantly. None of the other St. Bernard dogs in this large pack were involved, nor were the father or other two girls bitten.

The Father Superior in charge of the monastery was grief stricken and at a loss to explain why this occurred. This was the first attack on a human by one of their St. Bernard dogs since the founding of the Hospice of the Great St. Bernard in the 11th century. The father of the victim was very vocal and adamant in demanding the destruction of all the dogs, claiming they were all "wolves in sheep's clothing."[7]

The completely unblemished image of the breed for the previous eight centuries, the countless lives saved and humane service rendered by this breed all hung in the balance due to the actions of a single dog. It would take a month before the fate of all the St. Bernard dogs at the monastery would be decided. Fortunately, reason prevailed and the commandant of the Swiss gendarmes responded that the dogs would not be destroyed as they were not a public danger and it "must be recognized that the dogs rendered a great service to humanity throughout the ages."[8]

Sometimes, there is no satisfactory answer to an episode of canine aggression. The condemnation of an entire breed in response to the actions of a few dogs is always found to be based on emotion and not based on the breed's history, temperament or long standing record of cooperation and service to mankind.

Fox Terriers, Boston Terriers and Airedales

While large dogs are physically able to inflict damage on a wider range of victims, small to medium size dogs are able to inflict severe to fatal wounds on smaller victims. Neither Fox Terriers nor Boston Terriers are of sufficient size to show up in significant numbers in severe/fatal attacks. Nor were these breeds used in functions which would predispose them to be in situations where aggression towards humans was encouraged, yet there are rare cases of these breeds involved in severe to fatal attacks against humans.

Fox Terriers

The image of a feisty little Fox Terrier attacking the pant leg of a man passing on the street seems more comical than dangerous. However, when this same level of aggression is directed at a small child, the results are far from humorous.

A severe attack on a child by a Fox Terrier occurred in 1901. A 2-year-old boy was playing on the floor with the dog one evening when the dog began attacking the boy. The father rushed in to find the dog biting the boy on the legs. The little Fox Terrier refused to release the boy, and when the father kicked and pulled at the dog, the dog was separated from the boy along with 3 inches of flesh torn from the boy's leg. The child was taken to the hospital where an operation was performed to close his wounds. As this attack occurred in New York City during the middle of the summer, the excessive heat was noted in the article as a possible reason for the vicious attack by the dog against his "former playmate."[9]

Although there is no documented case of a Fox Terrier-related fatality in the United States, a case of an infant being killed by his grandmother's Fox Terrier is found in the United Kingdom in 1966 and a more recent case of a Fox Terrier killing another infant is found in Australia in 1979.

So while the size of the dog counts, what often counts more is intent or the level of bite inhibition in an individual dog. The same year as the Fox Terrier attack on the boy, another child was attacked by a Bulldog while walking home from school. There is no question that size alone would indicate that a Bulldog attack would be more damaging than a Fox Terrier attack. Yet this girl suffered only bruising on one arm and on the calf of one leg from the attack by this larger and more powerful breed. Clearly, the dogs in these cases had different intents and different degrees of bite inhibition. In many attacks, an individual dog's level of bite inhibition is what determines the severity of the wounds, rather than breed or size of dog.

Boston Terriers

The Boston Terrier is one of the few breeds to originate in the United States. Although the breed was slightly larger in the early part of the 20th century than it is now, the Boston Terrier was still considered one of the smaller breeds. The Boston Terrier was also an American favorite. In the United States, the breed was at the height of its popularity from 1929–1935. It is of little surprise that at the height of this breed's popularity it would be found in cases of attacks against humans.

As seen with the Fox Terrier, what some dogs lack in size can be compensated for in either intensity of attack, size of victim or by increased number of attackers.

A dangerous little Boston Terrier could be found in 1909 near Newburyport, Massachusetts. A 2-year-old boy was visiting his uncle and had wandered out to the backyard. The dog savagely attacked the boy, grabbing him by the neck and shaking him. The uncle rushed into the yard and had "great difficulty in forcing the dog to release the boy." The child died from a broken spine. Apparently, the dog was known to be aggressive, as the article reports that the little boy was "warned" not to play with the dog.[10]

A slighter larger child was overcome and killed in 1934 when two Boston Terriers attacked her in unison. This unfortunate 5-year-old girl was attacked in the street after she followed her father down the road to bid him goodbye on his way to work. As she was walking the short distance home, two Boston Terriers ran out and attacked her. She died a few hours later from her injuries.

Airedale Terriers

The Airedale Terrier breed again demonstrates that when a breed is extremely popular there will be a logical increase in attacks and bites.

This breed is perhaps not as well known as it should be for its service as a sentry and messenger dog during WWI. The Airedale is a medium-sized dog, weighing about 45 pounds. From 1910–1930, the Airedale was extremely popular in the United States. President Warren Harding (1921–23) and President Calvin Coolidge (1923–29) both owned an Airedale Terrier. No doubt the breed was sought out by many Americans. And no doubt there would be situations in which these dogs would be involved in attacks. Although the Airedale is not considered one of the larger or more powerful breeds, fatalities and severe attacks did occur.

In May of 1920, a small girl was killed when an Airedale bit her in the throat. The child was spending the summer with her parents at the home of the dog's owners in upstate New York. In 1923 and 1926, two more children were severely injured by Airedales in New York State.

In 1925, a 12-year-old Colorado boy was credited with saving the life of his sister from an attack by an Airedale. The boy and his baby sister were in a yard when the dog began attacking the little girl. The boy lifted his sister and held her up in the air as the dog tore at him, trying to reach the girl. The boy was bitten 12 times before help arrived.[11]

Even adults can suffer severe or near-fatal wounds by an enraged medium-sized dog. In 1921 it was reported that a man hunting in Pennsylvania was attacked and injured by an Airedale Terrier which had been living in the woods. The man's clothes and flesh were torn by the animal. The hunter stated that after finally beating the dog off him, he did not shoot it because he heard the whining of puppies. Nine puppies, about six weeks old, were later found by a posse sent out to search for the over-protective mother Airedale. Another hunter who had previously encountered the dog said the Airedale "was as savage as any wolf he ever saw."[12]

In Las Vegas, in 1931, a 16-year-old girl was credited with saving the life of her mother after an attack by her Airedale Terrier. The woman was reported to be terribly mangled by the dog she had raised from a pup. The woman had attempted to stop a fight between her Airedale and another dog in her backyard. She struck the dog with a stick and the dog turned upon her and knocked her to the ground, biting her viciously about the face. The woman, of slight build, was not able to ward off the prolonged attack. After the dog had bitten her numerous times in the face, she managed to turn facedown to protect her face from further injury. The dog continued his attack and fortunately the daughter returned home from school and was able to pull the dog off of the victim. The dog made no attempt to attack the daughter. The injuries included one ear almost torn off, the nose torn to the bone, her cheek ripped open, and numerous bites to the body.[13]

When a breed is popular there is an increase in all types of events associated with the keeping of dogs. In 1918, in San Francisco, the owner of a Pomeranian dog sued an Airedale owner. The Airedale had killed the valuable Pomeranian and the owner was seeking damages for the loss of his champion show dog. Indeed, the Superior Court jury awarded the Pomeranian owner $500 dollars. This was a small fortune in 1918 or, as the newspaper reported, $125 per pound (the Pomeranian weighed 4 lbs.).[14]

The examples of attacks by Fox Terriers, Boston Terriers and Airedales are presented not as an indicator of breed temperament, but to demonstrate two points: Small/medium dogs can exhibit occasional acts of extreme and dangerous aggression and the breeds of dogs involved in severe/fatal aggression change from decade to decade.

Savage, Vicious, Ferocious Dogs and Mongrel Dogs

Dog attack stories were of interest to the public one century ago and identifying the breed added another element of interest. It is not unreasonable to assume that in many, if not most, cases when a dog was simply identified as "vicious" or "savage," it was the result of not being able to identify the breed.

Most of these generic temperament descriptions undoubtedly were cases of mongrel or cur dogs.

This is demonstrated in cases when a dog attack story was carried in multiple newspapers. Some incidences of dog attacks were reported in a number of regional newspapers and the breed of dog was always referred to if known. For example, a fatal attack in Chicago on a young boy in 1885 was covered in at least six different newspapers from Chicago to New York. All accounts identified the dog as a Newfoundland or "a vicious Newfoundland." None of the reports neglected to identify the specific breed.

Mixed breed dogs have always made up a significant percentage of the dog population, so their appearance in severe/fatal attacks is a certainty. That these mixed breed dogs should be listed as "a ferocious dog, savage dog, large brown dog, or starving dogs" was only a matter of journalistic interpretation of what was a more valid description of the forces behind aggression than the simple term "cur" or "mongrel." Especially in large pack attacks, it can almost be guaranteed the dogs were a mixed lot of crossbred and cur dogs. Had the pack been five Newfoundland dogs or four Collies, this assuredly would have been reported as such.

In 1884, a 9-year-old boy had taken a bow and arrow for the purpose of hunting in the woods near his home. When he did not return for some time, his parents and neighbors began to search for him. He was found, barely alive, at the edge of a field. Looking at one of the neighbor's bent over him, he was able to say, "Your dogs bit me." No mention was made of how many or what kind of dogs the neighbor owned. The unfortunate boy was gravely injured and died soon after.[15]

An 1892 account tells of a fatal attack on a boy, Fred Ulrich, in Illinois. The boy was first attacked by one "savage brute" (presumably mongrel/cur dog) and, when a second dog joined the attack, the boy was overcome:

> "He was passing the residence of Mrs. H. H. Mitchell, when a savage brute kept
> by that woman attacked him. Ulrich made a good fight, and would have come
> out all right had not another dog, owned by William Walrod, also attacked him."
> *The Hamilton Daily Republican,* October 24, 1892

There are a number of stories such as these, with no identifiable breeds. These incidents were very shocking and distressing to the people of the time, and the level of shock was not dependent on the breed or type of dog involved. However, during the early 20th century a number of cases are found where the newspapers did identify the dog involved in an attack as a mongrel, cur, mixed or cross breed. Here again, the media is found providing information which helps define the behaviors of the dog(s).

In 1910, it was reported that an invalid woman who kept "a large mongrel for protection" was attacked and killed by the dog in her home.[16]

In 1917, a well-publicized report of a 9-year-old boy in New York City dying from a dog attack told of the boy trying to break up a dog fight between two mixed breed neighborhood dogs, when both dogs turned their fury on him, attacking and killing the unfortunate boy.[17]

In 1926, a news report tells of "starving mongrels" attacking and killing a man in Yonkers, New York.[18]

Stories about children and adults attacked by mixed breed dogs were reported with as much vigor and shock as found in accounts of the purebred dog attacks. The style and intensity of reporting found in unidentified breed attacks and identified breed attacks are virtually identical, with triggers, circumstances, relationship to victim and function of the dog reported if known.

CHAPTER 5

The Reporting of Dog Attacks in Early 20th Century Media

A fascinating aspect of 19th and early 20th century newspaper articles about dog attacks is the perception and portrayal of dogs as emotional beings. Dogs were described as jealous, treacherous, lonely, depressed, enraged, frustrated, angry, brave, heroic and noble. Although 19th century media reports could be dismissed by some as being anthropomorphic, doing so would be narrow-minded and counterproductive. Indeed, modern-day science is just coming to prove what has been obvious to dog lovers for centuries—that dogs are indeed emotional beings.

The media of the day understood the complexities of canine behavior and used emotional terms in an attempt to understand the motivations and reasons for dog attacks. At times, dogs involved in attacks on humans were simply described as savage or vicious, but other times the media in the late 1800s showed great insight and understanding of canine behavior. This apparent desire to understand the cause and effects of dog attacks led the media to reveal details of dog attacks not seen in more modern, sterile accounts.

While some accounts may have been a bit dramatized, nonetheless the underlying cause of the dog attack was clearly presented and appears to be a reasonable explanation of the forces contributing to the attack. An example of a keen understanding of dogs and their relationships with immediate family members versus more unfamiliar persons is given in the 1910 account of a dog attack in New York City:

"Solomon Ziskind, who has a wholesale leather store at Second Avenue keeps a big brindle English Bulldog called Rough, for his methods with undesirable intruders. Last evening ten-year-old Solomon Ziskind Jr., with his ten-year-old cousin, Bernard Romm was playing tag among the crates and boxes that littered the yard. The dog lay huddled in the shadow in the corner. He knew the Ziskind boy and didn't mind him, but his eyes followed the Romm boy wherever he went. Suddenly, the boy, dodging to escape his cousin, stumbled over the dog and fell. In another moment Rough leaped growling upon the little fellow…"

New York Times, March 22, 1910

The article goes on to describe the grievous injuries inflicted on the boy and the subsequent destruction of the dog. This account provides information understood to contribute towards canine aggression. Function (guard dog), wariness of strangers (cousin) and provocation (being tripped over) were recognized as factors that added motivation for this dog to attack. The dog was not in any way excused, nor the attack deemed any more acceptable because of these factors. The circumstances leading up to the attack were presented to show cause and effect.

Another case in 1897 describes an attack by a Newfoundland that "was a pet and not at all vicious." The dog was lying on the floor in the parlor of the house. The dog resided in the home with the owner and his 17-year-old daughter. The young lady was sitting in a rocking chair when "she brought one of the rockers down on one of the animal's paws. The animal sprang up with a yelp of pain and dashed about the room." The young woman called to the dog, and the dog responded by attacking her, biting her in the face, chest and arms.[1]

Another report clearly shows that dogs often have limits to the amount of roughhousing they will tolerate. The following case also shows how quickly one dog's actions can trigger a pack attack. In 1886, a 6-year-old boy was playing with four dogs belonging to his neighbors. Two of the dogs were Collies, one a Newfoundland, and the other an unidentified dog. The human and canine behaviors at work are clearly presented in this accounting of the attack:

"The Landers boy had often played with these dogs, as they have always been considered harmless. Taking for granted the gentle disposition of the dogs the child harnessed one of them, and, as he expressed it, began to 'play horse'. In chasing the dogs he fell and one of the Collies bit his wrist…and when the child attempted to rise they turned upon him and began to tear him in a fearful manner. A man who was passing was attracted by the boy's outcry, and after some difficulty succeeded in driving the dogs away, but not until they had literally stripped the child of his clothing and almost killed him."

Mitchell Daily Republican, November 7, 1886

The article concludes with the hope that attending physicians would be able to save the boy's life.

A newspaper article entitled "Attacked by Starving dogs" is clear in presenting the condition of the dogs and the behavior of the victim which clearly contributed to this attack. The attack occurred in Philadelphia in 1885. A 12-year-old girl was returning home from the butcher's shop carrying a package of meat when a pack of approximately 12 dogs began to follow and harass her. When the dogs began jumping and snapping at the meat she was holding, the girl became frightened and started to run. The dogs followed, quickly knocking her down. In the ensuing frenzy, not only was the meat consumed, but the girl was severely bitten about face, arms and legs with her clothes shredded and stripped off.[2]

A fair number of dog attack reports state clearly that the dog was teased or provoked by children. While girls seemed to do inadvertent things to cause a dog to attack, such as pushing the dog away or going near a dog with food or a bone, boys on the other hand seemed to provoke dogs quite regularly and intentionally.

In 1891, a group of boys were playing on a street in Wheeling, West Virginia. A yard off the street contained a kennel with six huge English Mastiffs inside. One nine-year-old boy approached the kennel and began teasing the dogs. It can only be assumed the fence made the boy feel secure enough to continue his tormenting to a dangerous level. The Mastiffs were huge, numerous and "became fearfully enraged." The dogs broke down the fencing and killed the boy.[3]

Some particularly sad cases involved boys teasing a dog and the dog taking its frustration out on an innocent girl who happened on the scene. In 1905, two boys were inciting a large dog to attack a smaller dog. When the little mistress of the small dog rode up on her bicycle, the large dog attacked the unfortunate girl. She was severely bitten, but survived her injuries.[4]

Dogs turning their frustration on innocent victims was not uncommon. Nor was it uncommon for humans to unreasonably expect dogs to tolerate all types of torment and still behave amicably. This article about a fatal dog attack in 1905 thoroughly vilified the dog, yet at the same time presented the details that drove this dog into a frenzy:

"The owner of a yard with a number of fruit trees purchased a large Bulldog to guard against the stealing of the fruit which are an attraction to the boys of the neighborhood. On an early May morning, Jack, the heavy headed Bulldog, lay crouched beneath a cherry tree, a stout chain limiting the circle of his movement. Boys of the neighborhood saw a chance to get at some half-ripe cherries in a tree near the fence, but found the dog menacing them. They then teased the animal until it was nearly frantic. Nearby, the little daughter of the owner was playing with a rubber ball. The baby's thoughts were busy on the ball, she did not notice how the wicked little eyes, red with rage, watched her. The child toddled in pursuit of a rubber ball that rolled into the bare spot which marked the limits of the dog's chain. The baby stooped for the ball, but, before she could pick it up, the dog had seized her by the head."

Perry Daily Chief, May 27, 1905

The account goes on to portray the dog as disloyal and vicious. So while all parties (the boys that teased the dog and the individuals recounting the story) recognized the factors that triggered this dog to attack, nevertheless the implication is that dogs should have no limit to their tolerance of human provocation.

This scenario is typical of fatal dog attacks. The older boys were able to read and understand the potential danger this dog had become. The 18-month-old girl was not capable of reading or understanding the danger of entering the chained space of this agitated animal.

Since most homes and businesses in the late 1800s were not enclosed by fencing, chaining a dog was often considered less dangerous than letting a potentially aggressive dog roam free. Even though it was a better option, it was also understood to increase aggressiveness. In an article describing the attack on a man by a Bloodhound, it was explained that the dog had been chained all five years it was owned. It was noted that the dog "was secured in his front yard by a strong boat chain, and being chained would naturally be cross."[5]

The article "Entirely Too Many Dogs/Many Children Bitten" printed in January 1901, shows that while the author is angry with dogs, he also understands that the problem is very much a human one:

> "A number of complaints have been received by the police lately about children being bitten by dogs. There seems to be no probability that there will be a cessation of these complaints until the authorities again tackle this dog problem in earnest…Of recent years various breeds of large dogs, such as St. Bernards and Mastiffs, have been introduced into Anaconda and they have flourished in such a way that there are now hundreds and hundreds of them. They are so large that an attack by one of them on a little boy or girl is a serious matter. Owing to their enormous size they cannot be beaten off and when once angered they are said to be very ferocious. It is not always, however, that it is these large dogs that spring upon people. The smaller ones are equally as bad.
>
> "Often times it is as much the fault of the children themselves as the dogs. The boys tease the animals by throwing snowballs and stones at them and by striking them over the nose and in other ways tantalizing them until the brutes become furious."
>
> *The Anaconda Standard,* January 13, 1901

The author goes on to discuss the frustration of the parents whose child has been bitten and the attempt of dog owners to hide the dog in cellars when police arrive to kill it. It is no small irony that these owners did not contain their dogs to protect them and the public to begin with; only after a child was bitten and the dog was in immediate danger of being shot by police did they think to contain the animal.

Clearly the media and the public of the late 1800s and early 1900s had a grasp on the causes and reasons for dog attacks. Obvious factors, such as excessive heat, teasing, chaining, and abuse, were included in news reports of dog attacks to explain behavior. However, not all cases involved provocation; some dogs attacked due to territorial or dominance issues, and there are always cases when a dog attack cannot be attributed to any motivations that can be understood by humans.

The reasons why dogs attack are often complex, but the answer to preventing dog attacks is relatively simple: Humane care and control of dogs is often all that is needed to prevent most dog attacks. Perhaps one reader summed up the dog problem best in 1905:

> "At this season of the year dogs that are suffering from the heat and the attacks
> of pestiferous insects, are ill humored and cross. That they should snap at
> children passing by or bite tormentors of more mature years is not
> surprising…Perhaps, (the dog), is not to blame for all the assaults which he
> commits. More blameworthy, possibly, is his owner. The dog owner's duty to the
> animal and the public does not end with the payment of the tax. If he does right
> he will protect the animal from the torments of the heated season and by keeping
> him off the streets, safeguard innocent people from the animal's hot weather
> temper. There are two sides to the vicious dog stories."
>
> *Fort Wayne Daily News*, July 21, 1905

CHAPTER 6

The Use and Misuse of Courage: The Bulldog

"The greatest pup in Mongaup today is a brindled Bulldog as brave as he is hideous. Every woman who meets the brindle pats it, seems disposed to kiss its ugly mug, and says: 'Good dog! Good dog!'"[1]

This is an excerpt from a *Washington Post* news story, in 1907, about a Bulldog that saved the lives of 20 women huckleberry-picking in a field in New Jersey. The women wandered near a fenced pasture in which a bull grazed. The bull became enraged at this perceived intrusion, breaking down the fence and charging the soon frantic women. One of the women had a Bulldog which had accompanied the ladies on their berry-picking adventure. Upon seeing the women running from the maddened bull, the Bulldog rushed into the fray. The dog intercepted and attacked the bull before it was able to reach the fleeing women.

As seen in the chapter on farm dogs, it was not uncommon for livestock to attack humans, or for faithful dogs to rush to their aid. Neither was it uncommon for dogs to be heralded or recognized publicly in the media for these deeds.

Dogs referred to as "Bulldogs" were extremely popular in the late 1800s and early 1900s. These all-purpose dogs appealed to a wide variety of owners. Bulldogs functioned as guard dogs, farm dogs, hunting dogs, police dogs, traveling companions, and house pets, as well as in such inhumane pursuits as dog-fighting, attack dogs, and/or as an object to give their owners a sense of power.

As seen with the Bloodhounds and the Northern breeds, more often than not, attempting to distinguish between similar yet distinct breeds is nearly impossible. During the 19th century the term "Bulldog" was a generic term used to identify a type of dog used for a host of functions. Even though there were separate breeds recognized as the Bulldog, American Pit Bull Terrier, and Bull Terrier, all these dogs were regularly referred to by many people and the media as simply "Bulldogs." Although each of these breeds has a common origin in a type of old English Bull-dogge used for bull baiting and/or pit fighting, each has their own separate history of breeding for a specific trait, appearance or function.

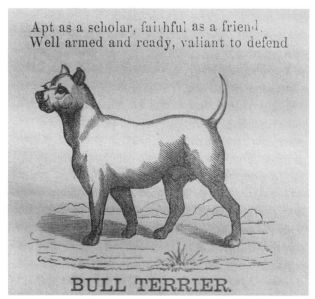

Apt as a scholar, faithful as a friend.
Well armed and ready, valiant to defend

BULL TERRIER.

Bull Terrier: "Is a cross from the Bull-dog and Terrier, and is one of the most useful guard-dogs now in use. In the woods he is an overmatch for the Badger, Fox, Skunk and Coon and none can excel him in activity, vigilance or sagacity. No animal is more abused, or less deserving of it" (Francis Butler, 1860).

Then, as today, there was much confusion, debate and misinformation as to the history and identification of the individual Bull-dog and Bull-terrier breeds. Less confusing and more revealing was the immediate function of the dog, and in the realization of that, the public and the media are found referring to dogs as either "Bulldog guard dog," "pet Bull-dog," "Bulldog used in the pit," or "farm Bulldog." These identifications were far superior to "Pit bull," "Bull Terrier" or "Bulldog" in explaining the behavior of dogs found in attacks or in the performance of heroic deeds.

The Bulldog had proven itself a valuable and dependable companion to the American people throughout the 19th century. Like most dogs, Bulldogs often endured hardship and abuse, yet were steadfast in their loyalty and devotion to their masters. Bulldogs were highly respected for these qualities, along with their fierceness. Fierceness was not considered a negative attribute a century ago, and many Bulldogs were praised for this particular trait. Fierceness was associated with courage and fortitude, and these characteristics were needed on farms, in the wildness and even in cities. Fierceness was not the same as ferociousness, and was not used to imply aggression towards humans.

Like any breed of dog that is popular and used in multiple functions, the Bulldog was involved in a wide spectrum of incidents and events, most advantageous to men, but some not so. Far too frequently in the human/dog relationship, humans place dogs in situations or environments where dogs have little option but to behave badly, and Bulldogs, because of their courageous nature, found themselves often in these lose-lose type of situations.

A strange kind of depravity is found a number of times in the late 1800s—that of men initiating a fight with a dog. This was seen in the staged match between a Siberian Bloodhound and a prize fighter in 1889. It was also seen a number of times with those who fancied themselves to be prize fighters. In another incident in 1889, two men were walking home one evening in Indianapolis. The men were discussing a boxing match which recently occurred. They passed by a house with a Bulldog in the yard. The less bright of the two claimed he could "knock the dog out in one round." The article goes on to say that "the brute accepted the challenge, and a fierce fight ensued, in which the man was terribly bitten about the neck and head. One eye was torn out and one ear bit off, and he would have been torn to pieces had not the owner of the dog come to his rescue." The article makes special note to describe the man as "perfectly sober" at the time.[2]

As bizarre as this case is, this man showed far more bravery than any of the traditional "dog fighters." Dog fighters flatter themselves that they are sporting men. But unlike a true sport which requires intelligence, stamina, or athletic prowess on the part of the human participants, only the dogs display any of these abilities in this "sport." The human agitators stand safely off to the side, needing no sportsman-like qualities other than being able to bend over and pick up the body of the animal which entrusted its life to this man.

As is the case with most breeds of dogs, few Bulldogs, American Pit Bull Terriers or Bull Terriers were expected to perform the original function associated with the breed. In the late 19th century most of the Bulldogs, Bull Terriers and American Pit Bull Terriers were *not* used for bull baiting or dog fighting, but were used to assist and accompany their masters in the daily tasks of living.

Early 1900s etching of a pet Bulldog and his two young masters. The caption reads: *"Black and White—the dog loves irrespective of colour or caste* (Photo credit: Kate Fraser).

From the Bulldog used for hunting to the Bulldog kept as a house pet, the breed's courage and steady temperament proved itself on a daily basis and in almost every circumstance. An incident which reveals much about the true nature of Bulldogs, even those dogs chained and deprived of adequate human attention, is found in the following 1882 account:

A Dog Steals a Negro Baby

"Yesterday morning a Negro woman in East Selma laid a very young child on a small pallet placed in the sun, where the wind would not strike it, and went to another part of the yard to commence her week's washing. Returning in a short while great was her distress and agony to find the child gone. A diligent search about the premises resulted vainly, and the mother was on the point of distraction when a faint cry was heard from the large dog house that stood by, a peep into which disclosed the baby stretched on the dog's bed—all right with the exception of a few scratches caused by being dragged over the ground, while the mischievous author of the excitement, an over-grown Bulldog pup, looked calmly on wagging his tail in an unconcerned way."

Selma Times, March 23, 1882

In 1903 a newspaper article tells of Bum the police Bull Terrier chasing crooks in New York City and leading his partner, Officer Shields, to the East River, where the dog began tugging at a man floating facedown in the river. The man was blind and had stumbled into the river. The Bull Terrier was credited with saving the man's life.

In 1906 an article entitled "Faithful Bulldog Copper Patrols Georgetown Beat" describes how "Jim, a handsome Bulldog" was rescued by a police officer from a burning building. The story goes on to explain how the Bulldog then became a member of the police force, patrolling a beat with his human partner and assisting in arrests. True to the Bulldog character, the canine police officer was reported to "love the excitement and dangers of police work."[3]

It was also not unusual to find *"fierce"* Bulldogs or Bull Terriers saving their masters/mistresses from *"ferocious"* dogs of other breeds. In 1905 an article entitled "Woman's Battle with Dog" has the subheading, "Pulled Down by Vicious Setter, Pet Bull Terrier Saved Her." The rest of the article goes on to explain how the Setter jumped at the woman, knocking her down, attacking and biting, before the woman's Bull Terrier rushed in and attacked the Setter dog.[4]

On the front page of the *Davenport Democrat* in 1924 is a photograph of two small boys sitting on a bench. One of the boys has his arm across the shoulders of a little Bull-dog, while the dog sits half on the bench and half draped over the boy's tiny leg. Another small boy sits beside them, his head swathed in bandages. The title of the article is "Pet Bulldog Saves Two Children from Mad Dog's Attack." The lengthy article goes on to describe in great detail the severe injuries inflicted in an attack by a mad Airedale Terrier on the two boys playing in the street. Queen, the little Bulldog, rushed out of the house when one of the children's mothers opened the screen door after hearing the boys' cries. The dog was credited with saving the lives of both children.[5]

Unfortunately, as we see time and again, there never seems to be a shortage of persons using dogs as an extension of their violent tendencies, and so Bulldogs, ever ready to please their masters, are found in situations of human initiated aggression. In 1871, there was a case reported of an Edwardsville man sentenced to six months imprisonment for inciting his Bulldog to attack his wife. The report reads:

> "The man having some grudge against his wife, locked the doors of the house so she could not escape, and then deliberately incited a large bull dog to worry the unfortunate woman. The details of her frantic struggle with the brute, which were given in evidence before a magistrate were unspeakably horrible. She was savagely bitten in many places by the dog, her husband doing his best to shut out all means of escape."
>
> *Edwardsville Intelligencer*, November 23, 1871

There are numerous other cases found of men inciting, encouraging or "setting their dogs" onto the unfortunate victims of their anger.

In 1905 we find an article about Bulldogs in which the author states; "A man is known by the Bulldog he keeps."[6] Indeed, the reverse is probably even truer: the temperament and behavior of many a Bulldog is known by the owner who keeps it.

The Bulldog's image experienced a rather sudden turn in the early 1900s when they left the farms, frontiers and pits and entered into urban apartment houses and began roaming in great numbers through city streets. Like the Collie, the Bulldog had much credit in the bank of public opinion in the later part of the 19th century. The Bulldog had proven itself among all levels of society as a hard-working, loyal dog. The Bulldog's occasional function as a fighting dog influenced the image of the breed negatively to some degree, but the many contributions the Bulldogs had made to early Americans as farm dogs and loyal protectors counteracted their fighting image.

It is no coincidence that President Theodore Roosevelt (1901–1909) owned a Bulldog during his term in the White House at the height of the Bulldog popularity. However, the bane of any breed is popularity. As seen time and time again, when a breed becomes exceedingly popular, especially if the breed has a negative function attached to it, there will be a significant increase in substandard and unsuitable owners. Such was the dilemma of the Bulldog in the early 1900s. Bulldog popularity soared in the first decade of the 1900s and Bulldogs were now found in great numbers in urban environments.

No surprise that we should find the highest number of fatal Bulldog attacks during the height of the Bulldog popularity (1900–1909). And no small surprise these attacks would be found clustered in the large cities, where these animals were often kept in apartment buildings or allowed to roam the city streets.

In New York City, a Bulldog killed his mistress after she savagely beat him the day before. As the woman lay dying from her wounds she remarked, "I beat the dog for disobeying me, and it was sullen all day." The woman also said she began to feel remorse for "whipping" the dog and had gone into the kitchen to get some meat for the dog when it attacked her. She died the next day from her injuries.[7]

During this same decade, we find the previously discussed case of the Bulldog chained to the cherry tree being teased by boys and killing a little girl who wandered too close to the dog.

In 1909 another tragic case of a Bulldog-related fatality could be found in New York City. A woman, Mrs. Liebess, who suffered from epilepsy, owned a Bulldog which lived with her in her apartment. Early in August the woman collapsed in a seizure. Her neighbor Mrs. Sness and her 15-year-old son, hearing a commotion, went to the woman's aid. Upon finding the door locked, Mrs. Sness and her son broke open the door. After they entered into the apartment, the Bulldog attacked both mother and son. Bedlam ensued as mother and son struggled to fight off the dog, with the owner still on the floor semi-conscious. Other neighbors responded to the scene but were afraid to intervene because they imagined the dog to be "mad." The unfortunate woman who attempted to help her neighbor died from her injuries from the over-protective and clearly agitated Bulldog. Her 15-year-old son survived.[8]

Besides a handful of fatal attacks, there were numerous severe attacks involving Bulldogs from 1900–1909. During this decade we find the Bulldog's reputation turning from a fierce dog to a ferocious dog.

One reader complained in 1904 about the tremendous boon in Bulldog ownership and the number of owners who were looking for a vicious dog:

> "In recent years, the bull dog fad has become very pronounced, it being
> considered the thing by many people in towns to own bull dogs—and the uglier
> and the more vicious the brute the more highly is he prized. Charlotte, for
> instance, is infested with bull dogs."
>
> *The Landmark*, June 10, 1904

Another reader complained of the number of loose dogs and of the owners who "seem to gloat over the fact of having a Bull Terrier that would take a man down if he came through the yard gate."[9]

While one faction of the public was encouraging the Bulldog to be a vicious guard dog, others were seeking Bulldogs out as pets, which led the old-time Bulldog breeders and dogfighters to bemoan the breed was losing its character (meaning fighting ability). In 1912, a dogfighter complained at a Bulldog Society Show that the Bulldog was "becoming increasingly popular as a woman's pet and was thereby losing much of its fighting quality." He further complains that "it is painful to see the coddling that goes on, the feeding of milk and the best quality of steak, sleeping indoors, and general effeminizing."[10]

Despite the confusion about function, despite an increase in severe/fatal attacks due to increased popularity with substandard owners and guard dog use, and despite the overall appearance of fierceness, the Bulldog never really found disfavor with the American public. The media continued to recount cases of Bulldogs performing heroic deeds during this decade (1900–1909) and in the decades to follow.

It is worthy of note that in 1911 the *Encyclopedia Britannica* felt the need to address the Bulldog's true nature versus the reputation the breed had acquired in the previous decade as a result of increased popularity with substandard owners. The edition defined the Bulldog as:

"The Bulldog is a small, compact but extremely heavily built animal of great strength, vigor and tenacity… Bulldogs were formerly employed in bull baiting and the tenacity of their grip is proverbial. Their ferocious appearance, and not infrequently the habits of their owners, have given this breed a reputation for ferocity and low intelligence. As puppies, however, Bulldogs are highly intelligent and unusually docile and affectionate, and if well trained retain throughout life an unusual sweetness of disposition, the universal friendliness of which makes them of little use as guardians."

Fortunately for the Bulldogs, much of this confusion about function and behavior abated when the public turned their attention to a newly emerging breed becoming known for its intelligence and watchfulness. In less than a decade, the German Shepherd would replace the Bulldog as the new status or fad dog.

With their popularity waning and with owners looking towards the German Shepherd as their new protector and intimidation dog, Bulldog-related fatalities and the number of severe attacks plummeted.

◆ ◆ ◆

The case of the Bulldog in the late 1800s and early 1900s is perhaps the best example of how function influences public perception.

During the 19th century, Bulldogs, more than any other breed, were used in the most extreme of negative functions (dog fighting, guard/attack dogs) and in the most positive functions (police dogs and in heroic deeds on farms). The media presented balanced reporting of both the devastation Bulldogs inflicted in attacks and of the contributions they made by saving lives and defending the public as police dogs and personal guardians. Additionally, the media often printed accounts of Bulldogs interacting with their owners and others in the more mundane or everyday activities. Due to this balanced reporting, and the use of

Bulldogs in many functions, both positive and negative, the Bulldog never received wide-spread public condemnation, even during periods of increased popularity when many owners allowed them to roam loose and behave aggressively.

During the first three decades of the 1900s, there were scores of accounts of Bulldogs saving their masters and mistresses from snakes, fires, drownings, gas leaks, burglars and charging livestock, and saving or alerting people to children fallen off of cliffs or wandering onto train tracks and highways. Even more enlightening about the attitudes and perceptions of the times are accounts in which individual incidents of Bulldogs not previously known to be noble were recognized for an act of humane service.

In 1919 a story is told of a "big, ugly Bulldog named Sinful Sam" saving a child from being run over on a highway in Berkeley, CA. The headline of the article reads "Bulldog Saves Life of Boy Playmate, Former 'Sinful Sam' Now a Hero."[11]

A most interesting and insightful understanding of function and image, as well as a clear demonstration that owners ultimately control and determine the behaviors found in their dogs, was chronicled in September 1900. This fascinating account entitled "Bulldog Saves Child's Life" with the subheading, "Thought it was Ordered to Attack Drowning Boy and Brought him Ashore," demonstrates with great clarity that even dogs used in negative functions can be viewed as good dogs and can do good deeds.

The account tells of an older man walking on the banks of St. Joseph River in Indiana accompanied by his Bulldog. The owner of the dog heard a cry for help and hurried around a bend in the river to find an 8-year-old boy drowning in deep water. The man admitted to being too old to swim, but instead urged his Bulldog to go after the child. He threw a rock in the direction of the boy and urged the dog to "go after" the boy. The article states:

> "The dog, it is believed, took this as a hint to attack the boy, and did so, seizing him by one arm and holding on like grim death while responding to his master's commands to come ashore.
>
> "Once ashore, the dog released the boy to his owner, who then pulled him up onto the riverbank."

The story concludes:

> "The dog is not credited with being actuated by a noble instinct, but the boy is thankful, nevertheless, despite a very sore arm."
>
> Special to the *New York Times*, September 14, 1900

This small incident clarifies the essence of dogs. It was implied this Bulldog was a fighting dog; nonetheless, when his owner commanded the dog to "attack" and "release" the boy, the dog obeyed and saved the drowning youth. Owners control the behaviors of their dogs, and whether the dog is used in a negative or a positive function is at the complete discretion of the owner.

A century ago, there was a more balanced view of both the dangers and contributions dogs made to the welfare of humans. The media portrayed what many people at the time seemed to understand: that good dogs occasionally behave "badly" and that even "bad" dogs could do good deeds.

By the early 1920s the vast majority of Americans would quickly forget the Bulldogs. Well over half a century would pass before any of these breeds would enter back into the collective consciousness of the American public. However, for over half a century in between, 1920–1970, millions of Bulldogs, Bull Terriers, American Pit Bull Terriers, American Staffordshire Terriers and all their mixed breed cousins served Americans well in every possible capacity and circumstance. From high-profile Bulldogs such as Stubby, one of America's foremost canine military heroes, and Petey, the famed *Little Rascals* Pit bull pal, to the millions of anonymous dogs whose owners either cherished, neglected, fought or horrifically abused them, Bulldogs served Americans consistently, courageously, faithfully, and peaceably.

WWI propaganda poster with dogs in military uniform representing rival European nations. In the center, an American Pit Bull Terrier represents the United States, with the caption: "*I'm Neutral- BUT Not Afraid of any of them.*" (Courtesy of Animal Farm Foundation)

CHAPTER 7

The Media Re-Shapes an Image: The German Shepherd

By the early 1900s, the large guard dog breeds, the Bloodhound, Newfoundland, Mastiff and Bulldog, were rather quickly being replaced by other breeds. It is with no surprise then that we find that severe and fatal attacks from these breeds dramatically decrease.

By the first decade of the 1900s, new breeds were being developed in other countries and imported to America. A few of these breeds gained tremendous popularity with the American people, becoming the new guard dogs, working dogs and companion animals. Perhaps no breed has risen in popularity so rapidly, become so consistently popular, served in so many capacities and dealt with so much conflicting criticism and praise as has the German Shepherd Dog.

The German Shepherd is a rather new import to the United States, with the first dog of this breed registered by the American Kennel Club in 1908. The start of a new century along with introduction of an entirely new breed allows for an old set of problems (breed, function, aggression) to be examined from a clean slate.

Like the Bloodhounds, Northern breeds and Bulldogs, attempting to obtain accurate breed identification of the German Shepherd in cases of aggression is, at best, a difficult task. Although the German Shepherd is a distinct-looking breed, the reliability of breed identifications in attacks where German Shepherds were named as the breed is relatively low. Police dog, German police dog, Shepherd dog, German Shepherd, Alsatian (still widely used in Europe and other parts of the world), Alsatian Wolf dog and, of course, German Shepherd Dog are all terms that have been used at one time or another to describe the breed of dog we know today as the German Shepherd.

The first reported fatal attack that may seem to suggest a German Shepherd is found in 1887, when a young boy was killed in Indiana as he tried to pet a "shepherd dog."[1] There is no doubt the dog involved in this fatality was *not* a German Shepherd, as the breed of dog we know as the German Shepherd had not yet been created. The term "shepherd dog" was certainly used to describe the function or class of dog (i.e., sheep dog, hound dog, terrier) and not a specific breed.

The generic term "shepherd dog" is seen again in another fatality in 1903, except this dog was further described as a "valuable shepherd dog." This case involved a farmer who was going into town and wished to lock the dog in the barn while he was away. The dog refused to enter the barn and when the owner tried to force the dog through the door, it turned on his master. The shepherd dog was relentless in his attack. The man's wife arrived and made a desperate attempt to save her husband. She hit the dog in the back with an axe, but this only maddened the dog further. She then swung a fateful blow that missed its mark, instead striking her husband in the leg. The man died a few hours later from blood loss.[2]

From 1887 through 1919, the only classification seen that even remotely suggests the involvement of a German Shepherd in attacks is the word "shepherd" dog. It hardly needs to be said that none of these cases can reasonably or reliably be attributed to the specific breed of German Shepherd.

Clues as to the possible breed involved in fatal/severe attacks are only slightly more revealing beginning in 1928, when it was reported that a 5-year-old boy in Minnesota entered into a building to play with three dogs kept there. The dogs, one of which was a police dog, became excited, knocking the boy to the floor. The situation escalated into a fatal attack.[3] But here again, function takes precedence over breed and the dog is described by what it does, "police work," rather than its specific breed. There exists the real possibility that this dog was not a German Shepherd, as it was not unheard of for Collies or Bulldogs to be described as police dogs during this time.

By the mid-1930s, the descriptions are more revealing, as German police dogs are found in reported cases of attacks. In July 1945, a young girl in Virginia was reported to have been attacked and killed by a "big, brown and very vicious German police dog."[4] German police dog was a very popular name for the German Shepherd from 1920–1945. This terminology does not allow for the suggestion of any other breed, unlike the description "police dog."

It was 1947 before the first dog involved in a fatality was officially named as a German Shepherd, when it was reported that a small boy was attacked and killed while sledding in Pennsylvania. By the 1940s the identification of German Shepherds involved in attacks appears to have some reliability, and even though fatalities were rare, there were a substantial number of severe attacks by this breed reported in the news.

◆ ◆ ◆

In direct contrast to the harm the media did to the reputation of the Bloodhound in the previous century, the media was directly responsible for salvaging the quickly deteriorating image of the German Shepherd in the beginning of the 20th century.

By the 1920s the German Shepherd had already gained tremendous popularity in the U.S. However, another phenomenon was gaining momentum just as quickly—the demonization of the German Shepherd. By 1920, the German Shepherd was well on its way to becoming the first "bad breed" of the 20th century. It is unclear as to the exact forces at work which were rapidly destroying the reputation of this newly formed breed.

In the first decade of the 20th century (1900–1909), there were a significant number of fatal dog attacks reported in the U.S. The only one of these that even remotely suggests a

German Shepherd was the attack mentioned earlier (in 1903, involving a valuable shepherd dog and a farmer).

By the second decade of the 20th century (1910–1919), fatal dog attack reports were few and far between. It is unlikely that canine behavior changed dramatically from one decade to the next. Perhaps it may be that with the First World War looming, the nation and the media were focused on issues of greater magnitude and dog attack stories took a back seat to national and international events.

With no authenticated cases of fatal German Shepherd attacks to be found from 1900–1919, it is difficult to surmise how the breed was developing such a bad reputation so quickly. But, by the start of the 1920s, the German Shepherd had developed a widespread reputation as a treacherous, deceitful and vicious dog, and was starting to overshadow the Bloodhound's long-standing image as the most ferocious breed.

No doubt there were non-fatal attacks on humans, and there appears to be a number of cases of predation (attacking livestock) with this newly popular breed. The fact that the breed was known in England as the Alsatian Wolf dog, and the term 'wolf' was attached to this breed in its beginnings, most assuredly contributed negatively towards their image. A common thread seen in maligning the breed is this reference to wolf blood. Up until very recently, people were very passionate in their hatred and fear of the wolf.

But what is clear is that by the 1920s there was a public perception that the German Shepherd had few redeeming qualities, and that the breed's only contribution to society was in increasing the number of dog attacks in the community. We find the public debate in full swing concerning the nature and disposition of the German Shepherd by the early 1920s. After a volley of letters debating the behavior of the German police dog was printed in the editorial section of the *New York Times*, Mrs. Dorothy Holden voiced her opinion in a response dated July 11, 1924:

> "I live in a neighborhood where there are at least ten within a radius of half a mile, and during the past year six women and children (including my own daughter) have been attacked by them without provocation—in two cases the victims were only saved from being torn to pieces by the intervention of the dogs' owners.
>
> "They do not seem to attack men or large dogs and if even a small dog shows fight they usually slink off. And for any usefulness they may have or endearing qualities, I do not notice…and with only a thin veneer over the wolf, they are certainly not to be trusted.
>
> "They are being imported in such numbers and are breeding so fast that they will soon be as numerous as the rabbits in Australia, and are a far greater menace.

"In conclusion, we live in a semi-besieged state of terror from these German police dogs, and the law does not seem to be able to help us, as their owners are wealthy."[5]

Indeed, this woman was not alone in her beliefs. In 1925, a New York magistrate proposed a ban on the German Shepherd dog in Queens. The City Magistrate of Queens requested that the County Health authorities ban German police dogs from the city, as they had been "branded a menace." Magistrate James J. Conway was also quoted as saying the German police dog was:

"…savage, vicious and bred from wolves…In the city at the present time there are thousands of these savage dogs. The police records show that there are 2,000 German police dogs in Queens…Hundreds of persons have been victims of dog bites during the past year, and the majority of biting dogs were police dogs. The dogs should be barred from the city."

The New York Times, January 7, 1925

It is not well-known, but the first official breed ban was against the German Shepherd. On May 2, 1929, the Australian government imposed an import ban on the Alsatian (German Shepherd) that was to stay in effect until March 1974. The ban was proposed due to the claim by the Graziers Federal Council of Australia and others that the Alsatian dog was a vicious dog with wolf blood in its veins. The Alsatian was also branded a sheep killer and the pastoralists (farmers) believed the dogs would mate with the dingo and produce a new strain of powerful and intelligent sheep killers.

A Montana reader was in full agreement after reading about the ban in Australia. His letter to the editor, entitled "Killer Dogs," speaks for itself. He expounds on his theory with the following comments:

"Australia has banned the German police dog and has ordered all in the country to be sterilized, due to the fact that this dog is not a shepherd dog, but a killer. The police dog is little less than a wolf."

The editorial goes on to describe attacks by German police dogs on livestock in Minnesota and concludes with:

"Why pay a bounty on wolves?…when we allow misguided citizens to import half-domesticated wolves from Germany and proceed to breed them and turn them loose on the already over-vexed sheepman. The sheep dog is a friend to man, but I would prefer the hyena to the German police dog."[6]

Just as the anti-German Shepherd movement was picking up speed, a number of extraordinary events occurred that turned the tide of public opinion on its proverbial head.

At the end of World War I, Air Force Corporal Lee Duncan returned to his California home with two German Shepherd puppies he rescued from a deserted bunker in France. The female puppy died soon after reaching the United States, but the surviving male puppy thrived and was named Rin Tin Tin. Duncan, an animal enthusiast, spent the next three years hounding movie studios to use his intelligent and well-trained dog in their productions. Finally, in 1922, Rin Tin Tin won a bit part in the movie *The Man from Hell's River*. The rest is history; Rin Tin Tin went on to star in another 25 films (most of them silent movies) in his 10-year career.

At the end of the 1920s, instead of printing editorials about vicious German police dogs, the newspapers were full of accounts of heroic deeds by German police dogs, as the German Shepherd craze was in full swing.

Another event occurred concurrently with the rise of Rin Tin Tin, which perhaps was not as well publicized, but certainly contributed to the turn around in public sentiment towards the German Shepherd. In 1928, Buddy, a female German Shepherd, became the first seeing-eye dog in the United States. This novel and humane function of the German Shepherd was another very positive image that helped dispel the rumors and allegations of wolf-like savagery associated with the breed only 10 years earlier.

The tide had turned so dramatically that in July 1934, when a young Long Island boy was killed by a chained German police dog, it was reported that the dog killed his young companion because he was "tied out" and "crazed by the heat." Another article describes the dog as "maddened by the heat." The implication now was that it was not in the true nature of the breed to behave this way; provocation or extenuating circumstances drove this dog to aggressiveness. This is quite a turnaround from the savage, vicious, treacherous depictions of the German police dog prior to the introduction of Rin Tin Tin and Buddy.

In addition to portraying the German Shepherd as a heroic breed, the media negatively manipulated other breeds to assist in bolstering the "new" positive image of the German Shepherd. A fascinating example of this was the 1925 release of the Rin Tin Tin movie *Below the Line*.

The movie begins with Rin Tin Tin being trained as a pit fighting dog. Early in the movie, Rinty (as Rin Tin Tin was familiarly referred to) falls from a train and is severely injured. He is nursed back to health and, of course, becomes devoted to the humans who have shown him kindness. In return, Rinty saves his human benefactors from all types of peril, one of these perils being an attack on the heroine by a pack of Bloodhounds.

A 1926 review of this movie shows with great clarity the reactions that Bloodhounds could still elicit from people. It also demonstrates that the shift in public attitude towards the German Shepherd had been so greatly influenced by the fictional Rin Tin Tin, that the public could also easily accept the death of a villain by an attack by the "new" heroic German Shepherd.

The title of this review is telling in and of itself:

Bloodhounds Rip into Rin Tin Tin in New Picture
"The Bloodhounds are loose! When that anguished cry shrieks out on the screen sub-title, you take a new hold on whatever is nearest you and prepare to try and stand the biggest thrill of all. For *Below the Line* has thrills from the opening flash. But, when the Bloodhounds get loose, excitement knows no bounds…The fight between the great shepherd dog and the pack of hounds is so vividly realistic that the producers of the picture have seen fit to explain, in a screen note, that it was filmed without any harm to the dogs involved."

The review of this film also describes the scene in which the villain is attacked and killed by Rin Tin Tin:

"…and you see Rin Tin Tin, the wonder dog come to the rescue. The dog kills the villain in a scene that carries with it the maximum of terror but with the minimum of repulsive detail."

Appleton Post-Crescent, July 7, 1926

In addition to Rin Tin Tin's severe aggression against the villain being acceptable in the context of the dog acting in the interest of a "worthy cause," the public's overall attitude towards certain canine behaviors was vastly different 80 years ago than they are today. A century ago, dogs were not expected to behave amicably all the time. Aggression was recognized to be part and parcel of what was the essence of the dog.

Americans have always loved their villains, be they of the two-legged or four-legged variety. And even though some breeds had developed ferocious reputations, it was nevertheless understood that dogs were complex beings, capable of behaving badly, while still serving their masters well. The concept of the familiar bond between owner and dog, along with the exclusivity on which this bond was based, was well understood and accepted by most people. This understanding allowed for the media to produce and the public to accept the concept of this movie. The idea that Rin Tin Tin could be an ex-fighting dog, wary and afraid of people, not only capable of severe/fatal aggression, but displaying fatal aggression towards a villainous human, while at the same time being a courageous and wonderful companion animal to the humans with whom he had formed attachments, was understood at some level to be the very essence of all dogs, be they Bloodhounds, German Shepherds, or Bulldogs.

One of the most fascinating aspects of the Rin Tin Tin movie *Below the Line* is not just simply how dramatically it assisted in the reversal of the German Shepherd's image from vicious to noble, but the dredging up and use of the old "ferocious" breed, the Bloodhound, to help accomplish this.

Rin Tin Tin

However, by the late 1940s, there was a slight trend towards the vilification of the German Shepherd again as the population of the breed was so great in the U.S. that it was unlikely that all those dogs were following in the heroic pawprints of Rin Tin Tin. But this sentiment was also squashed by another perfectly timed media event—television. Rin Tin Tin was reinvented on the television and brought into millions of American homes in *The Adventures of Rin Tin Tin*, which ran from 1954–1959. This was to start another huge wave of popularity for the German Shepherd and new issues with aggression would emerge in the late 1960s and early 1970s.

While the media was instrumental in salvaging the image of the German Shepherd, the breed itself is also responsible for the turnaround in public sentiment. The German Shepherd dog truly was, and still is, a versatile, intelligent, loyal and hard-working dog. The fact that this breed is used in humane and legitimate services to mankind (police work, military service, seeing-eye dog, movie star, shepherd of livestock, and more recently bomb sniffing, drug detection and search and rescue) are vital to helping the breed obtain and maintain a positive public image.

CHAPTER 8

The Myth of the Super-Predator: The Doberman Pinscher

How the Doberman Pinscher came to be considered a vicious breed is a fascinating study in the creation of a myth. A new, entertainment-hungry society was unmoved by the shop-worn vicious dog attack stories. Dogs have always attacked people and, as one journalist famously commented, "When a dog bites a man, that is not news, because it happens so often…"

To shock or interest an audience that had seen the atrocities of War World II would take more than your typical "dog bites man" story. And as was seen with the Bloodhound, villains and monsters (real or manufactured) are great entertainment. Jesse James, Lizzie Borden, Bonnie and Clyde, the Boston Strangler and Charles Manson are so familiar to generations of people because their evil doings are a thing of fascination and interest. And because no animal can compare with the wanton acts of cruelty and depravity of humans, we need to embellish or wildly exaggerate an animal's size or savagery for it to even begin to compare to the evil that men do.

We super-size animals to increase their capability to do tremendous damage and destruction, from over-sized apes *(King Kong)* and giant sharks *(Jaws)* to 40-foot crocodiles and gigantic ants. And if super-sizing may seem too far-fetched with more familiar animals (dog, cats, wolves), we instead instill them with supernatural or evil powers. We demonize them to increase their shock or entertainment value.

The German Shepherd dog had the right ingredients upon which an image of the super-predator could be created. Their association with the wolf was the prerequisite evil needed to separate this breed from "normal" dogs. The intelligence of the German Shepherd was never denied, even by those who despised the breed. Intelligence coupled with evil are perfect ingredients from which to build an image of supernatural abilities.

The breed was barely two decades old before this fear of a super-predator overcame the Australian government. Of course, their belief that German Shepherd dogs would mate with wild canids and create a super-intelligent, super-efficient sheep killer did not materialize in other countries which did not ban the breed. So while there were severe/fatal attacks involving the breed, the German Shepherd had the opportunity to prove itself as an excellent working dog and companion animal. The positive functions the breed became associated with and a hearty dose of fictional fame helped this breed steer away from becoming the first 20th century super-predator.

By the 1930s, the Bloodhound image as the most vicious breed had finally faded and with the new contender (the German Shepherd) knocked out of place, this left open the top contender spot of most vicious breed.

There would be no positive roles, humane functions or Rin Tin Tin to save the Doberman Pinscher. With the arrival of WWII, the Doberman would be dragged into the super-predator spot by the leash of Nazi guards. And the American public would do its part in keeping the Doberman firmly placed there for decades to follow.

The formula for creating a dangerous dog has been demonstrated (use in negative functions, abuse, poor socialization, chaining, dogs maintained as a pack, etc.). The formula for creating a dangerous breed is something entirely different. Since no breed of dog is inherently vicious, the creation of a "vicious breed" is in reality the creation of an image.

The Doberman—From Intelligent Watchdog to Nazi Killer Dog to Homicidal Guard Dog

In direct contrast to the controversy caused by the German Shepherd shortly after its introduction into the United States, the Doberman Pinscher's beginnings here started off quietly and uneventfully. Both German imports, the German Shepherd and the Doberman, were first recognized by the American Kennel Club in 1908. By the 1920s the Doberman was gaining popularity and was beginning to get the attention and respect of a fair number of Americans.

In 1929, *The Daily Northwestern* newspaper (Oshkosh, WI) ran a photograph of two impressive Dobermans side-by-side. The title over the photo was "Watchdogs for Chief Executives." The caption explained that President Hoover was to be the recipient of one of these dogs for his residence and Governor Kohler of Wisconsin was to receive the other dog for the protection of his home.[1]

The Doberman was quietly gaining respect as an effective and intelligent watchdog. No references to savagery or viciousness could be found describing the breed prior to 1940. On the contrary, almost all references and superlatives used to describe the Doberman were decidedly positive. Prior to WWII the adjectives repeatedly found describing Dobermans included: well-behaved, well-trained, super intelligent, sleek, handsome, beautiful, pedigreed, champion, watchful, alert, and brave, along with other references which allude to the Doberman's growing popularity as a show dog, respected watchdog, and obedience dog.

In the 1930s there was a relatively famous traveling show called "Willy Necker's Canine Carnival." The stars of this show were five exceptionally trained Dobermans who awed many audiences across the country with their intelligence and ability to perform tricks.

In 1932, a Doberman Pinscher named Myra was awarded a gold medal from the National Humane Society in recognition of her bravery. The Doberman was credited with saving the life of her 3-year-old master in Dayton, Ohio. The child was picking a rose from a bush in which a rattlesnake was coiled. The dog killed the snake, but was bitten in the process.

The mother of the child and the veterinarian who tended the Doberman's wounds made application to the Humane Society to honor the dog's bravery.[2]

By the end of the 1930s the Doberman seemed to have passed the courtship stage with the American people and it appeared the breed would meld into American society as just another intelligent and hard-working dog.

Then came WWII, with images of SS guards standing rigid and tall, their obedient Dobermans at their side and depraved accounts of concentration camp guards using Dobermans to torture and kill prisoners. These horrific images of Dobermans serving their sadistic masters in the subjugation and destruction of innocents were seared into the minds of the public, images many people can still conjure up today, 60 years later.

What is puzzling is that the German Army used other breeds as well as the Doberman Pinscher. Why the Doberman was the only breed to become directly associated with the atrocities of the Nazi soldiers is unknown. It is known that every concentration camp had an SS dog unit, and many of these dogs were indeed Dobermans. When the U.S. Army liberated Dachau, the American soldiers shot and killed all the SS dogs (Dobermans) kenneled there.

The fact that the United States Marine Corps also used Dobermans during WWII did little to negate the Doberman's association with Nazi Germany. Most of the Marine Corps' Dobermans were used in the Pacific theater of operations, ferreting out Japanese soldiers in fox tunnels and serving as sentry dogs and scout dogs. Dobermans were credited with saving hundreds of lives of American soldiers in the battle of Guam.

The Doberman was invaluable and highly respected by the soldiers of the U.S. Marine Corps and served their country with extraordinary efficiency and loyalty during WWII. Unfortunately, this did not weigh heavily in assisting the image of the Doberman. Perhaps if the Marine Corps dogs had not been nicknamed "devildogs," it may have alleviated some of the evil associated with the breed. But it is doubtful that anything could have impacted strongly enough to erase the image of a Doberman standing at the side of Nazi guards.

By 1950 the transformation was complete. The Doberman was almost universally known as a vicious, heartless, demon dog, a beast which took delight in killing, unpredictable and untrustworthy. Homicidal muscle dogs, Nazi hounds, crazed killers: There was literally no end to the emotional epithets. The reaction to the sight or utterance of the word "Doberman" was instant and emotional.

Although the Doberman had proven itself to be an extraordinarily trainable, intelligent and reliable working dog, its newly formed reputation excluded its use in positive functions. Before the dog could effectively work as a seeing-eye dog or in any other humane function, people needed to put aside their fears and emotions, and this is almost impossible with many people once they accept a belief.

An interesting case in 1952 demonstrates the typical reaction to a Doberman. The account is about a blind man who, rather unwillingly, is the recipient of a Doberman Pinscher seeing-eye dog. The report tells of Mr. Mike Chodak, a father of four children, who was having difficulty finding work due to his blindness. A friend urged him to get a seeing-eye dog which would allow him more independence and opportunity to provide for his family. Mike agreed and applied to the Pilot Guide Dog Foundation. After being accepted, he was notified that he needed to report to the Foundation's training school in Columbus, Ohio. After being evaluated at the school, Mike was assigned a dog suited to his particular needs. The article reads:

> "Needless to say when Mike was told that he had been assigned Baron, and that Baron was a Doberman Pinscher, he 'almost packed up and came home.' All he could think about were the four children at home and the countless things he heard about Dobermans. All the rumors, Dobermans were mean, they were vicious, they were untrustworthy, they minded only their master, they attacked for no reason at all, made it impossible for Mike to sleep at night."

The story goes on to tell of the confidence and trust developed between Mike and Baron, and how inseparable man and dog had become during training. Still, Mike feared introducing the dog to his wife and children. Upon returning home with Baron, Mike was amazed at how wonderfully the dog responded to his children, and commented on how rapidly "the dog and the children took to each other that in a very few minutes, the four youngsters and the dog were wrestling each other all over the living room floor."[3]

Most people did not have a Doberman thrust on them and did not need to go through the emotional process of discarding their fears and dealing with reality. This prejudice became

Young marine with Doberman during WWII (Official U.S. Marine Corps Photo #95252)

a constant obstacle in introducing the breed to new functions. Organizations that trained dogs for humane services then reasoned, Why take on this extra burden of "selling" the breed when other breeds could provide these services without "threatening" the public?

Now being shunned from legitimate and humane work because of its image, the breed had no avenue by which to rise above and beyond the original breed design (i.e., guard dog). As seen, guard dog status bodes poorly for any breed—it encourages breeding for aggressive traits and for use in negative functions which are often abusive to the dog and serve to instill fear in the general public.

No Doberman *Lassie* would arrive in American living rooms, showing the breed saving children from wells and romping with children. But, of course, there were thousands of Dobermans romping with children and protecting and saving their masters.

The Doberman would be kept in this position of super monster by a couple of real life incidents and by a huge number of rumors, myths, untruths and outrageous theories. While Doberman fatal attacks were very few and very far between, there were two cases of fatal attacks that had the terrible misfortune to occur within 5 years of each other, to both occur in New Jersey, with both victims being female owners, and both cases were covered extensively by both national and local newspapers throughout the country.

The 1955 case involved, not surprisingly, two Doberman guard dogs in Seaside Park, N.J. The owner, a 64-year-old woman, was walking the dogs on the beach when the dogs "turned on her" and killed her. The dogs were reported in the news to be "racing madly about her body."[4]

The 1960 case involved a 55-year-old woman in Northvale, N.J. The woman was the owner of the Aufenberg Kennels and there were approximately 40 dogs on the premises, many of them Dobermans. The Doberman responsible for killing his mistress was a 5-year-old champion male show dog. The woman was killed inside the house after an apparent struggle. The newspapers reported the dog was found near the woman "lunging about in wild circles."[5]

What seemed to be lost in the recounting of the 1960 attack was that this dog did not suddenly "turn" on his mistress. The woman had been advised by one individual to "keep the dog in check" after two persons had recently been bitten by the animal, and she had been advised by her doctor to get rid of the dog because of his aggressiveness.

Both these stories made references to what could only be described as psychotic behaviors by the dogs involved. The one case the dogs were "racing madly about her body" and in the other case the Doberman was "lunging in wild circles." This kind of reporting was virtually unheard of in all other fatal attacks. No doubt many dogs involved in fatalities were still in a state of heightened agitation after an attack, but except for being described as generally vicious or ferocious, extreme behaviors after an attack were almost never reported.

Certainly these dogs were vicious, but one can't help but wonder if the reporting of the behaviors after the attack were added to reinforce the pre-existing rumors of maniacal behavior or if these two stories were the beginnings of the "crazed" Doberman theory.

The dates when the rumors and theories of Doberman homicidal tendencies began to emerge are impossible to pin down, however, sometime during the 1960s these rumors of the crazed Doberman had taken on a life of their own. One of the most popular myths had the skulls of the Doberman too small to accommodate their growing brains—causing the dogs to go mad and their brains to explode. (Unbelievably, this rumor is still heard today—but it is mostly now attributed to the new "super-predator," the Pit Bull). Almost comically, two conflicting rumors were running at this same time: Dobermans only *obey* their masters and the strangely opposite rumor in which Dobermans only *kill* their masters. Slightly less popular, but still the belief of many people, was that the Doberman did not respond to human kindness, that the dogs were robotic killing machines, unmoved and unresponsive to the love and affection of humans.

Other breeds of dogs were involved in far more severe/fatal attacks during this time period. Hundreds of thousands of Dobermans were in the United States, living peaceful lives—certainly not mauling or killing anyone. The Doberman had proven itself an invaluable asset to the U.S. Marine Corps, was recognized as an intelligent seeing-eye dog and efficient tracking dog and had served thousands of Americans well in numerous capacities. None of this mattered. Like the Bloodhound, the image was set in the collective consciousness of the public and would not be shaken loose.

From 1950 to 1979, at the height of the Doberman's infamy and popularity, the breed was found responsible for the same percentage of fatalities as the "friendly" Retriever breeds (Labrador and Golden). The question then becomes, how did the Doberman maintain its reputation as the most vicious of all dogs when other breeds and types of dogs were involved in as many, or more, cases of severe and fatal attacks?

Either Dobermans were truly vicious, but terribly ineffective in causing injuries, or their image was not based in reality. Clearly, the Doberman is not ineffective at any function assigned to it. The breed is powerful, capable, and intelligent. It is doubtful the German Army and the U.S. Marine Corps, two very efficient-minded organizations, would use the breed if it proved ineffectual at the required tasks (which included aggression). This leaves the only other possibility: The Doberman's image was just that—an image.

Diane McWhorter is the Pulitzer Prize-winning author of *Carry Me Home: Birmingham, Alabama: The Climactic Battle of the Civil Rights Revolution.*[6] In a 2005 interview, Ms. McWhorter commented on the critical use of photo imagery in the Civil Rights Revolution during the 1960s.[7] She discusses how the use of a single episode of media-presented dog aggression could arouse and influence an entire population into accepting a cause or belief.

In discussing how the country finally came to rally behind the Civil Rights movement, Ms. McWhorter commented on the infamous photographs of children being attacked by police dogs, along with the use of fire hoses, during the Birmingham protest riots in 1963:

> "The photos of the dogs and the fire hoses nationalized the movement, no doubt about it. The actions photographed were such a graphic, primitive expression of the system. Ironically, the dogs were only out for no more than half an hour, and they never came back again…But the dogs got the job done very quickly! It is sort of a joke in the movement that a few dog bites—and not even that many people were bit—accomplished what a century of suffering and mayhem had not.
> "The pictures not only recalled Nazi Germany and their police dogs, but also *Uncle Tom's Cabin*, with the Bloodhounds chasing Eliza. They really spoke to the collective memory of the country."

All the speeches by civil rights activists, all the injustices and pleas for change and equality, did not impress the public nearly as much as a half hour of film footage showing police dogs biting and worrying protestors (specifically, child protestors). These few dog bites were perhaps the very least of the injustices bestowed upon African-Americans, but this brief imagery had more impact than a thousand speeches.

A fixed time and place (Nazi Germany during WWII), and a single horrifically negative function (attack-trained dog), would be the image associated with all Dobermans for decades. How quickly and effortlessly the public embraced the image of Doberman savagery is an unsettling example of transference. How long and insistent the public was in refusing to believe otherwise, despite evidence to the contrary, is an equally disturbing example of mass ignorance. The Nazi Doberman could have been so easily seen for exactly what it was—human savagery and human initiated evil.

It is doubtful the human ego will ever allow for the full acknowledgement that the terrible acts exhibited by these dogs were a direct result of the evil in us—be it the Cuban Bloodhound incited to attack a fleeing slave, a Doberman incited to attack a prisoner of war, or a Pit bull incited to attack another Pit bull. These *human* perversions of the human/dog bond have resulted in a public condemnation, prejudice and accepted cruelty against certain breeds because placing the blame on the dogs allows us to distance ourselves from the abominations found in our own nature.

◆ ◆ ◆

As with the Bloodhound and the Doberman and, later, the Pit bull, for every person who fears this breed there seems to be another who will seek it out for this exact reason. And so despite, or because of the Doberman's image of viciousness, the popularity of this breed soared during the three decades from 1950–1979.

In 1964 there were 4,815 new dog registrations for Dobermans filed with the American Kennel Club, making the Doberman the 22nd most popular purebred dog in the U.S. Five years later, in 1969, the Doberman rose to the 16th most popular purebred dog in the U.S., with 13,842 new dog registrations. Ten years later, in 1979, the Doberman would be the 2nd most popular purebred dog in the United States, with 80,363 new dog registrations.

At the height of their infamy, 1950–1979, well over half a million people obtained and registered a Doberman Pinscher. The Doberman Pinscher was consistently more popular during this time than the Golden Retriever, with more than double the amount of dogs being registered by the American Kennel Club.

While there were probably a substantial number of dog-savvy people who obtained a Doberman because they did not buy into the "crazed Doberman theories," there is no denying that many people who obtained Dobermans did so precisely because they did buy into these theories. An increase in a breed's negative image or reputation for aggression unfailingly yields an increase in the number of substandard owners.

Still, hundreds of thousands of Dobermans did not live up to their vicious reputation, despite the increase in substandard owners, despite the increase in irresponsible breeding to meet high demands, and despite their use as guard and protection dogs.

What was sorely lacking in real-life attacks for the media to cover was more than made up for in fictional accounts of vicious Dobermans. Any movie, TV or advertisement spot that required the portrayal of a vicious dog would be filled by a menacing, snarling Doberman, most times with lips pulled back to expose the maximum amount of teeth.

Fortunately for the Doberman breed, by the 1980s their "reign of terror" had run its course and people would set their sights on a new breed to become their next super-predator.

It needs to be pointed out that all the prior bad reputations assigned to individual breeds, from the bloodthirsty Bloodhound, to the treacherous German Shepherd, and the homicidal Doberman, did not come about as the result of newspaper manipulation or sensationalism. The media outlets which contributed so greatly towards shaping (or redeeming) bad reputations of these breeds were plays (Tom Shows), playbills, movies, television, advertisements and word of mouth.

Prior to the 1980s, newspapers never appeared to have a breed-biased agenda. Breeds were identified in the reports to add interest and detail. As seen, the newspapers were very keen on presenting triggers, circumstances and factors which may have contributed to a dog attack. The newspapers also printed many positive stories about dogs, and did not shy away from a good dog story because it involved a breed with a bad reputation.

Prior to 1980, the breed of dog was *not* the story; the attack was the story, with the breed an added detail.

Even in the two highly publicized cases of Doberman attacks in New Jersey in 1955 and 1960, the newspapers did not malign or discuss breed tendencies or imply breed viciousness. Other than describing the psychotic behaviors of the dogs after the attack, nothing else was remarkably different about these dog attack reports than any of the other dog attack stories reported in the newspapers.

Prior to the 1980s, theories and myths about Doberman skull size and wild rumors about viciousness were not taken up by the newspaper media—these outlandish theories were left in the schoolyards where they belonged. But, starting in the early 1980s, all of this would change.

A new breed of dog would start to be found in attacks and a new unscrupulous media would stir this into a storm of hysteria. Not only would the newspapers emphasize breed above all other elements in dog attacks, but the media would print outrageous rumors, myths and theories about anatomy and temperament that earlier generations of reporters had the good sense and professionalism to leave in the children's playgrounds.

CHAPTER 9

Setting Dogs Up For Failure: The New Guard Dogs

"Tis sweet to hear the honest watch-dog's bark
Bay deep-mouth'd welcome as we draw near home."

Lord Byron, *Don Juan*

Of all the functions that dogs perform, perhaps none is more rooted in the familiar bond than that of the guard dog. For thousands of years dogs have been praised and held in esteem for their service in protecting their owners from the dangers of unfamiliar persons or animals. However, as evidenced, this is the function which also dooms many dogs to failure, as it expects dogs to assess danger by human standards and morals. Another level of owner recklessness that dooms many dogs to failure is found when dogs are mismanaged to such a degree that they are permitted to harass, intimidate or attack other beings while roaming off their territory.

The following incidents of canine and human aggression are but a very small sampling of newspaper articles found during one single decade:

- "Policeman Uses Last Bullet to Kill Dog" is the headline of an article about a dog attack which sent three people to a hospital in Philadelphia and led to the pursuit of the dog by police. A police officer had finally barricaded the attacking dog inside a doghouse, but the dog tore down the boards blocking the entrance and lunged at the policeman. The officer shot the dog six times, after which the dog retreated back into the doghouse. Within seconds the dog "came flying out of the doghouse again" and it took another three bullets to kill the charging dog.
- Drug agents drove up to a duplex looking to make an arrest. The suspects rushed out of the house, loosening and ordering their dog to attack the officers.
- A girl is critically injured after three dogs attack her, tearing her scalp off and dragging her through the yard.
- A dog is shot twice after attacking two children and biting a police officer. The wounded dog runs from police and, after a protracted chase, they catch up with the dog. The dog attacks the police officers and it requires another seven bullets to stop the charging animal.

- A police officer is forced to shoot a dog that aggressively cornered him at a gas station.
- A mounted police officer is forced to shoot a dog attacking his horse.
- Police arrive to find a small girl being mauled by a dog. They are unable to release the child from the dog's grasp and instead are forced to shoot the dog at close range.
- Police are unable to locate a murder suspect. When answering a call for a vicious dog attacking a pedestrian, they capture the dog and trace it back to the murder suspect.
- A pack of dogs terrorize schoolchildren, chasing and biting three of them.
- A postal worker is severely injured when a dog bolts out of a house and attacks him.
- A man and his dog are attacked by another, larger dog. The man is injured attempting to save his little dog, but the small dog is mauled to death.
- A dog chained to a tree attacks and mauls a woman; she dies three days later.
- A boy is severely mauled by the dogs his parents use for breeding.
- An elderly woman enters into her backyard and is killed by her son-in-law's two guard dogs.
- An owner is arrested for releasing and siccing his dog on a police officer.

If asked to guess the breed of dog in all the above cases, most people today would be rather quick to venture that they involved a Pit bull, because these are kinds of stories we read about that breed today. However, all the above cases occurred from 1965 to 1976 and all the dogs involved were German Shepherds.

It is fairly obvious that the German Shepherd was the dog of choice for those who were looking for an intimidation dog or an attack/guard dog during the 1960s and 1970s. So it should be of no surprise that the German Shepherd would be found overrepresented in severe and fatal attacks during this time period (see Appendix B). But the German Shepherd never received the widespread public condemnation that the Bloodhound had in the 1800s or that the Pit bull receives today.

The explanations for this are rather obvious:

- The German Shepherd has consistently been used in positive functions by persons in authority (i.e., police, search and rescue, bomb detection, seeing-eye dog, etc.). These very public displays of the German Shepherd in positive functions were a tremendous asset to the breed image.
- The media never portrayed the German Shepherd negatively (as shown, the exact opposite was true).

- During the time of increased attacks with this breed, experts discussed and addressed canine aggression from a multi-faceted approach (examining owner, victim and canine behaviors as contributory factors in dog attacks).
- The Doberman Pinscher already held the top spot as super-predator.

Since the German Shepherd breed was involved in far more severe/fatal attacks than the Doberman, reason would have it that the Doberman should have been upstaged as most vicious breed by the German Shepherd during these two decades. However, image and reality are not dependent on each other. The German Shepherd had both a real-life and fiction-based image rooted in positive functions, which the Doberman breed was sorely lacking.

The Doberman Pinscher had no visible redeeming qualities to most people and so the image of viciousness could easily be maintained. Additionally, the German Shepherd did not have wild theories or outrageous claims about brain size, unpredictability and other myths associated with the Doberman.

Another very important factor occurring during the 1970s afforded much damage control to aggressive attacks involving German Shepherds. Despite increased incidence of aggression with certain breeds (specifically Great Danes, St. Bernards and German Shepherds) during this period, medical professionals (both human and canine specialists), humane society personnel and animal control officers were giving serious consideration to the forces behind what they perceived to be a growing dog bite problem.

After a series of very severe attacks in the early 1970s, a group of experts addressed the issue of the *"rising epidemic of dog bites in major American cities."* This was based on the fact that dog bites rose in New York City from 27,000 reported bites in 1965 to 38,000 reported dog bites in 1972. The opinion was that the increased number of dog bites was related to inner city ghetto growth, as low-income families acquired dogs they could not properly care for, while others obtained large guard dogs to protect against burglary and vandalism. The only reference to breed was the mention of a trend for families to switch from smaller pet dogs to the larger guard dog breeds, such as the German Shepherd and Great Dane.[1]

In 1977, a young boy in Atco, New Jersey was severely attacked by his grandmother's German Shepherd. The dog ripped off part of the crown of his head, severed his ear from the ear canal and mangled his mouth. The parents despaired at the numerous operations that would be required to reshape the boy's mouth to return it to some normalcy. The plastic surgeon involved in this case commented publicly about the increase in severe dog bites seen in the hospitals in Southern New Jersey and Philadelphia, stating "35 youngsters in one summer (1977) is way out of line." Also recounted was an incident of another young boy severely disfigured by his neighbor's Labrador Retriever mix and Great Dane. The surgeon commented on the deforming injuries inflicted on children by family pets "which had never shown signs of being vicious before."[2]

The experts consulted for this article (plastic surgeons and veterinarians) discussed the epidemic as being the result of the acquisition of guard dogs by inexperienced owners, the indiscriminate breeding of dogs and the inability of owners to properly care for or control their dogs.

Throughout the 1970s dog attacks were viewed as a multi-faceted problem, based on function of dog (guard dog), owner responsibility, loose roaming dogs, poor breeding practices, and the danger of children with unfamiliar dogs. The problem was discussed and viewed as a combination of factors at work, along with a need to educate the public in dog bite prevention. Neither experts nor the media suggested the eradication of the German Shepherd (or any other breed) as a solution to the dog bite epidemic. Nor was breed presented as the driving force behind aggression. More than anything, guard dog function was presented as the single most predominant factor in canine aggression, coupled with uneducated owners.

◆ ◆ ◆

The German Shepherd shared guard dog status with the Doberman Pinscher and Great Dane in the late 1960s and early 1970s. A person looking for a guard or attack dog during this period usually turned to one of these breeds. It was not uncommon to find some owners having more than one of these guard dog breeds at the same time. A fatality in 1967 involved a little girl killed by her stepfather's Great Dane guard dog. The stepfather also kept a Doberman and German Shepherd in the yard, neither of which participated in the attack on the little girl.

In only a five-year span, 1970–1974, these three breeds (German Shepherd, Doberman, Great Dane) together registered 735,469 new dogs with the American Kennel Club. Those examining canine aggression at this time understood the consequences of nearly 3/4 of a million of these large guard dog breeds going into the hands of many less than suitable owners in such a short period of time. It was the acquisition of these breeds as guard dogs or status dogs and their owners' subsequent lack of control over these animals which was correctly identified as the force behind attacks on humans.

Thirty years later, both the dog and human population in the United States had increased by millions, yet the population of these three guard dog breeds has decreased dramatically.

In the five-year time span from 2000–2004, there would be only 300,000 Dobermans, German Shepherds and Great Danes registered with the American Kennel Club. There were over 400,000 *less* of these three guard dog breeds registered in the U.S. than there were 30 years earlier (1970–1974). This was not because people no longer sought out guard dogs or status dogs; it is simply because people sought out new breeds to be their guard dogs. The new breeds were the Pit bull, and later the Rottweiler.

The now familiar trend repeats itself. As the German Shepherd, Doberman and Great Dane were no longer sought out as status or guard dogs, severe attacks and fatalities associated with these breeds decreased dramatically. As the Pit bull and Rottweiler dogs became the new guard and image enhancing dogs, attacks associated with these breeds increased. The fatalities are directly associated with the increased popularity of these breeds among substandard owners.

Unlike the American Pit Bull Terrier, the Rottweiler is recognized by the American Kennel Club. New dogs registered on a yearly basis with this organization provide some indication of an increase in the population of certain purebred dogs.

	5 Year Span 1975–1979 # of Dogs Registered	5 Year Span 1995–1999 # of Dogs Registered
Doberman	372,532	82,243
Rottweiler	9,961	355,797

Clearly, a new generation of owners looking for a status/guard dog turned to the Rottweiler as their breed of choice.

Owners who admire and respect other characteristics in the Doberman continue to own the breed, and these tend to be the more responsible and serious owners. Those owners looking for a new status breed obtained the newer version of the Doberman, namely the Rottweiler. These are potentially dangerous owners, because they purposely seek out what they believe to be the newer, trendier breed of dog in order to project an image of power. People who simply acquire the newest status/guard dog are very often unfamiliar with breed characteristics, have no genuine concern for obtaining or maintaining dogs with stable temperaments, and/or fail to ensure that breeding dogs are medically and behaviorally sound. Yet these are the very owners producing the next generation of guard/status dogs, as their dogs are usually intact and more often than not have been bred.

As history has demonstrated, the bane of any breed is popularity coupled with an increased use of the breed as guard dogs by substandard owners.

The following four examples are typical scenarios found in guard dog attacks and are actual cases of human fatalities:

Case #1
Elderly woman wanders into her backyard and is killed by her son-in-law's two
    guard dogs.

Case #2
Elderly woman wanders into her backyard and is killed by her son-in-law's two
    guard dogs.

Case #3
3-year-old climbs over fence and is killed by two guard dogs.

Case #4
4-year-old climbs over fence and is killed by two guard dogs.

Notice that Case #1 and Case #2 are identical in all respects: victim profile, function of dog, location, relationship (or lack) of victim to dogs, etc. Case #1 occurred in 1976 and involved two German Shepherds. Case #2 occurred in 1994 and involved two Rottweilers.

The 3rd and 4th cases are also identical in all respects, except for a one-year age difference between the victims. Case #3 occurred in 1972 and involved two German Shepherds. Case #4 occurred in 1997 and involved two Rottweilers.

The breed of guard dog is the only variable that changed over the decades. In 1975 the German Shepherd was the second most popular purebred dog in the United States with 76,235 AKC registered new dogs. In 1995 the Rottweiler was the second most popular purebred dog in the United States with 93,656 AKC registered new dogs. The Doberman was the 4th most popular purebred dog in 1975 and fell to 18th place in 1995. Clearly, Americans were looking to the Rottweiler (and Pit bull) to be their new status/guard dogs.

The truth is, regardless of breed, guard dogs are not suitable animals to keep in a residential area. Anyone believing ownership of such a dog is an asset faces the real possibility of being criminally and/or civilly charged when their guard dog causes injury to a person. They also risk the possibility of being attacked themselves if they are unable to exert control, physically and mentally, over these powerful animals.

As demonstrated throughout the last two centuries, guard dogs rarely attack and injure criminals or trespassers intent on evil doings—guard dogs attack neighbors, children, and persons looking to conduct legitimate business on or near the location of the dogs. And as seen a century ago, guard dogs are not averse to attacking their owners when treated harshly or when owners can not control these potentially dangerous animals.

While there may be a small number of very experienced and professional trainers able to handle, control and supervise their guard dogs adequately, almost everyone else lacks the resources, ability, strength, knowledge or time to properly control and supervise a dog trained or encouraged to behave aggressively as a guard dog.

A clear example of the difference between guard/attack dogs and companion animals is found in a case of a fatal attack involving three Rottweilers and their owner:

In 1998 an elderly woman broke her hip, which necessitated the use of a wheelchair. The woman had owned a female Rottwelier for the past eight years. More recently she had obtained two male Rottweilers, imported from Germany. Neighbors claim she took pride in the fact that both these dogs were professionally trained attack dogs. One day in September she was in her driveway when the two male dogs attacked her. She was dragged up and down the driveway before deputies arrived, shooting both dogs. The female Rottweiler was found "hiding" in the backyard near a kennel. The female dog had bite wounds on her body and a severe bite to her face. It is unknown if the female Rottweiler had attempted to intervene on behalf of her long-time owner or if the male dogs had simply attacked her during the fray and she escaped to the backyard. Either way, the female Rottweiler did not participate in the attack and she was clearly "frightened" by the behavior of the two male guard/attack dogs. The owner later died from her severe injuries.

This case demonstrates many components and factors found in severe/fatal dog attacks. Three large dogs take a considerable effort to maintain. In addition to the female Rottweiler, this woman needed to be able to control two intact, 2-year-old male Rottweilers with attack dog training. For even the most able-bodied person these dogs would be a formidable challenge to maintain control over and to care for.

Certainly, elderly or physically challenged individuals can safely keep a large dog, but increased risks may occur when multiple dogs, intact and trained for aggression, are kept by individuals clearly not able to control these animals should they become excited or aggressive.

◆ ◆ ◆

Since the beginning of the human/dog bond, people have used dogs to protect themselves from other beings. While dogs obtained to function as defenders or guards to their masters and his possessions have higher incidents of aggressive encounters with humans than dogs acquired strictly for companionship, there are other risk factors which need to be assessed before condemning the use of guard dogs.

There is no question that man inflicts far more grievous and frequent harm to his fellow man than dogs ever have or will. Guard and protection dogs have rendered a great service to mankind throughout history. Untold numbers of people have *not* fallen victim to other humans because they owned a guard dog that was perceived as protective or menacing. Millions upon millions of lonely people have benefited emotionally and physically from the security and comfort of having a protection dog by their side. While there are elevated risks associated with the maintenance of guard dogs (as compared to dogs maintained strictly as companions), the truth is that legions of guard dogs have contributed to our well-being without cost.

If we wish to continue to reap the emotional and physical benefits of owning guard dogs we must treat them humanely and owners must take responsibility for controlling situations where their dogs may be behaving appropriately by canine standards, but inappropriately by human standards.

CHAPTER 10

The Media Attacks a Breed: The Pit Bull

"Falsehood flies and the truth comes limping after, so that when men come to be undeceived, it is too late: the jest is over, and the tale has had its effect."

Jonathan Swift

In a 10-year span, from 1966–1975, there is only one documented case of a fatal dog attack in the United States by a dog which could even remotely be identified as a "Pit bull" (i.e. American Pit Bull Terrier, American Staffordshire Terrier, Staffordshire Bull Terrier, Bull Terrier, American Bulldog, English Bulldog or any dog resembling a "Pit bull" or "Bulldog").

So, how did the "Pit bull" find itself fully entrenched as the new super-predator by the early 1980s?

◆ ◆ ◆

By the middle of the 1970s there became an emerging public awareness of the cruel practice of dog fighting in the United States. Dog fighting began to get the attention of law enforcement and, hence, the media during this time and was being exposed as an insidious and growing problem throughout the country.

About the same time, in the summer of 1976, a California boy was killed by a dog. Newspapers from Louisiana and New Jersey to California reported this event, with each newspaper using a different breed description. The dog involved in this incident was alternately described as a Bulldog, Bull Terrier, or Pit bull. More than a few newspapers reported that the dog "locked its jaws on the child's neck." One newspaper could not make up its mind as to which breed caused the fatality so they simply mixed and matched the anatomy and alleged behavior of an American Pit Bull Terrier with that of the (English) Bulldog. The headline starts off claiming, "Five-year old killed by Bulldog" and in the next line identifies the dog as a "Pit bull." After now identifying the dog as a Pit bull, the article offers the following (incorrect) theory about English Bulldog anatomy that allegedly explains the "locking jaw" reported in this attack: "Because a Bulldog's lower jaw is longer than the upper jaw, it is physically impossible for the dog to let go while there is any tension on whatever it is holding in its mouth."

During this time, as police raided dog fighting operations, arresting dog fighters and seizing Pit bulls, the media began covering this growing subculture of drugs, guns, gambling and fighting dogs in earnest. Shelter personnel were interviewed about why the Pit bulls seized during the raids were being euthanized. Comments about the "killer instinct" of the Pit bull (unfortunately not defined as it was meant—dog-on-dog aggression) were found in these reports. Many of these shelter personnel lamented the destruction of these dogs and commented that despite their strength, tenacity and encouraged aggression towards other dogs, the seized Pit bulls were loyal, friendly and affectionate animals.

Unbeknownst to the media, law enforcement and shelter workers, the exposure of this cruel and seedy subculture and their descriptions of the Pit bull's fierce but loyal nature would strike a chord with a segment of the human population which has always been attracted to dogs they believe will enable them to impress or intimidate other humans. Exposing breeds of dogs involved in a negative function, through no fault of their own, will not increase their popularity with the average owner looking for a dog. Dogs portrayed in negative functions (fighting, guarding drug stashes, etc.) will only serve to increase their popularity with unsuitable owners who seek out dogs to increase their status as a person of power or intimidation.

The media's intention in first reporting dog fighting, police raids, and Pit bull seizures appears to have been legitimate and well-intentioned coverage of animal cruelty which rightfully should be exposed as criminal behavior. However, the media's first reports of two Pit bull-related fatalities in the late 1970s were filled with erroneous Pit bull anatomical references and sensationalized claims of Pit bull abilities. These glaring errors, along with the continuous exposure of Pit bulls used by dog fighters and drug dealers, would produce an immediate and predictable increase in the popularity of this breed with substandard and criminal owners. By the early 1980s the Pit bull was on the fast track to becoming the new super-predator.

Like the producers of the Tom Shows in the 1880s, when the 1980s media recognized that Pit bull attack stories elicited an emotional reaction from their audience, the media went into overdrive. The early 1980s find the media continuously churning out emotionally charged articles about Pit bull anatomy and behaviors that were based on rumors, myths and unproven claims by both experts and laymen. By 1982, Pit bulls were becoming a hot topic and the media would capitalize on this at every opportunity.

As the media delighted in reporting the Pit bull to be unpredictable and deadly, the population of Pit bulls accelerated each consecutive year. United Kennel Club (UKC) registrations show a 30% increase in registrations of American Pit Bull Terriers in a single year,(1983 to 1984).

The media would be in full lather by 1985 and nary an expert or laymen would pass up the opportunity to comment on the Pit bull issue in any public forum, with the Pit bull population continuing to increase in step with the hysteria.

In 1986 there were over 350 newspaper, magazine and journal articles printed about the Pit bull in the United States. The media image of the Pit bull was becoming so intense and magnified that it sometimes took precedence even over a person's actual experience with the breed. Owners with loving, affectionate Pit bulls were having them euthanized in fear they would "turn." One man who was "attacked" by a Pit bull in 1986 did not assess the temperament of the Pit bull by the dog which allegedly attacked him, but rather by the image of the Pit bull as portrayed in the media. The "attack" occurred when his neighbor's loose Pit bull came near the man's daughter, when he kicked the dog away, apparently the dog snapped at him. He easily warded off the dog with his foot and no injuries occurred. But it was reported in the media that the man "escaped serious injury." He is quoted as saying, "The Pit bull has the same instincts as a panther and should be treated as such. Some say if you train it enough, maybe it can become a pet. Well, so can a rattlesnake. But in the meantime, they're killing people, ripping their throats out." This comment came from a man who fended off an "attacking" Pit bull with only his foot.

The Pit bull hysteria would continue unabated in 1987 and the media, not above cannibalizing itself, would begin to report on the over-reporting of Pit bull stories. Two news stories in 1987 demonstrate with great clarity the extent of the hysteria about Pit bulls during this time. Some people became so frightened that they assumed any misfortune needed to be attributed to a Pit bull, while others used the hysteria and hype about Pit bulls in an attempt to disguise their own evil acts.

In 1987 a woman rushed her bleeding and partially paralyzed dog to a Veterinary Hospital in Kalamazoo. The woman claimed her small dog had been "mauled by a Pit bull." The dog had no visible bite wounds and x-rays were taken. It was discovered the dog had been shot and a bullet was lodged near the spine. The veterinarian commented that "unless Pit bulls are now carrying guns, the dog was probably shot by one of the woman's neighbors."[1]

Also in 1987, an Oakland, California, man called the police to report his 19-month-old daughter had stopped breathing. The man tried to convince police the family Pit bull had attacked and killed the little girl. There was absolutely no evidence the child had been attacked by the dog. The investigating officer stated the dog blamed for attacking the child "was so young, it barely had teeth." The father was arrested on suspicion of murdering his daughter. The Pit bull puppy was taken into custody by Animal Control.[2]

In 1987, *Rolling Stone* magazine did a remarkable and graphic exposé on teenagers, inner city gangs, violence and the horrific abuse of Pit bulls, entitled "A Boy and his Dog in Hell."[3] This investigation into inner city youth showed that not only were Pit bulls being used as an extension of their owners' depravity, but were extensions of their teenage owners' egos. When Pit bulls lost an arranged street fight they were subjected to unimaginable cruelty and violent deaths, because they became a source of embarrassment or failed to uphold the machismo image of their owners.

Addressing the societal ills identified in the *Rolling Stone* report—crime, poverty, animal abuse, ignorance, greed, depravity, and man's lust for violence—is a far too daunting and disturbing task for most people. So much easier on the human psyche to address the situation with Pit bulls as *Sports Illustrated* did that same month. On July 27, 1987, the entire front cover of this issue was a photograph of a Pit bull, mouth open, teeth bared, over which in bold print was the headline, "Beware of this Dog." The lengthy article inside the magazine gave lip service to the abusive "sport" of dog fighting, while alternately portraying the Pit bull as vicious and unpredictable.[4]

Here we also see the beginnings of outrageous examples of Pit bulls involved in attacks being described as "family dogs." One of the "family" Pit bulls described in this *Sports Illustrated* article was actually one of four dogs chained behind a trailer in Oklahoma. All the dogs (three chained Pit bulls, and one chained Chow) had scars consistent with dog fighting. The owners/parents were charged with criminal neglect for allowing their 2-year-old daughter to wander out to these "family" dogs.

But no article could compete with the blatant fear mongering and horrendous portrayal of the Pit bull that *Time* magazine ran this same month. In an apparent attempt to top all others in shocking the public into reading their Pit bull article, they ran the headline "Time Bomb on Legs."

Horror author Stephen King could not have created a more frightening monster than this portrayal of the Pit bull. The second sentence of this article reads, "Never in the delirious dream of a disordered brain could anything more savage, more appalling, more hellish, be conceived than the dark form and savage face" (of the Pit bull).[5] The rest of the article descends even further, vilifying the Pit bull as a creature that revels in a "frenzy of bloodletting," and described as "lethal weapons" with "steel trap jaws" and as "killer dogs," and the new "hound of the Baskervilles." An unproven, unreferenced claim of Pit bulls biting with 1800 *psi* is included. The article then goes on to describe the formula used to torture, abuse and create a dangerous dog.

The author of this article is blithely unaware or unconcerned with his role in perpetuating the problem. While this type of journalism may be entertaining, the demonization of dogs by the media has serious consequences. Demonizing certain breeds only furthers their appeal to the most extremely abusive of owners while feeding into a public hysteria and frightening off any potential suitable owners for this breed of dog.

This same month, July 1987, still another major publication, *People Weekly,* would also contribute to the hype and hysteria about the Pit bull with their article, "An Instinct for the Kill."[6]

Even when other breeds of dogs were involved in attacks, the media would "spice" up the story with a reference to Pit bulls. In 1989, an Akita attacked and severely mauled a 5-year-old girl in Massachusetts. The article describes the attack and claims the Akita is "a breed that resembles the Japanese Pit bull."[7]

The Centers for Disease Control (CDC) report *Dog Bite-Related Fatalities From 1979–1988,* released in September 1989, would seal the fate of the Pit bulls with pseudo-statistics.[8] The CDC breed "statistics" were actually numbers derived largely from newspaper stories and from the media's identification of dogs involved in attacks. The report then discussed canine aggression almost exclusively from a focus of breed. Factors such as the function of the dog (guarding/fighting/breeding), reproductive status, sex of dog, victim behavior, and owner behavior were not addressed.

The primary focus of the study was breed of dog and victim profile (age/sex). While the media was quick to quote the CDC findings on the percentage of Pit bull attacks, virtually no coverage was given to one important finding in this study. A number of times in report, the CDC identified the risk of infants left unsupervised with dogs. In summarizing their findings the CDC wrote, "In particular, parents should be aware that very small infants left alone with a dog may be at risk of death." This finding with the potential to save lives was ignored. The number of Pit bulls found in attacks was of much greater interest.

The 1980s media and epidemiological focus on breed was a drastic departure from the multi-faceted approach of the early 1970s. Now, the story of dog attacks began and ended with breed of dog. Politicians, the media, and even some "experts" discussed and debated the problem of canine aggression only as it related to the Pit bull. Pit bull history, anatomy, and temperament were all dissected and examined at length. Little to no mention was made of the factors that had been recognized for centuries as contributing to canine aggression. The heat-stressed, chained dog that attacked a child in 1965 was now being reported as the "family Pit bull" which mauled a child. Almost no one cared to know anything about a dog attack, apart from breed.

Yet the courts and law enforcement have often demonstrated that incidents of severe/fatal aggression were the direct result of negligent, dangerous and/or criminal behavior by the dogs' owners. In the 1980s an unprecedented number of owners (Pit bull and non-Pit) were beginning to be charged criminally when their dogs were involved in a fatal attack. During this period, fully 25% of all owners of Pit bulls involved in fatalities were convicted of some type of criminal offense related to the attack. Law enforcement and the judicial system not only recognized that owners were the direct cause of their dogs' involvement in attacks, but pursued the matters criminally. Unfortunately, then (as today) many other owners escaped convictions due to the fact that many local or state laws did not adequately address negligent and/or abusive dog owners.

Nevertheless, four Pit bull owners during the 1980s were convicted of involuntary manslaughter and received prison sentences after their dogs were involved in a fatality. Another Pit bull owner received a 5 year prison sentence for reckless injury to a child when his 4-year-old stepson wandered near one of his Pit bulls chained to a utility pole. His defense, "That boy knew better than to get near that dog," probably did not help his case. (He was allowed to serve this sentence concurrently with a 10-year sentence he had already received for drug possession.) Other owners of Pit bulls (and other breeds) were convicted of crimes ranging from child endangerment to criminal negligence.

So while politicians, the media and others were clamoring about Pit bulls behaving unpredictably, the courts found and proved that indeed many of these attacks were very predictable.

Finally, in 2001, the American Veterinary Medical Association (AVMA) convened a Task Force on Canine Aggression and Human-Canine Interactions to address the continuing dog bite problem and to assist in avoiding "ineffective responses" following a severe dog attack in a community.[9] This in-depth study reported that "dog bite statistics are not really statistics, and they do not give an accurate picture of dogs that bite." Unfortunately the findings and information presented by these learned experts has been largely ignored by many communities when addressing dangerous dogs.

◆ ◆ ◆

If the media acknowledged their over-reporting of anything Pit bull in the late 1980s, one would imagine they would be able to recognize their intense over-reporting on Pit bull related matters today. Apparently not.

During the middle 1990s, as the Rottweiler appeared to be replacing the Pit bull as America's new guard/protection/intimidation dog, the Pit bull's popularity with unsavory owners who sought out dogs for negative functions appeared to have waned. No surprise, Rottweilers then overtook the Pit bull in severe and fatal dog attack statistics.

With a new monster looming on the horizon, the media briefly took their focus off the Pit bull. It seemed the Pit bull had finally run its two decade course as America's favorite super-predator and the unfortunate Rottweiler was positioned to suffer a similar fate.

In 1997, there were "only" 400+ newspaper headlines with the words "Pit bull" in them (down from 850+ in 1987).

In 2000, the third and latest CDC report on dog bite-related fatalities in the United States released another set of pseudo-statistics claiming the Rottweiler caused the most fatalities for the years 1997 and 1998. But, again, the CDC report counted the number of Pit bull-type dog attacks from their previous two studies (dating back to 1979 and still using media sources for breed identifications) and released a total for Pit bull-related fatalities during the last two decades, from 1979–1998.[10]

The unbridled media coverage of this report could only be described as orgasmic. Within a month after the release of the CDC report, hardly a person in America did not come to know that Rottweilers and Pit bulls caused the most human fatalities over the previous two decades.

It didn't matter that the odds of dying from a dog attack during the year 1996 were 1 in 11,534,087, while the odds of being struck by lightning during the same year were 1 in 4,210,857.

Nor did it matter that some of the dogs included in this study were terribly abused or were invited to act so aggressively by their owners. Dog breeds involved in fatal attacks were big news.

If the intense media focus on an event which occurred to one person in every 11 million exaggerated the risk of a fatal dog attack, things would get much worse for the Pit bull.

The War on Pit Bulls—Politicians Declare the Pit Bull Public Enemy Number One

In 2003, a 23-year-old woman was at work as an administrative assistant in Denver when Animal Control officers arrived at the home she shared with her mother. The officers explained to the woman's mother that they were there to confiscate her daughter's two dogs. The mother, confused and unsure as to what was happening, allowed Denver's Animal Control officers to enter her home and seize her daughter's two pet Pit bulls, Lady and Man.

Thus began this young woman's abrupt introduction to the world of Denver's Pit bull politics. It is no surprise this woman knew nothing of the ban on Pit bulls in the city of Denver, as she was only 9 years old in 1989, the year Denver concluded that the solution to canine aggression was to rid the city of Pit bulls. Now with her dogs seized and at Denver Municipal Animal Shelter, the only way to save them from death was to take them and move outside the city limits. Reluctantly, she moved, consoling herself that she was still close enough to visit and check on her mother regularly.

And so she did. For the next few months she frequently drove back into the city to visit her ailing mother. One day she took her two Pit bulls into the city with her, both for companionship and because her mother loved the dogs and their presence gave her comfort and joy. The young woman arrived at her mother's house and was inside with the dogs when, not half an hour later, Denver Animal Control officers appeared at the door. The young woman explained to the officers that she no longer lived in Denver and provided proof of her new residence. She attempted to explain that she was only visiting for a few hours with her mother. Pleading with the officers, she said she knew the dogs could not live in Denver, but she believed she could still bring them into the city to visit as long as she was able to prove the dogs resided outside the city. Nevertheless, Animal Control officers entered the home and seized the two dogs. Sometime during the next 24 hours, while the distraught young woman was making phone calls and trying to contact people in order to find out how she could get her dogs back, Denver Animal Control killed her pets.

Two years earlier, at the age of 21, when this woman received the young female Pit bull from her boyfriend, never did she imagine that the dog would be taken from her and destroyed. She believed if she was a good owner and did everything right—her Pit bulls were house dogs, never allowed to run loose or even be in the yard unless she was there also—the dogs would be safe. Additionally, the dogs were well-behaved, sweet, friendly and had never harmed anyone—what could possibly go wrong?

What went wrong was that these dogs were born Pit bulls. And as of 1989, Denver had passed a law making it illegal for a dog to be born a Pit bull.

How did Denver come to conclude that it is wrong to be a Pit bull? We've seen that starting in the 1980s the media introduced many of the ingredients necessary to frighten the public into believing that Pit bulls were dangerous. But while it is one thing for the public to buy into fear mongering, hysteria, misinformation and unproven claims, it is quite another matter for laws to be passed based on unsubstantiated claims and media-driven rhetoric.

Laws banning Pit bulls were introduced by another element that entered into the Pit bull debate during the 1980s, disseminating misinformation and unproven claims while manipulating the fear fostered by the media: The Politician.

We would like to believe that our laws are passed based on scientific data, proven theories or the testimony and evidence provided by, if not the majority, at least a respectable number of experts or professionals. This has never been the case with breed specific-legislation or the decision by officials to ban or restrict particular breeds of dogs. Experts are rarely consulted and even when they are invited to speak, their testimonies are more often than not discarded in favor of newspaper headlines or the emotional testimonies of a few victims.

Hundreds of examples can be given of politicians who flatly refuse to believe canine experts who have extensive personal and professional experience with dogs. The following example is typical of the responses politicians give when faced with the issue of canine aggression as presented by someone who has spent a lifetime working with aggressive dogs or studying canine behavior.

During a roundtable meeting about Denver's proposed Pit bull ban in 1989, a dog expert was attempting to describe and explain the nature and workings of canine aggression to a Denver councilwoman. The man was a professional dog trainer and had personally handled and trained over 100 protection trained dogs (of different breeds). He was explaining how all dogs can display the same types of aggression and how all dogs will respond aggressively to certain stimuli.

The councilwoman flatly refuted his knowledge of canine aggression, commenting, "You can't tell me that if there was a Pit bull loose and a small terrier loose, that they are going to respond in the same manner, because that is not true."

The expert dog trainer assured the councilwoman that it was true and stated, "You could be attacked by a Schnauzer the same way that you could be attacked by a Pit bull."

Again she rebuffed his knowledge of canine aggression based on her self-appointed expertise and knowledge of the subject matter, with the response, "I'm sorry but people run away from Pit bulls. People don't run away from Schnauzers."

Perhaps worse than the "Pit bulls are dangerous because people run from them" argument, are comments such as the following, so often used by politicians and delivered by Denver's Director of Environmental Health:

"I'll tell you the difference between Pit bulls and other breeds: They have lower levels of fighting inhibition; they have a tendency to attack without provocation because they're bred to do that. They will continue to fight until they're either dead or exhausted, no matter how bad you've hurt them, because they have been trained to do that. They don't signal when they're going to attack…"

This is the standard description used by almost all politicians when discussing how Pit bulls are different and need to be banned.

It is incredible that these politicians do not see what they are doing by asserting these claims: They are deliberately ignoring the testimonies of legitimate professionals (veterinarians, humane society personnel, dog trainers, breed clubs) and choosing to believe and to validate the boasts of a criminal, inhumane, machismo group of dog owners who for a hundred years have touted extraordinary abilities about their dogs in order to increase their personal and financial worth. The claims like those quoted above are almost word for word the claims of dog fighters.

Additionally, the city of Denver entered into evidence outrageously flawed statistics and then drew totally inaccurate conclusions about the "differentness" of Pit bulls based on these meaningless numbers (see Appendix C).

During the late 1980s and early 1990s, newspapers were hyping the Pit bull for all it was worth. Many politicians quickly jumped on the bandwagon, enacting laws and ordinances in response to the hysteria. Denver would be joined by Miami, Cincinnati, Kansas City, Toledo, and dozens of smaller cities in enacting bans on Pit bulls in the late 1980s.

But things would get much worse for the Pit bull as, by the end of the 20th century, there would be another 200+ cities, communities and counties which enacted breed bans or restrictions against them or any dog that may be viewed as having "Pit bull characteristics." Not only was ridding the community of Pit bull-looking dogs touted as a cure-all for dog attacks, but at least another 26 breeds of dogs would be banned or restricted as "dangerous" in communities across the country. The arbitrariness of these "dangerous breed" determinations cannot be overstated. Some breeds with no documented cases of severe or fatal attacks in the community (or even throughout the country) were banned. Some communities touted their breed bans to be a pre-emptive strike, banning an entire breed *before* it had a "chance" to attack. Others merely looked up the history of a breed and determined the dangerousness of the dogs according to the original function of the breed. Other community leaders offered no reason for the "dangerous" determination of certain breeds on their ban/restricted list.

The beginning of the 21st century shows little respite for the Pit bull (and other breeds) as the media and some politicians have partnered up to create a tag team of misinformation and hysteria about canine behavior.

◆ ◆ ◆

The 21st century media has introduced the public to a host of new canine experts: Kory Nelson (Denver, CO), Michael Bryant (Ontario, Canada), Virginia (Ginger) Rugai (Chicago, IL), Rep. Paul Wesselhoft (Moore, OK), and Peter Vallone Jr. (Astoria, NY). These "experts" can easily be found in newspaper articles discussing the history, anatomy, nature and temperament of the Pit bull. The only problem is all these "Pit bull experts" have other full-time jobs—as politicians.

Yet, somehow they have managed to acquire the sum total of knowledge about dog breeds, canine behavior, epidemiology (the study of dog bites), canine population statistics, Pit bull history, Pit bull temperament, Pit bull anatomy, and Pit bull aggression. Not only have they acquired all this knowledge, but they have analyzed it and discovered the solution to canine aggression which has eluded full time canine experts throughout the last century.

Their analysis of the data has led them to definitively conclude that the dog attack problem is caused by: the Pit bull.

And this is supported by their assessment that either:

• Pit bulls are ticking time bombs
• Pit bulls are land sharks, or attack like sharks
• Pit bulls feel no pain, or are impervious to pain
• Pit bulls are inherently or uniquely dangerous
• Pit bulls exhibit behaviors unlike any other breed of dog, or are "different"
• The Pit bull's history of dog fighting makes the breed uniquely dangerous

These assessments are incredible in the breadth and depth of their ignorance of Pit bulls (and all breeds of dogs), the function of dogs in the history of the human/canine bond, and the human and canine behaviors which contribute to incidents of aggression.

The fact that government officials in some of these cities and provinces can enter your home to seize your property (Pit bulls or mixed breed dogs that may look like Pit bulls) based on these grade-school-level assessments of canine behavior is a frightening reality. Yet, outrageous comments about Pit bulls and canine behavior are broadcast across the country, enabling these very same legislators to garner support for their one-step solution to canine aggression.

Perhaps worse than failing to address the real reasons for dog attacks, is the fact that these politicians seem blissfully unaware of the insidious results of making such outrageous claims about Pit bulls and Pit bull behavior. History has repeatedly shown that publicly portraying a breed of dog as exceedingly ferocious or dangerous will only serve to increase the breed's popularity with dangerous owners. Public statements that Pit bulls are "land sharks" or "ticking time bombs" will not increase the breed's popularity with responsible owners, but only serve to increase the breed's popularity with owners who are purposely seeking out a "dangerous" dog. The claims of these politicians have only perpetuated the problem by demonizing breeds of dogs and then making them even more desirable and more sought after by people who will mismanage and abuse these animals in such a way as to put the community at risk.

◆ ◆ ◆

At perhaps no time in history has mankind been as ignorant of natural canine behavior as we are today. Perhaps at no time in history has mankind been more ignorant of the essence of the familiar bond between owner and dog—the bond which drives and directs most canine behavior. And perhaps at no time in history has man publicly forsaken or denied his command of the canine species.

It has even been suggested that Pit bulls are no longer domesticated animals. Maquoketa, Iowa, has made it unlawful to keep certain animals. The list includes all types of wild and exotic animals from lions and baboons to hyenas. Pit bulls are included in the list between Piranha fish and the puma (mountain lion).

A claim that Pit bulls are different or unlike other domestic dogs is a direct refusal to acknowledge a factual relationship which has formed over tens of thousands of years—a relationship which man has controlled, directed, and mastered with great efficiency over the centuries.

In a society unparalleled in its access to information and ability to control our natural environment, we now claim that we are unable to master our dogs. Supremely adept in the art of transference, humans have now absolved themselves from any control or culpability in the creation and maintenance of the Pit bull. We've thrown up our hands and cry out that we are now the victim of this breed. They have forced us to destroy them. It is not our fault; the beast has gotten away from us.

How easily we forsake the dogs rather than take responsibility for their behavior is a sad testament to how well humans fulfill their commitment to the canine/human bond. This is perhaps the ultimate act of betrayal which humans have inflicted on our canine companions—the refusal to own what is ours, what we have created.

It is no mere accident that Pit bulls are labeled "different." It is also no small coincidence that Pit bulls are compared to sharks. This is a psychological ploy that has been used for centuries to disassociate or distance one being from others of its own kind in order to subjugate, abuse or annihilate them.

With humans, color of skin, religion, sex, language, and country of origin have all been used at one time or another as the basis for categorizing the "inferiority" or "differentness" of another group of persons. Once a mental distancing or disassociation is accomplished, it "allows" for abusive or atrocious behaviors to be visited upon these dissimilar beings.

For those with their own agenda, this psychological ploy has been used (wittingly or unwittingly) with great effectiveness against the Pit bull. By stripping away the traits that humans recognize and cherish in their dogs (loyalty, obedience, devotion, faithfulness, predictability, trustworthiness), the Pit bull has been separated from all his canine brethren or stripped of his "canineness."

We would like to believe our society has advanced from the mass persecutions and ethnic cleansings that our fellow humans have ruthlessly practiced since the dawn of history. However, fear coupled with ignorance are still powerful mind-numbing agents, allowing seemingly rational people to be swept up by currents of panic-stricken accusations and led into notorious miscarriages of justice. From the Salem witch hunts to McCarthyism and the Communist red scare, Americans have proven we are not immune to the suspension of reason and the sacrifice of innocents to quell public hysteria.

History now clearly shows there were no witches in Salem, nor was our country overrun and infiltrated by communists, and eventually history will bear out that Pit bulls are dogs just like any other dogs. But before that can happen we must come to realize that we are in the midst of a social hysteria about Pit bulls.

Today, police chase down fleeing Pit bulls in the street, firing dozens of wild shots in response to media-fed rumors of supernatural Pit bull abilities. Politicians coach and nurture this fear with their own brand of rhetoric used to assist in the passing of quick and ineffective legislation created to pacify communities ignorant of the real cause of dog attacks. Hundreds of animal shelters throughout the country kill unclaimed Pit bull-looking dogs, as they are deemed "unadoptable" solely on their physical appearance.

This has occurred because we have allowed the Pit bull to be "stripped of his canineness"—not by genetics or by breeding, but by wild theories, rumors and myths. We have succumbed to the fear propagated by individuals and organizations with agendas totally unrelated to community safety or dog bite prevention.

CHAPTER 11

Pseudoscience and Hysteria Triumph

"There is nothing to fear except the persistent refusal to find out the truth, the persistent refusal to analyze the causes of happenings."
(Dorothy Thompson, 1894–1961)

There is an incredible amount of information and misinformation available both in paper form and on the Internet about the history, function and temperament of the American Pit Bull Terrier. This plethora of information consists of everything from factual data to hysterical diatribes and unsubstantiated theories about Pit bull temperament and anatomy.

Politicians, prosecutors, attorneys, newspaper reporters, TV and radio station personalities, breeders, trainers, animal control officers, veterinarians, shelter workers, dog fighters, street thugs, and just about anyone able to speak has an opinion or personal theory about the strength and temperament of the American Pit Bull Terrier. These opinions and theories are based on a dizzying mixture of personal experience, media-induced images, rumors, myths, speculation, fear mongering, and personal or political agendas.

Separating fact from fiction is time consuming and tedious work. It is much easier for most people to embrace information which supports their pre-existing belief. For example, if your neighbor has a gentle and friendly Pit bull, you may be more inclined from personal experience to believe information presented which supports this view of the breed. If your neighbor is a drug dealer and has three Pit bulls lunging from chains or barking madly behind a fence, you may be more inclined to believe information supporting the vicious nature of Pit bulls.

Professionals, too, can have diametrically opposed viewpoints and opinions about Pit bulls. Police officers are more inclined toward encountering bad owners (criminals and their aggressively encouraged dogs) and often see only the "bad" Pit bulls. Veterinarians often have a positive image of Pit bulls since in their profession they more frequently encounter these dogs in stressful situations (pain, fear, with strangers) and recognize the extreme tolerance found in Pit bulls.

If you have no personal experience with Pit bulls, then your only information is acquired from newspapers headlines, and it is not difficult to understand how people have formed a very negative opinion of Pit bulls with the media as their only source of knowledge about the breed.

Not until false claims, both of anatomical and behavioral issues, are cast aside, not until breed identification issues are addressed, and not until the circumstances that contributed to dog attacks are examined can aggression be addressed in a way which may provide viable solutions and offer preventive measures to decrease the number of attacks on humans. Solutions to canine aggression are doomed to fail if they are based on "facts" not founded on evidence or on unproven claims of canine anatomy or behavior. Unfortunately, much of the information presented about Pit bulls falls under the category of pseudoscience. Pseudoscience can best be described as information presented as fact, with the appearance of a scientific basis, which, however, is found upon examination to have no evidence supporting such claims.

Claims of anatomical abnormalities, for instance, seem to have a ring of truth about them. The fact that a tangible physical feature is the source of a theory or "fact" would seem to suggest there is tangible physical evidence to support this. In other words, the jaw of an animal is a tangible feature; it can be seen, touched and examined. Claims of abnormalities in such a visible feature seem to be based in reality because, seriously, why would these claims be quoted and widely believed if they can so easily be disproved?

Pit Bulls and the Locking Jaw Myth

The Doberman was purported to have anatomical abnormalities (brain size vs. skull size) which rendered it dangerous and unpredictable, setting it apart from other breeds of dog. To upstage the Doberman another breed would also need an anatomic abnormality which set it apart from other breeds in its ferocity. The Pit bull arrived on the scene in the early 1980s with not one, but multiple rumored anatomical features which quickly outclassed the Doberman in their ability to frighten and shock the public.

The first anatomical claim to fame about the Pit bull was the myth of the locking jaws. This theory suggests that the Pit bull has a unique jaw and dental structure which allows it to "lock" onto their victim.

While Pit bulls do have a specialized and manipulated trait which allows them to exhibit tenacity and perseverance in maintaining their grip (from their Bulldog ancestor), this is not sufficient to propel the breed into super-predator status. After all, while Pit bulls (and Bulldogs) had this ability to hold for well over a century, prior to 1980, other breeds were considered far more vicious than the Pit bull. All breeds of dogs have a particular trait or appearance which sets them apart from other breeds. The new breed that "we love to hate" would have to have much more impressive credentials than just a specialized ability to hold on tenaciously; they would have to have an evil design which would allow for this ability. And an inescapable locking jaw is just such an evil- sounding device.

This is a classic example of a belief that has no factual or scientific basis. The locking jaw mechanism is a myth. But this myth was as easily bought into by the public as was the myths about the bloodthirsty nature of the Bloodhound and the Doberman brain size. It is not terribly difficult to see how easily this was accomplished and how fervently people hold onto their beliefs once they accept them.

The myth of the Bloodhound's "bloodthirsty ferocity" was a rather easy sell. The breed was mostly used to track down unsavory persons or in the cruel pursuits of their masters. Being chased or set on by dogs taps into humans' instinctive and primal fear of being prey. The name "Bloodhound" certainly held a negative connotation and many people confused or misunderstood the true definition of the term. Bloodhounds were defined as a hunter *of* blood, not a hunter *by* blood. To some, this distinction may seem trivial, but in reality there is a vital difference. The Bloodhound tracked warm-blooded animals, but was not following a "blood trail" (not thirsting after blood). As discussed previously, the Tom Shows did much to reinforce this bloodthirsty image.

A generation later, with images of Dobermans and Nazi Germany still fresh in the minds of the public, anyone taking even a cursory look at a Doberman's rather narrow skull could easily buy into the "skull too small-dog goes mad" theory. The media showing any attack or guard dog as a snarling Doberman helped fix this image of viciousness.

In the 1980s, the broad head and square jaw of the Pit bull easily sold a whole new generation of people into the "locking jaw" theory.

All these theories sound like they have a scientific basis, and that there must be evidence on which these beliefs are based. The truth is, there isn't. There are no scientific studies or evidence which validates any of these widely held beliefs. On the contrary, there are several written statements by experts definitively refuting the locking jaw theory.

Dr. Howard Evans (Professor Emeritus, College of Veterinary Medicine at Cornell University, Ithaca New York and author of the world's definitive work on canine anatomy [*Anatomy of the Dog*]), in conjunction with Dr. Sandy deLahunta, one of the foremost dog neurologist in the country, along with Dr. Katherine Houpt, a leading dog behaviorist wrote the following statement about the "locking jaw" in Pit bulls:

> "We all agree that the power of the bite is proportional to the size of the jaws and the jaw muscles. There is no anatomical structure that could be a locking mechanism in any dog."

Research on the functional morphology of the jaws of various dog breeds conducted by Dr. I. Lehr Brisbin of the University of Georgia showed that:

> "there were no mechanical or morphological differences between the jaws of American Pit Bull Terriers and those of any of the other comparable breeds of dogs which we studied. In addition, we found that the American Pit

Bull Terriers did not have any unique mechanism that would allow these dogs to lock their jaws."[1]

Clamps with Front Teeth and Grinds/Chews with Back Teeth Myth

This is a carry-over from the old 1800s Bulldog myth. Jack London may have unintentionally contributed greatly to this myth with the publication of his novel *White Fang*. In his classic theme, wild animal versus dog, we find a wolf pitted against a Bulldog. In London's telling of this lengthy and protracted battle, the Bulldog's fighting technique in defeating the wolf is described in part as, "the jaws shifting their grip, slightly relaxing and coming together again in a chewing movement." The wolf is described as at a loss to defend itself against the Bulldog's tactics as he "did not know the chewing method of fighting, nor were his jaws adapted to it."

But, as one reader in 1908 pointed out, Mr. London "displays an innocence (about dog fighting) which does him credit." The reader, apparently intimately familiar with dog fighting, explains in great detail how the Bulldog is not truly a fighting dog, and that the breed's function and physical appearance was designed to bait or hold onto bulls and not for fighting. The author then describes the creation and capabilities of what he believes to be the true fighting breed, the Bull Terrier ("A Question of Bulldogs and Fakers, President Roosevelt and Jack London Seem to Forget That the Bulldog is Not Really a Fighter," *New York Times*, November 1, 1908).

The grinding/chewing jaw capability is just another of the many myths which surrounded the Bulldog a century ago, and which has carried over into the new Pit bull mythology. Neither Bulldogs, Pit bulls, nor any other breed of dog have a jaw structure that would allow for gripping with their front canine teeth and simultaneously grinding or chewing with their back molar teeth.

Pit Bull Bite Force Calculated in *psi* (pounds per square inch) Myth

Another physical ability alleged to set the Pit bull apart from all other breeds of dogs, and even surpass the capabilities of many wild carnivores, is the claim of massive biting power, measured in *psi*, or pounds per square inch of force.

A disturbing number of newspaper reporters, attorneys, politicians, physicians, and testosterone- driven websites discussing Pit bulls advance outrageous claims of Pit bull biting power in terms of *psi*. Claims of 1200 *psi,* 1800 *psi,* 2000 *psi,* and even 2600 *psi* are quoted and bantered about regularly in discussions on Pit bulls. And like the locking jaw mechanism, though widely believed, none can cite a reputable source for this information.

Extensive research on the subject of Pit bull biting force reveals only one medical journal reference on the *psi* of Pit bulls. The information (or rather misinformation) is startling and unsettling in that it is printed in a scientific journal without supporting data. "Mauling by Pit Bull Terriers: Case Report"[2] is an article presented in 1989 by four medical doctors on the multidisciplinary management of a child presented with extensive soft-tissue damage as the result of an attack by four Pit bull terriers. The authors of this article state: "Pit bulls bite with greater force than most dogs (up to 1800 lb/in 2)." They cite their sole reference for this claim as: Boenning, D.A., Fleisher, G.R., Campos, J.M.: "Dog bites in children." *Am. J. Emerg. Med.*, I: 17–21, 1983.

Examination of this cited report, "Dog bites in children,"[3] reveals an extensive medical article written on the management and treatment of dog bites in children. *No* mention or reference whatsoever is found to Pit bulls, biting force, or dog breeds within this article. Their source cited for the *psi* claim is nothing more than a red herring.

The authors of the original report ("Mauling by Pit Bull Terriers") make other unsettling and unsubstantiated claims about Pit bull anatomy when they state, "Once they have their victim in a hold, they do not merely maintain the 'bite', but continue to grind their premolars and molars into the tissue while the canine teeth stabilize the hold."

Despite the proclamations of these human doctors, this simply is not true. Pit bull anatomy, jaw structure, dentition, biting/chewing behaviors and abilities are no different than any other breed of dog (perhaps with the exception of the some of the brachiocephalic or extremely short nosed breeds). Pit bulls, and all other breeds of dogs, have an upper jaw (maxilla) and a lower jaw (mandible), neither of which have movable parts (or joints), meaning that if the back molars in the upper jaw are moving so are the front canine teeth in the upper jaw. The front canine teeth cannot be unmoving (or stable) while the back molars are moving (grinding) as they are fixed on the same bone (maxillary bone). The same is true of the lower jawbone or mandible.

Misinformation and unsubstantiated claims about Pit bull anatomy and abilities published in medical journals is profoundly disturbing. Once inaccurate and unsupported data is published in a science journal, all future studies which reference this source become fundamentally flawed. Doctors who treat human patients, in reporting on dog attack cases in medical journals, continue to reference each other in a never-ending succession, building on one false and unsubstantiated claim made in 1989. These unproven claims have even been entered into official court documents as "evidence" of the "destructiveness" of the Pit bull bite. Needless to say, any conclusions about the type of injuries inflicted by Pit bulls found in a medical journal article that cites this inaccurate source (Pit bulls bite with a force of 1800 lb/in 2) are invalid.

Recently, Dr. Brady Barr of *National Geographic* did a study on animal bites. Domestic dogs and humans were tested along with wild animals. The results seem more feasible and within the parameters of reason. The force of bite in the test subjects was recorded as:

Humans: 120 pounds of bite pressure
Wild dogs: 310 lbs
Lions: 600 lbs
White sharks: 600 lbs
Hyenas: 1000 lbs
Snapping turtles: 1000 lbs
Crocodiles: 2500 lbs
Domestic dogs: 320 lbs. of pressure on average

A German Shepherd, American Pit Bull Terrier and Rottweiler were tested using a bite sleeve equipped with a specialized computer instrument. The American Pit Bull Terrier had the least amount of pressure of the three dogs tested.[4]

In addition to the *National Geographic* study, other reliable sources have done studies on the *psi* of non-specific breeds of dogs. It is generally agreed that all dogs bite at approximately 200–450 *psi* (the higher end numbers apply to larger dogs).

While these results seem within reason, bite force in animals is difficult to measure accurately. Variables which cannot be controlled include: the individual animal's motivation to bite into a testing device and how hard the animal chose to bite. It is not possible to know if animals are biting with full force or if a bite is inhibited.

According to Dr. I. Lehr Brisbin of the University of Georgia:

"To the best of our knowledge, there are no published scientific studies that would allow any meaningful comparison to be made of the biting power of various breeds of dogs. There are, moreover, compelling technical reasons why such data describing biting power in terms of 'pounds per square inch' can never be collected in a meaningful way. All figures describing biting power in such terms can be traced to either unfounded rumor or, in some cases, to newspaper articles with no foundation in factual data."[5]

Fortunately, an emergency room doctor in New York, seemingly unaware of the debate and rumors of *psi* biting force in Pit bulls, allowed common sense to prevail when presented with a patient with severe bites. It was reported in the newspapers in the fall of 2003:

A 37-year-old man entered Harlem Hospital (NYC) seeking treatment for bite wounds. The man claimed he had been bitten by a Pit bull dog. An emergency room doctor, after examining the wounds, determined the injuries to the man could not have come from a dog bite, Pit bull or otherwise. The wounded man abruptly left the hospital. Police officers later arrived at his apartment to find the animal responsible for the bites was a 400 lb. Bengal-Siberian tiger the man was keeping as a "pet" in his Harlem housing project.[6]

Hormonal Reactions, Chemical Imbalances, Brain Size and Other Neurological Nonsense

None of the claims about chemical imbalances or brain pressure warrant serious discussion. These are outlandish assertions serving only to embellish the super-predator image of the Pit bull and appear to be myths simply transposed from the Doberman onto the Pit bull.

Recently, a newspaper article stated that "some experts even believe that the presence of hormones in children of puberty age can set off Pit bulls."[7]

As with most of these outrageous claims, the source ("some experts") is not cited. The questions which could be put to these "experts" are: How has it happened that Pit bulls, exclusively, have come to acquire this ability to detect and react to pubescent hormones? And the even more compelling question: Since pre-teens and teenagers (male and female) are vastly underrepresented in fatal dog attacks, what evidence supports such a theory? (Pre-teens and teenagers are in one of the age groups least likely to be attacked and killed by any dog. Children under the age of six and the elderly are overwhelmingly the most frequent victims of severe/fatal dog attacks by any breed.)

Nonetheless, newspapers and editorials print this baseless nonsense. Suffice it to say, these are all untrue and there is no evidence whatsoever to support any claims of a chemical, neurological or puberty-based aggression exclusive to Pit bulls.

Pit Bull Attacks are Like Shark Attacks—Pit Bulls are Land Sharks

A first impulse is to simply dismiss these allegations as nonsensical because, like the exploding brain myth, they are so outlandish as to not warrant serious discussion. The fact that the city of Denver introduced the claim that "Pit bull attacks are like shark attacks" as evidence for breed-specific legislation demonstrates how this kind of misinformation and shoddy research can wind up as "fact" in official court records. The fact that "educated" and not-so-educated people in positions to legislate and enact laws are making these claims necessitates addressing this theory as if it truly had any merit.

From the Poodle to the Pit bull, all domestic dogs are descended from the same ancestor—the wolf. But the Pit bull has seemingly accomplished an astounding genetic feat. It has singularly been able not only to surpass all traits found in its direct ancestor (the wolf), but has allegedly been able to bypass its own species and class and cross over to join the ranks with entirely different species and classes of animals (lions/tigers/sharks).

Not only do Pit bulls allegedly attack and bite like tigers, lions and sharks, but the implication is that they have also taken on the behaviors of these wild animals. In the interest of not belaboring similar inane theories (Pit bulls are like tigers/lions), only the shark issue will be addressed, as this is the most commonly seen comparison to Pit bull attacks.

Shark Anatomy/Jaws, Teeth (Class: *Chondrichthye*)

Sharks are cartilaginous fish. The shark's jaw exhibits characteristics unique in the animal kingdom. Unlike almost all other animals (and all mammals), the shark is equipped with two mobile and independent jaws, enabling it to attack large prey and tear off extensive pieces of flesh. This jaw structure allows for tremendous extensibility, enabling the animal to swallow some prey whole.

In addition to a unique jaw structure, the shark has a set of teeth of which the anatomy and manner of replacement is unique in the animal world. While there are over 400 species of sharks and they differ significantly in dental formula, all sharks have at least five sets of teeth, covered to varying degrees with buccal mucous membrane. One set of teeth sits on the ridge of the jawbone, with at least 4 rows of teeth lined up behind the first, functional row. If one or more of the teeth on the functional row are broken or torn out, the corresponding teeth in the next row will rotate up to replace them.[8] For example, the White Shark has 46 teeth arranged in seven rows (not all of which are functional) for a total of 322 teeth.[9]

While shape and size of teeth vary among shark species, all sharks have serrated teeth. These teeth are edged or lined with smaller teeth, which are razor-sharp, rendering each tooth a veritable saw.

Canine (Pit Bull)/Jaws, Teeth (Class: *Mammalia*)

Dogs are mammals. Unlike the shark, the dog does not have two mobile and independent jaws. The only mobile bone in the mammalian skull is the mandible, or lower jaw. The dental formula for the dog is 2 (I 3/3, C 1/1, P 4/4, M 2/3) for a total of 42 teeth.

Anatomically, the comparison between dogs and sharks could not be any more far-fetched. The dog does not have a jaw structure which allows it to swallow prey whole, nor does its jaw structure contain independent jaws (upper and lower). Unlike the shark, the dog's upper jaw is firmly attached to the skull. The dog's teeth are not serrated with razor-sharp edges, nor do they have rows of teeth positioned behind a primary set of functional teeth.

Perhaps the persons who made the claim that "Pit bull attacks are like shark attacks" will say that the comparison was not to be taken so literally—that they meant it as the "manner of the attack," "the nature of the attack," "the behavior of the attack" or "the injurious nature of the attack" when they compared Pit bulls to sharks.

The manner, nature, behavior, and injuries inflicted by sharks during an attack are driven by predation or feeding. Biting off large chunks of flesh, tearing and ripping are methods by which the shark obtains food. The comparison would have to end here, as no one can seriously believe Pit bulls view humans as a food source.

If an argument is made that the comparison was not to be taken literally at all, but was simply a metaphor, the question then becomes: *How can comparing Pit bulls to sharks help in the understanding, or prevention, of canine aggression?*

Well, it can't.

Which leads to the following questions:

- What is the purpose of comparing Pit bulls to sharks?
- Is this approach an effective way to address canine aggression?

Since Pit bulls do not behave, attack or have anatomical features which allow for any meaningful comparison with sharks, this cannot possibly be an effective way to address canine aggression. This leaves the remaining question about the purpose of this comparison.

While some politicians appear to know very little about canine anatomy and aggression, and even less about shark anatomy, they do know how to promote themselves as "effective" and "concerned" lawmakers. The "facts" released about Pit bulls by some politicians are not really facts, but rather tactics—tactics that alarm and frighten the public into buying into a quick and ineffectual approach to a complex human problem.

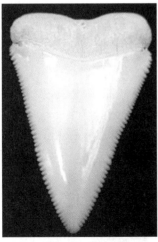

Shark Tooth - Great White

L 1.78 inches x W 1.20 inches

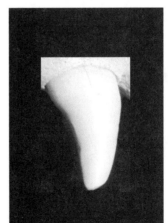

Canine Tooth - 70 lb. Dog

L 0.79 inches x W 0.47 inches

Photo Credit: megalodonsharkteeth.com

Statements comparing Pit bulls to sharks tap into a primal human fear of being attacked and eaten by large predators. These references are emotionally charged, attention-getting devices, capable of frightening a large segment of the public into believing that they are more likely to be killed by a roaming land shark (Pit bull) than by driving to work in the morning. A jittery public sighs in relief when politicians tell them not to fear, for they have the problem within their grasp. They have legislation which will rid the streets of these menaces, soothing the very fear they helped to create.

This is certainly not to suggest that all politicians are unconcerned with finding real preventive measures to control dangerous dogs. But those who instill fear in order to promote their agenda are either grossly ignorant of canine behavior or have questionable motives. Either way, this will not produce effective legislation to protect the public from dog attacks.

Pit bulls are Impervious to Pain and Therefore More Dangerous During an Attack

Because Pit bulls have historically been bred to have an increased tolerance for pain, it would not be unreasonable to conclude that this would be a factor in severe/fatal dog attacks. There are also some documented cases where Pit bulls appeared highly tolerant of pain and focused during an attack.

But sweeping statements like this are never based on documented evidence of significant populations. Behaviors such as extreme tolerance to pain can be found in groups of dogs within a population, but it is equally easy to find groups of dogs within the Pit bull population which have normal or even increased sensitivity to pain. Increased tolerance for pain is an unnatural or artificial trait within the breed and as such needs to be constantly selected for. Therefore, the number of Pit bulls that are extremely tolerant to pain would depend largely on the recent breeding practices of humans, which cannot be determined.

There are documented cases of Pit bulls that were extremely difficult to disengage from an attack. There are documented cases of Pit bull attacks which were thwarted when the dogs were struck with bats or shovels. There are documented cases of Pit bull attacks which ceased when the animals were struck with sticks, curtain rods, hands, feet or other relatively ineffectual objects. And there are many cases of Pit bulls attacking without much conviction, with the dog retreating at the shouts or mere appearance of another person. But these situations only demonstrate that there are many variables within any breed.

It is well-documented that other breeds of dogs, upon attacking in a severely aggressive manner, are also difficult to disengage. This could be seen as far back as the previously mentioned 1903 attack with the shepherd dog, during which the arrival of the wife, who struck the dog on the back with an axe, "only maddened the dog even further." Even though the dog was frenzied, the arrival of the woman might very well have saved her husband's life, had she not struck him in the leg with the axe.

Many severe Pit bull attacks did not result in a fatality, precisely because of direct interference or thwarting of the attack. Attacks that resulted in a fatality overwhelmingly involved unsupervised children or elderly persons alone with the dog(s), regardless of breed.

The probability is not that a Pit bull attack will result in a fatality because the dog could not be "beaten off" the victim, but simply because there was no one of significant force to do exactly that.

While it may seem logical that increased tolerance to pain would be a significant factor in Pit bull attacks, in reality it is not. Most dogs do not respond to pain while in the frenzied state of a severe attack. This is a behavior observed in many different breeds of dogs and is found repeatedly in many of the earlier examples given of dog attacks. However, forceful and direct intervention, by either separating or shielding the victim from the dog(s) has prevented many a severe attack from becoming a fatality in both Pit bull and other breed attacks.

Again, this distinction is important, because claims of Pit bulls being highly tolerant of pain easily turn into the misconception that Pit bulls feel no pain. Recently, Chicago Alderman Rugai, in commenting on the reasons for introducing breed-specific legislation in her city, was quoted in the *Chicago Tribune* as saying, "Pit bulls feel no pain…"[10] These kinds of outrageous comments do incalculable damage. Aside from the obvious repercussions Pit bulls may suffer from this, humans can suffer as well.

One hundred years ago the media was reporting that dogs would attack in response to pain, thus educating people in the avoidance of attacks. Yet today the very persons who clamor so loudly about their desire to save people from dog (Pit bull) attacks disseminate information which is the antithesis to dog bite prevention.

Pit Bull Attacks are Unprovoked—Pit Bulls Attack without Warning

This subject will be discussed in more detail in the chapter on media and interpretation of behavior as it relates to all breeds of dogs. However, as it relates to Pit bulls, this is just another unsubstantiated claim which has been used to classify Pit bulls as "different." Pit bulls are alleged to attack "without provocation" as a result of their breeding and use as fighting dogs.

Outrageous claims about Pit bulls and provocation are found regularly. Statements that "most" Pit bull attacks are unprovoked can be found from politicians, physicians, and others unschooled in canine behavior and unfamiliar with the circumstances preceding dog attacks. There are numerous reasons why claims of Pit bulls (or any breed) attacking without provocation are baseless.

The classification of an attack as unprovoked is usually based on the declarations of a negligent owner who does not care to understand canine behavior, an owner who is unable to read (understand) canine behavior, a busy owner who is too preoccupied with the tasks of daily living to see the signs and signals dogs usually display, or persons who deliberately misrepresent the facts to limit their culpability.

Dogs have evolved over thousands of years (both from their ancestor the wolf, and as domesticated dogs in a human society) to be social animals. Social animals communicate by body language and with vocalization. Dogs do this with stares, body stiffening, positioning of ears, tail and head, and growling, to name only a few. Pit bulls do this as much as any other breed of dog.

Only hubris allows humans to declare that a few generations of selective breeding of a small population of Pit bulls (for fighting) can erase what thousands of years of evolution have created.

While we certainly can find cases in which a Pit bull seemingly attacked without displaying any warning signals, again this is not a phenomenon exclusive to Pit bulls, and it certainly is not representative of most Pit bull attacks. Additionally, since so many severe and fatal dog attacks (all breed) are on young, unsupervised children who cannot read or understand canine warning signals, this certainly leads one to question how these types of claims of "attacking without warning" can be taken seriously. As previously stated, there was only one recorded fatality by a Pit bull-type dog in the United States from 1966–1975. The first fatal Pit bull attack we find after this decade occurred in May 1976, when a 6-year-old girl wandered over to a Pit bull chained under a carport at an apartment complex. It is worthy to note that neighbors stated they heard the attack and "heard the dog growling," but assumed it was growling at another animal and did not respond. Only too late did they realize that these very clear signals of aggression were directed towards the child.

The overwhelming majority of Pit bulls in the United States cannot trace their lineage directly back to game-bred fighting dogs. And fortunately most Pit bulls are not used for fighting but live, to varying degrees, in social environments where signals of fear, aggression, excitement, contentment, and friendliness are sent and received on a daily basis. Because humans attached to these dogs cannot, or care not, to read these signals does not mean they do not exist. Contrary to what the media and most owners of attacking dogs would have you believe, severe/fatal attacks by Pit bulls are usually the end result of an escalation of a series of obvious aggressive behaviors.

It is more within the nature of humans to lie about events that point to their culpability than it is within the nature of dogs to attack unprovoked. So, we find owners less than truthful about prior incidents of aggression or improper treatment of dogs when they are facing legal or civil action after their dog has severely or fatally injured someone.

No owner is going to admit a Pit bull attacked a child because it was kept on a heavy logging chain for five years, bred two times a year, was worm-infested and parasite-ridden, was teased by children and lived a miserable, lonely existence in the far corner of the backyard. The owner is going to tell police that the dog never showed any signs of aggressiveness. And if owners' comments are unreliable, media accounts of these events are even more so as they are all too content to describe these dogs as "family pets" and print the abusive owners' cries of ignorance and denial.

Another reason why statements about dog attacks being unprovoked are unreliable is because rarely do they take into account the familiar aspect that is so important from a dog's perspective. What may be provocation for one dog will not be provocation to another dog, depending on the relationship between the dog and the person. A clear example of this occurred in Tennessee in 2003 when a 4-year-old boy accompanied his grandfather to a nearby home. The boy had a Rottweiler at home, with which he was known to play very roughly. It was not uncommon for the boy to jump upon his dog and attempt to ride on the Rottweiler's back. Like true family dogs, the Rottweiler tolerated this child's rambunctious play good-naturedly.

However, the home they were visiting also contained a Rottweiler along with another large mixed breed dog. Neither of these intact, male dogs had any history of aggression but, unfortunately, the boy went into the yard alone and it is believed he attempted to play with these dogs in the same fashion as he would play with his pet Rottweiler. Clearly, the reactions of these dogs if the boy attempted to climb onto their backs would be different than the boy's pet Rottweiler. Did the boy mean to harm the dogs? Did he intentionally provoke them? Of course not. But from the dogs' perspective this easily could have been perceived as a threat.

And for those who proclaim that dogs should tolerate all these conditions and that the provocation was not serious enough to justify an attack, their opinion matters little. It was

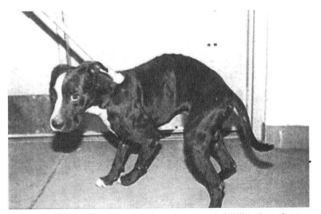

*In 2004 the media reported this "Pit bull" attacked and killed a 4-year-old boy. It was **not** reported that this chained, intact male dog was visibly underweight with numerous old scars on his head and neck. Veterinarian examination revealed the dog was heartworm positive, flea-infested, and suffering from internal parasites (hookworms). He was anemic with a low-grade fever and was diagnosed as having very poor body condition and muscle mass. Stress and wear marks along the teeth suggest the dog did not receive adequate nutrition during development. The dog was poorly socialized and very fearful.*

the dog's perception which ultimately decided if the provocation was serious enough to warrant an attack. Owners and non-owners alike need to anticipate a dog's reaction or perception of provocation before an attack or deal with the consequences afterward. And this applies to Pit bulls as much as any other breed of dog.

Pit Bulls are "Ticking Time Bombs"

"Pit bulls are ticking time bombs."

> Michael Bryant, Attorney General, Ontario,
> in defense of his legislation to ban Pit bulls

"…the breed should be terminated as simply being a time bomb waiting to go off."
> Kory Nelson, Assistant City Attorney, Denver, Colorado

These comments are almost always used to support the claim that Pit bulls are vicious, unpredictable and need to be restricted or banned. This is blatant fear-mongering. It is as baseless as saying that "Pit bulls are land sharks," "Pit bulls have chemical imbalances" and other claims used by those who are so grossly unschooled in the subject of dog attacks and canine behavior that this is the only way they can address the issue.

These statements are even more troubling when they are made by people who claim they have the interests of the public at heart, the very same people responsible for enacting laws to control dangerous dogs under the guise of safeguarding the public. Should the public feel safer when politicians enact dangerous dog legislation based on the "ticking time bomb theory" of canine behavior?

Would we accept this one-dimensional, emotional argument from our children's fourth grade teacher? Could a teacher tell a classroom of children that the Civil War started because men are inherently aggressive, or World War II started because men are evil? Would this be an acceptable teaching and learning tool? Do we solve problems or address issues effectively this way, or do we learn from examining both the major and subtle forces which preceded a war, or a dog attack?

A Breed Apart—or "Attacks Unlike Any Other Breed"

Pit bulls are often accused of being inherently different from other breeds of dogs, both in anatomy, temperament, manner of attack and ferocity of attack. In any discussion about the dangerousness of Pit bulls, the most frequently used evidence is the number of fatalities attributed to this breed and the description of the injuries to victims. But are Pit bull attacks, in terms of physical injury to the victim and the potential to cause death, actually different than those of other breeds?

Consider the cases of double human fatalities due to dog attacks. While fatal dog attacks are extremely rare, cases in which dogs have attacked and killed more than one victim during an attack are almost unheard of. However, over the last century, throughout the world, there are found twelve reported cases of double human fatalities during a single episode of a dog attack (four in the U.S., two in Canada, one in Mexico, one in France, one in Hungary, one in North Korea, one in South Africa, and one in Kenya).

While most fatal attacks involve severe aggression, the aggression and ferocity of an attack by dog(s) resulting in the death of two victims during a single episode would have to be utterly extreme in nature and force. Yet, of the twelve cases of multiple deaths resulting from a single episode of a dog attack, not one of the dogs involved in these incidents was identified as a Pit bull, a Pit bull-type dog or any other Bulldog-type breed.

Clearly, other forces are at work in these types of attacks that are unrelated to breed.

Consider also that during the 20th century there have been over 450 documented cases of fatal dog attacks in the U.S. by non-Pit bull breeds. This would certainly suggest that either other breeds exhibit aggression similar to Pit bulls, or Pit bulls are exhibiting aggression similar to other dogs.

One of the characteristics often used in claims that Pit bull attacks differ in nature and force from other breed attacks is the shake, hold and tear "manner of attack." In enacting a ban on Pit bulls in 1989, the city of Denver "proved" that Pit bulls inflicted more serious wounds than other breeds because they tend to attack the deep muscles, to hold, to shake, and to cause ripping of tissue.

As far back as 1875, descriptions of dogs holding, shaking and tearing their victims could be found. The word "torn" is actually the most frequently found description of dog bite wounds during the last century.

A fatal attack on a little girl by a large mongrel occurred in 1875. The dog is described as having "teeth fastened into the child, and was shaking her furiously."[11]

In 1893 a vivid description was given of a woman killed by a Mastiff. The article reports that the woman was viciously attacked and lying on the ground when help arrived.

> "Mrs. Morrison was lying on the ground unconscious, and the angry brute, with his teeth buried in her flesh, was standing over and worrying her. When the men approached the dog seemed to grow more furious. An attempt was made to beat him off with clubs, but he refused to let go his hold, and at each blow from a club he shook his victim so that it was feared he would kill her. After some delay a pistol was obtained and the brute was shot, but only after he received a second bullet did he release his hold on the woman" (*The Daily Advocate,* February 15, 1893).

The next year, a fatal attack by a Newfoundland is described in great detail. In Chicago, a young boy, Tommy O'Hara, was playing with a Newfoundland when the dog turned and attacked the boy. The report describes many of the typical behaviors found in severe/fatal attacks:

> "During the progress of the terrible attack on the child, a small brother and sister appeared on the scene and the maddened brute turned on them momentarily and inflicted cruel wounds. But his rage seemed to be against the boy Tommy, and he turned again and seized the little one in his teeth, shaking him until he was almost lifeless." *(Herald Dispatch*, March 3, 1894).

The canine behavior of holding and shaking during a severe attack continues to appear in recorded dog attacks throughout the century. In 1965, a 4-year-old boy died after being attacked by a Labrador Retriever. The dog was tied to a picnic table and when the boy approached the dog, the "black Labrador seized and shook him." Adults nearby could not intervene quickly enough to save the boy from the fatal head injuries inflicted by the dog.

There are untold numbers of other cases involving many breeds and types of dogs involved in these behaviors (tearing, shaking, and holding) during an attack, seen consistently over the last century. Throughout the history of the human/dog bond, owners have witnessed their puppies or adult dogs vigorously shaking and tearing at everything from stuffed toys to captured small animals. For the city of Denver to claim this is a behavior exclusive to Pit bulls demonstrates how statements made with no factual basis can easily wind up in "official" court records, especially in a climate of fear and hysteria.

Statements that Pit bulls inflict wounds unlike those of other dogs display unfamiliarity with postmortem reports of victims of other breed attacks. It is not necessary to provide the graphic details of autopsy results of Pit bull victims versus non-Pit bull victims. The fact is, they are indistinguishable. It is impossible to examine an autopsy report of a dog attack victim and determine what breed of dog inflicted the injuries. Clearly, other breeds can and do inflict injuries so grievous and profound as to cause fatalities.

For centuries farmers have been plagued by livestock losses due to predation by loose roaming dogs. As recently as the 1970s, newspapers were full of stories of dogs attacking all types of farm animals, from two Labrador Retrievers breaking into a pen and killing 900 chickens in Oregon to a pack of large mixed breed dogs attacking a herd of 26 young Holstein bulls in Maryland, killing one and severely mauling another.

Wild animals also regularly fall prey to loose roaming dogs and, during the previous decades, local newspapers were often reporting the yearly number of deer kills caused by dogs. As people lose touch with the natural world we allow ourselves to be convinced by sensationalized newspaper headlines that only certain breeds are capable of participating in these types of attacks.

In 2001, a woman witnessed four domestic dogs attacking a large buck off a rural North Carolina roadside. The dogs circled the deer, then began jumping and tearing at the flesh from the deer's neck. Distressed at witnessing this attack, the woman immediately called authorities. Officials responded, capturing three of the dogs and shooting the gravely injured buck. The owner of two of the dogs expressed surprise and dismay in learning that his two Labrador mixed breeds had participated in this brutal attack. However, faced with reality, the man was forced to acknowledge that the breed of dog mattered little, as Labradors, like all dogs, are predators, and all dogs have the potential to behave "badly," especially when operating as a pack.

Dogs capable of killing a 150-lb. buck or bringing down a 500-lb. steer would have little trouble inflicting fatal wounds on a 2-year-old child. Whether the breed is an 80-lb. Labrador or an 80-lb. Pit bull has little to no bearing on the injuries. The determining factors are the intent and the bite inhibition of the individual dog.

To address fatal attacks as a Pit bull-specific problem invalidates the hundreds of deaths caused by other dogs. This approach renders any lessons we may have learned from all non-Pit bull attacks useless or of no intrinsic value in the understanding of canine aggression. There are lessons to be learned from all fatal attacks—lessons which can only be gleaned from examination of all the available data, not just the cases which involve a single breed.

The Pit Bull Dominance Factor—Or, If a Pit Bull (or Rottweiler) is in the Pack, the Other Dogs Don't Count

This is perhaps the single best argument for the unreliability of breed statistics. It also happens to be the single most compelling argument for the extreme bias of the media.

While the media and others are guilty of broadly interpreting and applying the term "Pit bull" to dogs of very questionable breed, the omission of dogs other than Pit bulls (or Rottweilers) in the reporting of attacks is nothing short of disreputable. The media (and others) repeatedly give no recognition to breeds in multiple dog attacks unless they are of Pit bull or Rottweiler descent, even when it is proven the non-Pit bull or non-Rottweiler dogs participated in the attack.

To demonstrate how single-minded the media is in reporting breeds, and how inaccurate statistics can be on dog attacks: In the past four years alone (2002–2005), eleven dogs involved in fatal attacks with *no* Pit bull characteristics were counted as Pit bulls, while their "true" breeds were not reported, and three dogs that were clearly not Rottweilers were identified as Rottweilers. Even more distressing is that in the media's haste to report Pit bull or Rottweiler attacks, three human deaths were attributed to dogs (two cases were reported to be Pit bull attacks and one case was reported to be a Rottweiler attack) when, in reality, the cause of death of these individuals was later determined to be from causes other than dog bites.[12]

Even if we increased the accuracy of breed identification (hence statistics) by subtracting the number of falsely reported "Pit bulls" and adding corrected breed identifications, the results are still unacceptable.

Even though, in the above examples, photographs of the animals were examined and animal control personnel and law enforcement were consulted for the breed identifications, the breed identifications were still admittedly guesswork. It is as unreliable to classify/count Pit bull mixes as Pit bulls as it is to classify/count Labrador mixes as Labrador Retrievers.

Bear in mind, all previous "statistical" studies on fatal dog attacks (Winkler, Pinckney, and the CDC) have relied on newspaper articles for breed identification. The frequency of media-reported errors in breed identification is so great (and biased) as to render all numbers on breeds obtained from media sources invalid.

The CDC Studies and Pit Bull "Statistics"

The oft touted and well-known study by the CDC (Centers for Disease Control) "Breeds of dogs involved in fatal human attacks in the United States between 1979 and 1998,"[13] has been quoted, misquoted, cited, misread, and misunderstood on a regular basis by politicians, attorneys, the media and others looking for a sound-byte or quick solution to a complex problem.

The CDC study, if read in its entirety, explains in detail the inherent problems in attempting to calculate breed involvement in fatal attacks. The CDC further explained that a major flaw in their study was the inability to factor in total breed populations relative to breed related fatalities. The CDC concluded that fatal attacks are so rare as to be statistically insignificant in addressing canine aggression.

Despite these inherent flaws, the numbers of particular breeds involved in fatal attacks, as put forth in the CDC study, are continuously used as "evidence" of the danger of certain breeds of dogs. Ignoring the claims of the CDC that the number of dogs involved in fatal attacks cannot be used as a basis for legislation to address dangerous dogs, many individuals, organizations, courts, and communities continue to cite the numbers of breeds involved in fatal attacks found in the CDC studies.

The number most frequently cited from the CDC study is that 66 fatalities (more than any other breed/type) were attributed to Pit bull-type dogs over a 20-year period from 1979–1998 (or approximately three deaths per year from dogs reported to be "Pit bulls"). This number has repeatedly been used as "statistical evidence" as to the dangerousness of Pit bulls.

However, consider the statistics on child deaths from physical abuse versus child deaths from dog bites. In both of these examples, the first two statements are factual:

Fact: In 2002 over 420 children were killed as the direct result of physical abuse by a parent or a guardian (*this number does not include death from neglect*).[14]

Fact: The majority of physical abuse deaths of children were inflicted by fathers or father-type men (stepfathers, live-in boyfriends).[15]

Conclusion: *Therefore, fathers are "statistically" the most dangerous of all persons.*

Fact: In 2005, sixteen children were killed by dogs.

Fact: The majority of the dogs responsible for these fatalities were Pit bulls, Pit bull-type dogs or Pit bull mix dogs.

Conclusion: *Therefore, Pit bulls are "statistically" the most dangerous of all dogs.*

Why does the first conclusion sound ridiculous and the second sound reasonable?

We've all been exposed to fathers, either our own or other people's, and we know from personal experience that they are not all potential child killers. Also, even though most people are not statisticians, on some level we understand that variables are missing or other factors are not taken into account before coming to this obviously faulty conclusion.

Not all people are exposed to Pit bulls and therefore have no frame of reference of personal knowledge which would make the second conclusion appear as absurd as the first.

People unfamiliar with Pit bulls often rely on information presented to them through the media to make an assessment about the nature of Pit bulls. But when the media or politicians talk about vicious Pit bull attacks, and hundreds of people write in telling of their friendly Pit bulls, no one wants to hear it. Reporters and politicians have been heard to say, "Don't tell me about your friendly Pit bulls." In reality what they are saying is, "Don't inform me of the behavior of one thousand or ten thousand Pit bulls, because I want to base my theories on the behavior of 10 or 20 dogs and then present this to the public as evidence of my belief." The non-Pit bull owning public then accepts this skewed and biased presentation as reliable information, and the second conclusion does not appear as absurd as it really is.

Anyone admitting that the first conclusion (fathers are the most dangerous persons) is an invalid one based on the data presented has to acknowledge that the second conclusion (Pit bulls are the most dangerous dog) is also invalid based on the data presented. Yet, this is the exact data and faulty conclusion which are used to prove how dangerous Pit bulls are.

No reasonable person can believe that the extreme behaviors of a small group can be used to define an entire population, whether it is fathers or Pit bulls.

Additionally, to demonstrate how most people's belief that Pit bulls cause the most child fatalities are skewed by the media, the years 2002, 2003 or 2004 could not be used in the above comparison, as the Pit bull was NOT the breed responsible for the majority of child fatalities during any of those years.

Temperament and Unpredictability

Perhaps the most difficult problem facing the Pit bull today is the image that the breed is unpredictable and unstable. This has come about largely through the intense media focus given to a number of cases in which owners have encouraged or permitted their dogs to engage in dangerous behaviors. These are the dogs that then become representative of the breed.

However, for every Pit bull that attacks someone, there are tens of thousands of his brethren that tolerate all the conditions humans place them in, from loving homes to horrific conditions of abuse, without ever biting or attacking. There are no highly publicized reports or scientific journal articles on the behaviors of these dogs. The tolerance of Pit bulls in extremely abusive situations is almost never reported or given recognition by the scientific community or the public. Only a few of these long-suffering dogs can be found as a footnote in a report on a completely unrelated matter or in newspaper articles or reports of dog fighting and cruelty investigations. *Yet, the behaviors of these dogs are the behaviors which define the breed*—the hundreds of thousands of dogs that reside in homes with small children and elderly persons, from doting owners to distracted owners, from abusive owners to demented owners.

Millions of examples can be given of loving, loyal Pit bulls, but these are usually of little interest to most people. The following examples are the type that does interest us; though these stories are of monsters and monstrous acts: only it is not the Pit bulls who are the monsters.

In 2004, a sad story begins with the discovery of a dead child inside a bag on the steps of a New York City church. Investigation reveals the dead boy was placed there by his father, who claimed he did not call 911 because he had outstanding warrants. Further investigation has the father admitting to hitting the 3-year-old to "stop" the boy's seizures. Photographs of the apartment where this child lived with his three siblings reveal filthy, roach infested rooms, with dirty water covering the bottom of a corroded tub, and flies buzzing around decaying food.[16]

Prior to his death, this 3-year-old child, with cerebral palsy and a history of seizures, resided with the most minimal care in an uninhabitable apartment along with four loose Pit bulls.

In 2003, a 15-month-old girl died in Lucas County, Ohio. The newspapers reported the child had suffered multiple broken bones, a head injury, and abdominal trauma. The coroner also found the child had recent exposure to cocaine and there was evidence of cigarette burns on the child's buttocks, near her armpit and on the sole of one foot.

The mother's boyfriend was charged with inflicting the toddler's injuries. The environment this child lived in prior to her death was one of domestic violence, extreme child abuse, drug abuse, alcohol abuse, and criminal activity. The man accused of inflicting the injuries to this child owned a Pit bull. The dog's name, Ice, was shaved into the fur on the dog's back. The man's estranged wife told authorities he injected the dog with steroids and this aggressive dog was incited to attack family members at the direction of his owner. Yet, in this horrific climate of abuse and encouraged aggression, it was never the Pit bull which harmed this desperate child. The boyfriend, with the silent consent of the mother, was alleged to have abused and tortured this child until it ultimately resulted in her death.[17]

There are thousands of these types of stories, enough to convince the skeptics and bore the believers. However, these stories are not accessible to most people and so the extreme tolerance and stoic nature of these dogs goes unnoticed, while hundreds of articles are printed about the errant behavior of a handful of dogs involved in attacking a person.

Pit Bull Identification

"Those who disagree with the ban will say that there will be identification problems. I don't doubt there will be some issues on the margins, but, by and large, I think most people know what a pit bull is. The *Toronto Star* did a caricature the other week. They had a pit bull on it. I won't say what was underneath the caricature, but everyone who saw that picture knew, everyone who read that caricature knew what that was. That was a pit bull. It didn't say 'pit bull,' but you knew when you looked at it that it was a pit bull. That's what it was."[18]

Attorney General Michael Bryant

This rambling and surreal method of breed identification was uttered by Ontario's Attorney General in his speech during hearings to ban Pit bulls in the Canadian province. And if perhaps comparing a dog to a cartoon character (caricature) is unsuccessful in helping identify whether a dog is a Pit bull or not, the Attorney General offered another method:

"I've said before and I will say again, if it walks like a pit bull, if it barks and bites like a pit bull, wags its tail like a pit bull, it's a pit bull. That is going to apply, I'm sure, to the vast majority of identification cases."

If these methods appear to border on the absurd, the proof of this was established when the Attorney General was asked to point out which dog was a Pit bull when shown photos of different dogs. Unable to do so, he referred to this as a "trick."

Apparently the Attorney General isn't the only one "tricked" by the Pit bull. Those in the media also believe it is easy to identify a Pit bull, and when they are equally taken to task as to their methodology, resort to similar excuses. Those who have knowledge of dogs and dog breeds understand that breed identification in dogs anything less than purebred is often difficult, if not impossible.

Even with purebred dogs, many people could not correctly identify certain breeds. These breeds need not be exotic or rare. Most people would not be able to identify an Australian Cattle dog, an Anatolian Shepherd, or distinguish between a white Boxer and an American Bulldog. Even experienced shelter workers, veterinarians, and rescue organization personnel are at a loss to identify certain cross breeds. Mixing similar-looking, yet distinctive, breeds, such as the Mastiff, Bullmastiff, Bulldog, Boxer, American Pit Bull Terrier, American Bulldog, Presa Canario, Coonhound, Weimaraner, Rhodesian Ridgeback and even the Chesapeake Bay and Labrador Retriever, would yield a dog that even experts would have difficulty identifying correctly.

Mixing Malamutes, Huskies, Wolf Dogs, German Shepherds, Samoyeds, Eskimo dogs, or any of the Northern-type breeds would equally yield a dog in which it would be next to impossible to guess the exact parentage or even predominant breed.

However, the media has been able to solve the seemingly complex identification problem with Pit bulls. The application of the "one drop rule" has made identifying a Pit bull an easy task for many in the media. The "one drop rule" has long been the standard used in America for determining race. This racially biased theory was based on notions of bi-racialism (the world is viewed as divided simply into White or Black races). The "one drop rule" emerged from the Old South and defined any person having any trace of black/negro blood as black/negro. Having even a single drop of black/negro blood determined one's race to be black/negro. The implication was that African-Americans were inherently inferior; therefore any trace of "black blood" was a pollutant.

The field of population genetics now rejects the "one drop rule," recognizing that this system was based on social issues and not based on biology or science. But today the canine equivalent of the "one drop rule" is applied to any dog appearing to have any characteristics (blood) of a Pit bull. The notion here is also that any Pit bull blood "pollutes" the dog, regardless of degree or ancestral fractions.

The canine world is currently viewed as made up of Pit bull and non-Pit bull dogs. The same principles which allowed for discrimination against African-Americans are now applied to dogs. Determining a dog to have Pit bull blood allows for the dog to be classified as genetically and socially inferior, allowing for segregation and discrimination. Dogs clearly of very mixed parentage, if involved in attacks, are repeatedly described in the media as Pit bulls or Pit bull mixes. The insistence on classifying dogs as Pit bull or pit bull mixes, even when unable to reference the source of this identification, is clear evidence of the media bias.

These very poorly socialized, fearful dogs were repeatedly identified as "Pit bulls" by the media—even though they were identified by Animal Control as Labrador mixes. These dogs were part of a pack of six dogs that mauled to death their owner's elderly neighbor in 2001. All six dogs were intact, with one of the females giving birth to puppies shortly after the attack. The pack had a history of aggression and were so unsocialized they could not be handled by shelter personnel.

◆ ◆ ◆

From the Bloodhound-type dogs to the Northern-type breeds to the Pit bull-type dogs, accurate identification of specific breeds involved in aggression has always been unreliable at best. However, there is always other information which can be recorded with precision and which yields valuable insight into the circumstances which directly contributed to an attack. For instance, debating whether the dogs that killed a child in 2005 were Pit bulls, Pit bull mixes or simply mixed breed dogs is an exercise in futility, yielding no definitive results. The information about this attack that can be recorded accurately is:

- An intact, male dog, found as a stray, usually chained, was brought into the basement for the night.
- A female dog, usually chained, was brought into the basement with a litter of newborn puppies.
- The dogs were used by the child's parents for a negative function—guard dogs.
- An unsupervised, 2-year-old child was allowed to enter the basement with the dogs.
- The owners/parents had a history of drug abuse (use of drugs the night before the attack).
- The house was found to be "uninhabitable" and condemned.
- The owners/parents had a history of animal abuse (two of their previous guard dogs had died from heat exhaustion).

Whether the dogs involved in this attack had any Pit bull characteristics is highly debatable. The facts listed above are *not* debatable, and this is the tangible evidence which needs to be examined and addressed when searching for the causes and solutions to dog attacks.

This dog was repeatedly referred to as the "family Pit bull" in the media—and is the female dog cited in the case above. Photo credit: Michael Kestner and the *Virginian-Pilot.*

CHAPTER 12

Fighting Dogs:
Branded with the Sins
of Their Masters

"And, like a dog that is compell'd to fight,
Snatch at his master that doth tarre him on."

William Shakespeare, 1564–1616
(*King John*, Act IV, Scene I)

William Shakespeare wrote this verse nearly three hundred years before the existence of any of the breeds recognized today as the American Pit Bull Terrier, American Staffordshire Terrier, Bull Terrier or Staffordshire Bull Terrier, all of which were not established until the 19th and early 20th century. Though Shakespeare was hardly an expert on dogs, he understood the vital component in the relationship between men and dogs that seems to elude many people today. That is: When we encourage or expect our dogs to behave badly, we cannot feign surprise if they do, nor can we ignore the owners who are directly responsible for the behaviors of these dogs.

In breeding dogs some humans have created and continue to select for traits that will increase their tendencies to inflict injuries and to fight one another for the exclusive purpose of our "enjoyment." To claim that the dog is dangerous because we seek out, select for and encourage these behaviors is just another example of the transference of cruel human traits and behaviors unto our dogs.

Both the dog fighters who claim that "Pit bulls love to fight" and the politicians who claim Pit bulls are "inherently dangerous" because of their fighting history are equally obvious in their attempt to absolve humans from any guilt and responsibility for the plight of the Pit bull in our society. Consider the claims of both of these self-serving groups against the real situation of the "fighting" Pit bull:

90 Days of Reported Cruelty in the United States
(January 2005–March 2005)

- A woman is arrested in Texas for felony cruelty to animals after three dead Pit bulls are found in her yard. Two other Pit bulls were barely alive in a storage area without food or water. One dog was so emaciated it could not walk. The surviving dogs had scars indicative of dog fighting.

- A Louisiana man is arrested on animal cruelty after animal control officers found a pile of dead dogs and starving live ones chained in his yard. Seven Pit bulls were found dead, some still chained. Three chained Pit bulls were still alive. There was no food on site and all living dogs were severely malnourished.
- Deputies in Hancock County, LA, received a call about dog fighting. They arrived at the residence to find 35 Pit bulls "living in poor conditions." The owners claim they were "only" breeding the dogs.
- A Pittsburgh, PA, man who mailed videotapes of fighting Pit bulls to a government investigator becomes the first person convicted at trial under a 1999 federal animal cruelty law.
- Police officers find two men fighting their Pit bulls in an arranged dog fight between two public housing complexes in Annapolis, Maryland.
- Five men face felony charges in a night raid that one official called the biggest dog fight event he'd ever seen in Texas. Ninety Pit bulls were removed from the grounds in eastern Bexar County. Taken to the humane society, the dogs elicit only sympathy from shelter personnel as one dog is shown walking gingerly in a cage due to his severe wounds. The Pit bull, 15 pounds underweight, is wagging his tail and welcoming the attention of reporters and TV cameras. His front paws are bent inward, as if he were bowlegged from the elbows down. This is thought to be caused by having his front legs broken and not being taken to the vet for treatment, as dog fighters naturally do not take fighting dogs in for medical attention. The dog was also covered with quarter-sized splotches of pink flesh and scabs dotted over his body.
- Floyd Boudreaux and his son, Guy Boudreaux, are each arrested on 64 counts of dog fighting, 64 counts of animal cruelty and one count of possession of anabolic steroids, a schedule III narcotic. Hundreds of fighting roosters were also on the Youngsville, Louisiana, grounds. Both men were accused of fighting the dogs and breeding, training and selling the Pit bull terriers for fighting. The Louisiana Society for the Prevention of Cruelty to Animals called Floyd Boudreaux "the grandfather of dog fighting" for his work as a breeder since the 1950s.
- A Mobile man is convicted of dog fighting and steroid possession. During the trial, witnesses testified that about 20 of the 23 Pit bulls found on the man's property were disfigured with injuries. All the Pit bulls were dehydrated and emaciated to various degrees. The dogs had been kept on heavy logging chains.
- Franklin County undercover detectives execute a major dog fighting arrest in Ohio, after two dog fighters were caught on tape talking about horrific methods used to kill "losing" dogs.
- A Pit bull is found dead in a trash can behind a restaurant in Indiana. The dog's mouth was bound with duct tape and the mauled condition of the Pit bull's body convinced authorities the dog was used as a bait dog by dog fighters.

- Deep in the woods of rural central Florida, officers find half a dozen Pit bulls chained to trees. There is no shelter, food, or water for these dogs bound with heavy logging chains.
- A Wisconsin man is charged with fighting Pit bulls in his basement.
- Six people, including a law enforcement officer, are sentenced to community service and probation for dog fighting in New Orleans. All six persons are able to expunge their records after serving their sentence (i.e., community service) and paying a $125 fine.
- A suspected dog fighting ring is found in Detroit. Police found seven Pit Bulls, growth hormones used on the dogs, syringes and dog fighting training equipment. One official commented, "There was blood everywhere in the basement. I don't think the dogs were ever let outside." Five adults and six children were at the residence at the time of the raid.
- A New York teenager is arraigned on charges of torturing animals and dog fighting after numerous Pit bulls, starving and with open wounds, are found at his home. Several Pit bulls were found in pens in the yard and nine Pit bulls were found in the basement. All the dogs were emaciated, scarred and had fresh, untreated wounds.
- A Richmond man is convicted on a charge of dog fighting after twelve Pit bulls on heavy logging chains, a treadmill, illegal veterinary drugs, dog fighting videos and other paraphernalia is found in his Virginia home.
- A Long Island man is arrested for training fighting dogs when police were alerted to his website. Although the website claimed to offer "gentle and effective training for puppies and dogs," this was hardly the case. Officials found 12–15 fighting dogs in his garage in unsanitary and cruel conditions.
- Two men are charged with dog fighting after deputies found them cleaning up and taking apart a portable dog fighting arena in South Carolina. Deputies seized fifteen Pit bulls from the property. An animal control officer stated, "The dogs should weigh 50 pounds or more, but most of them didn't weigh half that."
- An 18-year-old in Tyler, Texas, is arrested for dog fighting and theft after a police investigation found him stealing dogs from backyards, taping their mouths shut and tossing the stolen pets to his nine Pit bulls. Police found the remains of six dogs on the property, believed to be stolen pets.
- The son of a former Ku Klux Klan grand dragon is arrested after staging a Pit bull fight in a makeshift arena in the living room of his home. Madison County officials found two Pit bulls with fresh wounds that were bleeding and another Pit bull with old scars on its head.
- In only three days more than 80 Pit bulls are seized in Anderson County, Texas. Authorities believe the dogs had been used for fighting. At least nine Pit bulls were found dead, still chained to trees. Six Pit bulls had their ears completely cut off, and the infections resulting from this required immediate medical attention. All the

dogs were extremely underweight, malnourished and being kept in deplorable conditions. Some of the chained dogs had no shelter and were huddled in a ball, shivering. The owners of these dogs were charged with varying crimes, including: cruelty to animals, possession of a controlled substance, unlawful possession of a firearm by a felon, and assault on a public servant.

- For five days, Simon the Pit bull lay in the bottom of dumpster, near death. The Pit bull was thrown in the trash bin near a Portage Little League baseball field in Indiana. The dog had a gaping wound in his head and multiple lacerations and bite marks over his entire body. Officials believe he suffered abuse for a long time. His teeth were broken off, his left eye was injured and the dog was "skin and bones."

Consider the population of Pit bulls and Pit bull-type dogs in the United States during these three months (January 2005–March 2005):

There were the 380+ horrifically abused Pit bulls listed above. There were thousands more fighting dogs whose owners were not apprehended by law officers and reported in the news during these 90 days. During this time there were also other Pit bulls that were subjected to horrendous injuries or unspeakable acts of depravity by humans, unrelated to dog fighting. There were also thousands more abusive owners, who may not have necessarily been fighting or inflicting depraved injuries on their dogs, but nonetheless kept them in extremely abusive environments. There were also hundreds of thousands of negligent owners, reckless owners, ignorant owners, irresponsible owners, average owners, good owners and great owners of Pit bulls.

There were millions of Pit bull-type dogs experiencing every type of positive or negative emotional and physical circumstance humans are capable of imposing on dogs—and only two of these Pit bull-type dogs responded by fatally attacking a human during these 90 days.

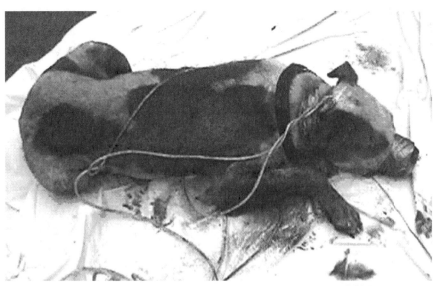

Pit bull found inside a dumpster in Indiana in 2005

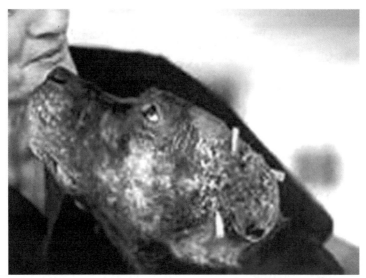

A terribly abused Pit bull responding to humane treatment.

As for the claim of dog fighters that Pit bulls "love to fight"—and the claim of some politicians about the "inherent dangerousness of the breed"—no sane person could witness the horrific condition surrounding many of these dogs and believe either of these statements have an ounce of validity.

> "The world is a dangerous place, not because of those who do evil, because of those who look on and do nothing."
>
> Albert Einstein

In March 2005, a Mobile, Alabama, man was convicted of dog fighting and steroid possession. He was found with 23 Pit bulls chained in his yard. Twenty of the Pit bulls were emaciated and disfigured from injuries. All the dogs were scarred and wounded. His wife was also arrested and went to trial on these charges. The jury, while convicting her husband, acquitted the wife.

During the trial, the wife of the dog fighter testified that "She didn't know about the dogs on her property and never saw them."[1]

The woman claimed ignorance of 20 starving, disfigured Pit bulls chained in her own backyard.

As a society, we are no different than this wife of a dog fighter who claims no responsibility or knowledge of events occurring in her own backyard. Yet dog fighting is pervasive. No town, city, county or state is immune. Dog fighting is found from the backwoods of Louisiana to the urban streets of Chicago. The Anti-Cruelty Society (SPCA) of Illinois reports that a survey of Chicago's school children has found that students are almost universally aware of dog fighting in their neighborhood, with 1 out of every 6 children admitting that they have attended a dog fight.[2]

These fighting Pit bulls are kept in garages, basements, backyards and even have occasion to run loose. These dogs then pose a direct danger to children—not because they are Pit bulls, but because they are individually abused, encouraged to be aggressive, poorly socialized and have not had the opportunity to form positive attachments to humans. As demonstrated, this is the classic formula for creating a dangerous dog.

Many an article has been written about a suburban mother's outrage over her children being traumatized after witnessing a Pit bull killing a cat or attacking another dog. These mothers are given a voice, both in the media and in community hearings, on dangerous dog legislation and these complaints are often used as "evidence" of the dangerousness of Pit bulls to support the banning of the breed.

Nary an article has been written about an urban mother's outrage over the trauma her children endured from witnessing an organized dog fight in a ghetto apartment or an informal dog fight in a back alley.

Do all these urban mothers not care that their children witness this terrible violence and cruelty to animals, or is it the media that cares not to report the outrage of less affluent members of our society?

Urban mothers and other persons in Chicago do care very much about the horrors of dog fighting. Recently, Chicago's Mayor Daley began a city-wide public service labeled the "Born to Lose" campaign, for the purpose of targeting dog fighting. In 2002, the city of Chicago designated an emergency code for people to call and report animal fighting, and in 2003, the city received and responded to 1,093 animal fighting complaints.[3]

◆ ◆ ◆

Only when, and if, society becomes committed to applying the energy and resources needed to actively and forcefully penalize dog fighters and animal abusers can there be any hope of reducing aggressive dogs in the community.

Horrifically abused Pit bull picked up by Chicago police

◆ ◆ ◆

The Pit bull's history of being bred for dog fighting is used by some politicians, experts, courts of law, the media, and even Animal Control personnel as proof of the "dangerousness" of the breed. There are many books and much information to be found on the history of dog fighting and the history and development of the Bulldog breeds. But, briefly, the history of the American Pit Bull Terrier begins at least two centuries ago, in England, where a type of working Bulldog was found to be useful to butchers in holding and controlling animals at market or to be slaughtered. This function (the ability to hold a bull) was also used solely for entertainment in the brutal spectacle of bull and bear baiting and was popular in England until it was outlawed in 1835. Since human history is steeped in violence and the exploitation of other beings, outlawing the bloody "baiting sports" had only minimal effect. Although the practice of bull and bear baiting did wane after these events became illegal, the use of dogs for ratting (pitting dogs against rats) and dog fighting increased. Adding Terrier genes to these working Bulldogs was found to create a lighter, athletic and more agile dog which proved more efficient in fighting smaller or equal-sized adversaries.

Some of these Pit bull-dogs or Bull-terrier dogs were brought over to America prior to the Civil War. The traits which were found to be useful in bull baiting and fighting were also found to be of great use in the hard-scrabble life of many frontiersmen. So while a segment of Bulldogs were being bred and maintained as fighting dogs, most 19th century Americans were busy eking out a living and using their Bulldogs in functions other than the cruel (and illegal) blood-sport of dog fighting. However, here is the point when the history and beliefs about the Pit bull splinters and becomes skewed.

There has always existed a core segment of the population that bred, maintained and used Pit bulls for dog fighting. The very essence of this blood sport required the participants to promote or record the breeding, traits and abilities of their dogs. Dog fighters chronicled extraordinary claims about their dogs because it served their egotistical and financial needs. Often times, the "best" history available about the American Pit Bull Terrier has come from a criminal based, self-aggrandizing minority of dog owners who recorded their claims and boasts about their dogs in order to increase their personal status or worth.

The untold number of average persons who owned Bull-dogs or Bull-terrier dogs functioning in everyday, legal activities have not provided a chronicle of legends and claims about breed temperament and abilities, so today the contributions these dogs have made and the high regard Americans had for the Bull and Terrier dogs have largely been lost or forgotten. Yet, Pit bull-type dogs were a highly respected and recognized part of American culture for the better part of the 20th century. Pit bulls and Bulldogs were prominently displayed in advertising, literature and in the cinema. Buster Brown and his Bulldog, Tige, started off as a comic strip in 1902 and later became affiliated with the Brown Shoe Company, and the Bulldog become a well-known advertising icon. Even more famous and recognizable during the better part of the 20th century was Petey, the famous Pit bull pal in the *Our Gang* comedy series (later known as *The Little Rascals*). So famous was Petey that, even today, many people can still recall the Pit bull with a black circle painted around his eye tagging along in the comedic misadventures of Spanky, Darla, Buckwheat, Alfalfa and the other child stars of *The Little Rascals*.

So today, while much of the history of the Bulldog/Pit bull is only a brief remembrance of some of the more famous and high profile dogs of days past, access to late 19th and early 20th century newspapers has now allowed for renewed insight into the popularity, function and behaviors of the Bulldogs found in the general, non-fighting-dog population of dog owners. These records show that many Bull-dogs or Bull-terrier dogs continued to work in their old function as farm/stock dogs, while many more became guard dogs, hunting dogs, traveling companions and family pets.

While professional dog fighting men may have been breeding for traits believed to increase fighting abilities, they were certainly the minority of breeders/owners. Bulldog-type dogs were exceedingly popular in the late 19th and early 20th century and even became so popular in cities that complaints could be found in the newspapers about the large number of Bulldogs roaming through the streets. Certainly all these Bulldog owners were not breeding their dogs for fighting abilities.

While dog fighters certainly shaped and contributed to breed appearance and some behaviors, they cannot make claim to "owning" the breed. The original baiting, gripping, Bulldog had been used for many centuries to control stock animals, before being specifically bred for dog fighting. And even after dog fighters began breeding Bulldogs for fighting traits and behaviors, they cannot make claim to controlling the population.

Those who choose to define all behaviors of the Pit bull solely by their history as told by dog fighting men are in essence choosing to believe the claims made by a century-old, criminal-based, cruel, self promoting minority of Pit bull owners, while at the same time refusing to believe the claims or examine the behaviors found in the much larger, legal, non-fighting community of Pit Bull owners.

Even if we were to believe the claims of dog fighters about the extraordinary ability of the Pit bull, one cannot conclude that this translates into aggressiveness or dangerousness towards humans. Over the centuries, the majority of dog breeds were originally created, encouraged and maintained to harass, worry, chase, fight, hunt, or kill other species of animal, from small vermin and large game animals (deer, boar) to other large predators (wolves, bear). Dogs are predators: all dogs are equipped and have the innate ability and drive to hunt, fight and kill. Throughout history most types of dogs were bred for specialized aggression or behaviors towards specific prey (Irish Wolfhound, Scottish Deerhound, Rat Terrier, Foxhound, etc.). A dog encouraged, either by artificial selection and/or by training to excel in hunting, fighting or killing other animals, has never been considered a precursor or basis for aggression towards humans.

All breeds of dogs are created by men, therefore any breed-specific trait or ability is the result of artificial selection. Highly selective or artificial traits, if not constantly selected for, are easily lost. It has long been the lament of working dog enthusiasts that when a breed becomes popular with the general public and breeding for appearance or pet qualities takes precedence over breeding for ability, the dogs quickly lose their edge or ability to outperform other breeds at a particular task or function. Individual breeds will retain some specialized traits, but they become muted or less viable. Pointers will still point, retrievers will still retrieve, sheepdogs will still herd and fighting dogs will still fight, all to some degree. But the uniqueness of the trait or specialized ability to perform a particular function becomes blunted. These behaviors then begin to revert back to more normal or natural levels found in all canids.

Those who claim the Pit bull is destined by its genetic code to behave a certain way are denying the very fact that man has selected for these traits, continues to select for them and could just as easily select against them. It is this claim that Pit bulls cannot revert back to normal behaviors; that they are permanently altered as to render them unable to behave like "normal" dogs, which is the basis for the flawed argument of "inherent dangerousness."

The Pit bull breeds are maintained by a constant and continuous selection for traits. To claim we can no longer control the appearance, behaviors or traits within the breed, or that the breed has "gotten away from us," is absurd. We can easily fashion the Pit bull to exhibit increased or decreased behaviors. We can test for temperament and select for reduced aggression and drive before breeding dogs. Once dogs are born, we can continue to select and direct behaviors by neutering, training, socializing and practicing humane treatment and maintenance. If dogs still exhibit undesirable or aggressive traits it is still entirely possible to effectively control and supervise the animal so that it does not become a potential danger to others.

Every part of the Pit bull, from conception to death, is within the direct control of owners.

Any way in which the Pit bull differs from any other breed of dog is the direct result of our behaviors (or lack thereof). To claim we are now hapless victims of the Pit bull's strength, temperament or anatomical traits is denying the indisputable fact that breeds of dogs are man-made, while at the same time failing to acknowledge the very essence of the human-dog bond—dogs will perform functions or behave in ways to serve their owners.

CHAPTER 13

Sensationalism Replaces Common Sense

Towards the end of the 1970s, two incredible transformations in human and canine behavior occurred in perfect unison:

- Children suddenly stopped teasing dogs.
- Dogs suddenly started attacking without provocation.

In less than a decade, human children thoroughly evolved into empathetic little beings, thoughtful of the feelings and mindful of the needs of other forms of life. Adults also became paragons of morality and empathy, ceasing all forms of provocation and abuse towards animals. Just as quickly as children and adults evolved en mass into considerate beings, dogs reverted to their ancestral roots, discarding their long held attachments to mankind and attacking humans in wild abandon. Dogs seemed no longer affected by heat, pain, or frustration, and began attacking only from a natural viciousness.

Or so the media would now have us believe.

Half a century ago, the newspapers relished a good dog attack story as much as the media today. But here is where any similarity between the newspapers of a generation ago and the media of today ends. As recently as 30 years ago newspapers were still printing circumstances believed to have been a trigger or contributory factor in dog attacks. All manner of insightful details were given which explained canine behavior. This type of reporting filled two vital needs: It provided both entertainment and information on individual cases of dog attacks, but even more importantly, this type of reporting provided subtle information for the prevention of dog attacks.

Behaviors from small infractions, such as pushing or shoving a dog, to major abuses, like hitting dogs with pipes, were observed as triggers for a dog attack. These details were given in addition to some of the larger forces at work, such as the chaining of dogs, owners permitting dogs to roam loose or children attempting to interact with unfamiliar dogs.

The reporting of dog attacks and the overall attitude of the people a generation ago seemed to maintain a healthy balance between the danger which some dogs presented versus the overwhelming tolerance and good nature of most dogs. If anything, dog attack reports in the middle 20th century demonstrated an even more acute understanding of canine aggression and the limits to a dog's tolerance than the colorful dog attack reports of the 19th century.

While 19th century America was rather unforgiving of dogs no matter how extreme the provocation which made them bite, mid-20th century attitudes were more tolerant of dogs and episodes of biting.

There are scores of cases reported during the 1960s and 1970s in which dogs were euthanized only after a third or fourth bite on a child. Children were known to provoke dogs, and dogs were recognized to have limited tolerance. A 1971 newspaper story which demonstrates this is entitled, "Patient Dog Bitten 6 Times by Boy." The story goes on to tell of a family trying to find a new home for their German Shepherd because they could not stop their two-year-old son from biting the dog. Six times the boy had bitten the dog so hard that the animal bore scars from the boy's teeth. The parents commented, "Not once has the dog retaliated. We felt we couldn't try the dog's patience any longer."[1]

Another article clearly demonstrates the understanding of the behavior of dogs in pain and the true forgiving nature of dogs. A 1948 article tells of a boy, Jimmy, walking in the woods with his dog, BoBo, and the poor animal stepping into a steel-jawed leg trap. The boy could not bear to see his dog howling in pain and attempted to free him. But each time he approached the dog, the distressed animal snapped at him. The article then describes the thoughts of the boy:

> "For a minute he wondered what he should do—run for help and let Bobo suffer until he got back, or try to get Bobo free, even if it meant getting bitten.
> Jimmy decided to risk the bites. He reached in toward the trap's jaws. Bobo bit him—three times. Jimmy winced but kept trying to open the trap. Finally he did.
> Bobo jumped out—and immediately began licking Jimmy in gratitude."[2]

Another case reveals both the overall and immediate events which led to a dog attack. In 1972, the parents of three children went out to dinner, leaving a babysitter in charge. The babysitter left the house, leaving a 9-year-old in charge of his two younger siblings. The children decided to make popcorn and accidentally spilled the scorching hot kernels on the back of their German Shepherd dog. The dog reacted violently by attacking the children.[3]

An account of an attack by a German Shepherd police dog provides an excellent visual impression of how the attack occurred:

> "Not even a fellow member of the police force can get away with treading on the tail of Wolf III. Wolf III, German Shepherd member of the police canine corps, was sitting by his master, Patrolman Funderbruk, near an escalator of the City Hall subway station. Another patrolman was standing with his back to Wolf III, when people getting onto the escalator forced him to take a step backward, right onto the tail of Wolf III.
> Wolf III whirled about and sank his fangs in the patrolman's leg. The officer was treated at Philadelphia General Hospital and released."[4]

From the early 20th century until the late 1970s, hundreds of dog bite stories describe events which contributed to dog attacks/bites. Children are found throwing blankets over dogs' heads, pelting them with snowballs or rocks, shoving dogs, running in fear from dogs, poking dogs with sticks, yanking bones out of their mouths, inciting dogs to attack other animals, and generally trying the patience of even the most tolerant of dogs. Dogs are found biting in reaction to being scalded by burst radiator pipes or after being tripped over. We find a case of a chained dog watching children in the yard chase a rabbit, and the frustrated dog biting a child running past him. There are scores of cases of children trying to hug, pet, kiss or "caress" chained dogs and being severely bitten in the process.

Experts asked to comment on cases of dog attacks during the 1960s and early 1970s almost unanimously agreed the problem rests with owners failing to control their dogs, children attempting to interact with dogs unfamiliar to them, and the use and procurement of large dogs for guard/attack dog functions.

But by the 1980s the events contributing to a dog bite virtually disappear from newspaper reports. Dogs were now reported as biting without provocation and even some of the "experts," relying on media accounts for their information on dog attacks, began to erroneously blame specific breeds.

It was the great misfortune of the Pit bull to be the new "fad" dog and thus the new dog found in incidents of attacks at the very same time when the media stopped reporting triggers or events which precipitated an attack. This would not only prove to prejudice the public against Pit bulls while creating a myth of breed unpredictability, but would also play an important role in the general public's loss of knowledge about canine behavior.

In 1950, a man was rushed to a hospital in Pennsylvania in critical condition from loss of blood. The man was able to tell doctors that he had fainted while in the backyard with his Dalmatian. A neighbor found the man with the dog alongside him. The Dalmatian had chewed his master's hand off at the wrist and the man had lost a critical amount of blood. This poor old gentleman loved his dog to the last. Before dying from shock and loss of blood, he insisted the dog was only trying to rescue him and only injured him in an effort to drag him into the house. One of the last things the man said before dying was, "He's a good dog."[5]

Whether this dog was indeed trying to rescue his master or was exhibiting some other, less altruistic behavior is unknown. What can be gathered from this sad story is the prevailing attitude towards dogs. At the time, many people's perceptions towards dogs were the same as could be seen 50 years earlier; that even good dogs could do "bad" things and that even "bad" dogs could be found doing good deeds.

Consider an incident reported in 2002. An elderly woman was found dead in her daughter's home. The woman appeared to have several dog bites on her. A Pit bull and a Pit bull mixed breed dog were in the house with the deceased woman. The police and coroner reported the dogs had caused her death. The newspapers, always on the alert for a Pit bull attack, ran the following headlines and stories:

"Killer Pit bulls Rip Granny to Shreds" *(New York Post*, December 11, 2002)

"Grandmother mauled to death by family's Pit bulls" (*Newsday*, December 10, 2002)

One article claimed that one Pit bull was "covered in blood." This same Pit bull in another article "appeared to have blood" on him (the him was actually a female dog). One neighbor claimed, "the dogs were vicious, they barked a lot and looked vicious." Another neighbor claimed they were nice dogs. One newspaper printed a photograph of one of the dogs clearly agitated (teeth bared) in the new and stressful surroundings at the animal shelter. The dogs would be impounded for the next eight months.

The daughter, the owner of the dogs, could not believe they would have killed her elderly mother. She hired an independent forensic pathologist from the renowned Henry Lee Forensic Institute to review and re-evaluate the findings of the initial autopsy report. Only then was it discovered that the woman had died from a cardiac arrhythmia, and the few bite wounds on her body were non-lethal and post mortem.* Her death was attributed to natural causes and it was determined the dogs did not participate or contribute to her death. There was a dangerous dog hearing which resulted in both dogs being released back to the daughter.

No retraction or correction was ever printed about this "Pit bull attack." This incident remains permanently archived in the newspapers and on the Internet as a "Pit bull-related fatality."

---

*Note: It is well-documented that dogs will, on occasion and for unknown reasons, inflict post mortem bites on their deceased owners. This has been documented with breeds from Poodles and Dachshunds to Labradors and mixed breed dogs.

◆ ◆ ◆

In a society of violent video games, Internet pornography, schoolchildren shooting their classmates, husbands killing wives, court TV, gang warfare, drug abuse, serial killers, terrorist bombs and mothers drowning their children, we are becoming increasingly more difficult to shock. Our monsters need to be increasingly terrible in order to keep pace with a society easily bored by our own species' violent acts. Since dogs have for thousands of years befriended, sacrificed and served mankind in selfless devotion, it would require constant and wildly exaggerated claims of ferocity and supernatural abilities in order to convince most people to view them as a significant danger.

The intense and persistent media and political attention given to Pit bull attacks has skewed our perceptions so dramatically that we no longer have a balanced view of the dangerousness of a very few dogs against the extreme tolerance and contributions that millions of other dogs provide. And this has been accomplished by constant over-sensationalism of anything Pit bull related. The barrage of headlines with the word "Pit bull" in them appears to be very convincing evidence of the vicious nature of Pit bulls. But are these reports legitimate evidence of aggressive behavior within the breed?

There are simply too many outrageous examples of media manipulation and fear-mongering to list. Not only are there different types of biased reporting, but the media has been relentless in pursuing all things "Pit bull." Despite claims to the contrary, there is no question the media vastly over-reports Pit bull attacks as compared to other breed attacks.

-   In September 2003, a young boy was killed by a Husky-type dog in Alaska. The incident was covered briefly in only two Alaskan newspapers.
-   In December 2003, an elderly woman was killed by a "pack of Pit bulls" in Florida. (None of these dogs were actually Pit bulls—four were identified by animal control as Lab mixes and two were Pit bull mixes.) This story was covered in over 200 major U.S. newspapers and television stations, and was reported in newspapers in Australia, the United Kingdom, South Africa and Canada.
-   In 2004, a man was killed by his large mixed breed dog in California. The briefest mention of this attack (less than 50 words) could be found only in the local newspaper.
-   A month later, a child was killed by a Pit bull in Michigan and this story ran in over 100 national and international newspapers.

Nor is this extraordinary media blitz confined to the American media, as a Pit bull-related fatality in the United Kingdom in January 2007 generated over 1,120 articles on this tragic, but singular event.

In 2004 this dog killed his owner when the elderly man attempted to stop the dog from lunging at another dog on the other side of his fence. The only media coverage given to this attack was a 50-word article in the local paper.

The over-reporting of injuries to children by Pit bulls versus other forms of grievous injuries to children are possibly the most disturbing type of reporting. We are justifiably upset when a child is the innocent victim of a dog attack. Dogs that inflict severe/fatal injuries on children are certainly dangerous dogs. However, the level of fear and outrage towards dogs after such an incident is not proportional to the real risk of severe injury and death.

In Illinois, on November 5, 2005, three Pit bull-type dogs rushed out of a house and attacked two children. One child was severely injured and the other child was very critically injured. Even the owner was severely bitten in an attempt to control his dogs. During the next few days, there were over 250 articles printed on this incident. The story was covered in Canada, Japan, Australia, Russia, India, Italy, on FOX News, CNN news, and in over 200 national newspapers. Though one boy suffered grievous and life-threatening injuries and remained hospitalized for over a month, the child did survive. The media continued to report on the long and difficult recovery of this boy over the next month. (Eight months later, in August 2006, another 60+ separate newspaper articles were published covering this very same attack.)

The same week as the non-fatal Pit bull attack on the children in Illinois, at least eight children suffered other types of horrific injuries and abuse from a parent or guardian, which resulted in the death of seven of these victims. None of these extreme child abuse injuries/deaths warranted more than one or two small articles run only in the local newspapers.

This type of over-reporting of Pit bull attacks versus acts of extreme human violence towards children demonstrates how media bias can easily distort the public's perception of the dangerousness of dogs, while minimizing the more frequent and devastating injuries suffered by children.

◆ ◆ ◆

Errors and random breed identifications by the media have been discussed; however, one further example will demonstrate that even when the breed has come to be identified accurately due to intense public and political interest in a case, the media will still make gross errors when referring to breeds of dogs involved in attacks.

The 2001, San Francisco death of Diane Whipple is unquestionably the most publicized dog bite fatality in the history of the human/dog relationship. Thousands of articles were written on the initial attack and the subsequent murder trial of the owners. An entire book was written on this single dog bite-related fatality *(The Red Zone)*,[6] and another entire book was published on the victim *(Death of an Angel)*.[7]

In many severe/fatal attacks, the first newspaper reports in the day or two following the attack include breed identifications that are unreliable and inaccurate. Initially, the breed involved in this case was identified as Bullmastiffs or Pit bulls. Due to the unprecedented amount of interest in, investigation into and coverage of this case, the breed of dogs involved was later correctly identified to be the Presa Canario. Photographs of these dogs ran in dozens of newspapers and even the dogs' names became familiar to many people (Bane and Hera).

Yet, incredibly, four years and thousands of articles later, some in the media still refer to this as a Pit bull-related fatality. In the coverage of a Pit bull attack in Illinois in 2005, the regional newspaper printed the following quote as additional "evidence" as to the vicious nature of Pit bulls:

> "A San Francisco couple was charged with involuntary manslaughter when a Pit bull they were watching mauled a woman in the hallway of an apartment complex in 2001."[8]

And if over-reporting and erroneous reporting of Pit bull attacks were not enough for the media, they have concocted a new and novel way to titillate their readers. Incredibly, the media now reports Pit bull "almost attacks" or "escape from attacks." The reporting of "almost or escaped" attacks is a phenomenon never witnessed before in the newspaper reporting of the interactions between dogs and humans.

Approximating on the low side, 350,000 persons are attacked and bitten by dogs seriously enough to require medical attention each year in the United States. This translates into at least 950 persons PER DAY receiving a significant bite by a dog.

Incredibly, the media will often report an "almost" attack or an "escaped" attack by a Pit bull in which absolutely no injuries were inflicted on a person. The only conclusion which can be drawn from this is that the media views an "almost" Pit bull attack to take precedence over a real attack by another breed of less interest.

This type of reporting is most often found in communities or areas in which Pit bull bans are being considered. Instead of reporting bites by other breeds to present a more balanced and realistic approach to dog bite prevention, the media feeds the flames of hysteria with reports of Pit bull "almost" attacks.

In 2005, California was in the process of considering state-wide dangerous dog and/or breed specific legislation. An example of journalistic hysteria during this time is found in the San Jose media, which ran the headline "Elderly Man Narrowly Escapes Pit Bull Attack." This article goes on to tell about an elderly man taking out his garbage when he spots two loose Pit bulls. The man claims that "he saw them, and they saw him and then they came after him." He is reported to have run from the dogs and escaped into his house. (This is obviously the one and only trait Pit bulls are not reported to have—the ability to outrun elderly gentlemen.)

This same article goes on to report another "Pit bull attack" involving two Pit bulls and a man walking his small dog. The man was reported to have not been injured, and his small dog received minor injuries.[9] How or why the man and his small dog "escaped" from this "attack" by two Pit bulls is not reported.

In Louisville, Kentucky, in 2005, after a fatality by a Pit bull and another fatality by two mixed breed dogs (which were, of course, reported as Pit bulls), the news also began grasping at Pit bull straws for stories. Since Louisville was considering breed-specific dog laws in reaction to these two tragic cases, the newspapers attempted to keep Pit bulls in the news by reporting "almost" attacks. The story "Pit Bull Traps Boy, 4, on Car Roof" tells the not-so-harrowing story of a boy placed on the roof of a car by his father when a Pit bull "charged" them. The father "fended the dog off with a pole and a lawn chair." No one was reported to have been bitten, scratched, mauled, clawed or otherwise come into contact with the dog. But, the article made special attention to note the dog was "confirmed to be a Pit bull."[10]

Even in communities that are not focused on enacting Pit bull legislation, some in the media cannot pass the opportunity to print any encounter between a person and a Pit bull(s).

"Two Teenagers Escape Serious Injury after Pit bull Attack near Hanover" is a headline that ran in 2005. This story claims the Pit bulls "attacked without warning" and that the dogs were "vicious." The only problem with this story is that no one was truly attacked, bitten, knocked down or mauled by any of these six Pit bulls. Two teenagers walking down a street in Hanover stated that "six Pit bulls came out and started attacking us. We kept walking." It was reported that neither youth was "seriously hurt" and, after being examined by a doctor, the "scrapes" were deemed to be so minor as to not require any treatment.[11]

Six dogs (Pit bulls or otherwise) surrounding and jostling a person can be an unnerving and worrisome event. Especially in today's climate of fear surrounding Pit bulls, these two teenagers were justifiably worried. But are two upset teenagers a newsworthy event? Also, these teenagers did not "escape serious injury," nor were they "attacked," because it is obvious these dogs were exhibiting appropriate bite inhibition. Even in this large pack, acting independently of their owner, clearly excited, and with two unknown and very nervous-acting teenagers, these dogs did not inflict any bites. More accurately the headline should have read, "Negligent Owner Allows Dogs to Frighten Teenagers."

It has gotten to the point where any Pit bull witnessed near a person in distress is assumed to be the cause of that distress. In March 2004, police received a call about a Pit bull mauling a man in Fort Madison, Iowa. The dog was lying beside his owner, who was dead from a self-inflicted gunshot wound to the chest. The dog did not bite, attack or cause any injury to this man, but was simply lying beside his fallen master. A dog of another breed would have been heralded for devotion to his deceased owner.

Since persons being severely injured or killed by automobiles are so commonplace as to not elicit much reaction from the reading public, one media source seriously misrepresented the facts of one incident to grab the interest of their audience. "Man Struggles to Recover from Pit Bull Attack," "Update on Pit Bull Attack" and "Pit Bull Attack Victim Leaves Hospital" were three separate news stories run from April 14 through April 29, 2003.[12] The first line of one of these articles reads, "After a vicious dog attack families of the victims often suffer the most." The first line of the follow-up article reads, "A Rockford man has now left his hospital bed after being attacked by a vicious dog."

These articles are a shameful and gross misrepresentation of the facts. The facts of this accident are that a man was walking into a restaurant when a Pit bull began "chasing him." Unfortunately, in running away from the dog, the man ran into the street and slammed into a passing van. The man's injuries were the result of coming into contact with a motor vehicle, not with the dog.

Additionally, Pit bulls attacking cats (and even rabbits) are now being reported in newspapers, usually accompanied by highly emotional quotes from parents claiming fear for the safety of their children. The reporting of such cases as Pit bull related aggression conveys either questionable motives or a shocking level of ignorance about very natural, albeit unpleasant, canine behavior (i.e., chasing and killing small prey animals).

Even the most innocuous events involving Pit bulls are deemed not only newsworthy but threatening. Chicago, Illinois, was in the midst of a much-publicized proposal to ban Pit bulls in late 2005. A neighboring suburban community swept up in the latest media-driven Pit bull hysteria was also considering a ban of Pit bulls. The area newspaper tells of the experience and testimony of one man at the town council meeting. The news story is headlined, "Pit Bull Angers Resident." The article goes on to tell of one resident's anger and fear of Pit bulls resulting from a loose Pit bull stealing food from his bird feeder. The man addresses the council, stating that the town needs to "do something before there is another incident."[13]

With thousands of legitimate and serious injuries inflicted both by other breeds of dogs and by parents on children each day in the United States, we need to examine why our society views a Pit bull attacking a cat or an "almost" Pit bull attack as more newsworthy.

◆ ◆ ◆

The media barrage of all-things-Pit-bull has defiled the image of the Pit bull so profoundly that it has resulted in a public perception that only certain breeds of dogs can be aggressive towards humans (and other animals).

Time and again other breed attacks are reported only if the attack was so extreme it could not be ignored. The overwhelming majority of serious and even severe attacks by other breeds are either unreported or underreported as compared to Pit bull attacks. Proof of this is found in human interest stories in which attacks by non-Pit bull dogs played a role. Often, non-Pit bull or non-Rottweiler dog attacks are not reported on their own merit, but only as they relate to how the attack impacts another part of a person's life. The following examples are taken from only one year, 2005:

A highly publicized case of the first face transplant was reported in November of 2005. This was a significant medical and media event. How the woman came to need this operation was revealed to be the result of a severe mauling by her Labrador Retriever. The woman, while unconscious, had her nose, lips and chin torn off by the dog. The attack occurred months prior to the operation and was apparently of no interest to the media at that time.

Another attack by a large mixed breed dog (listed as a Shepherd mix) was only reported in the media a month later when the mother was arrested on a charge of child abuse after she failed to get medical attention for the severe injuries caused by the dog. The dog had bitten one of her children in early 2005, and a social worker had advised the mother to remove the dog from the home. A few weeks later the dog bit another child in the home, inflicting a laceration 7 x 2 centimeters long on the top of her head. The attack became publicized due to the consequences of the bite becoming infected and the mother being arrested for child neglect.

An October 2005 attack was not reported until December 2005 in the story of a hardship case of a man who could not afford to pay the bills incurred as a result of a dog attack. Two months earlier the man had attempted to stop a Chow dog from attacking two girls on the street and in the process he was attacked, losing part of his finger and receiving severe bites to his arm. Unable to work after these injuries and with no insurance, the story tells of the unfortunate financial circumstances of this man.

A September article discussing the outcome of a lawsuit and jury-allotted award to the parents is the only report found of the severe injuries received when a 4-year-old boy was attacked by a caretaker's dog. The dog, a Golden Retriever-Basset hound mix, had clamped its teeth on the boy's head and swung the child back and forth repeatedly during this attack.

In December 2005, a brief article was published in reference to the recovery and solicitation of funds to help a small girl who was the victim of a severe dog attack. The article is about the family's gratitude to all the kindness people had shown them and their injured daughter. At the time of the article the child had been released from the hospital and was facing "several more surgeries, including major reconstructive surgery to her face." One sentence describes how her injuries came to be: "The fourth-grader was injured last Tuesday by the family's Labrador Retriever, who has been with the family for 3-1/2 years. Details regarding the incident were unavailable."[14]

The attack itself was not reported in the media when it occurred and is only mentioned in this article about the family's appreciation of people's support.

The obvious harm of such unbalanced reporting of different breed attacks is illustrated in a comment made by Chicago Alderman Ginger (Virginia) Rugai. In attempting to pass Pit bull breed-specific legislation in 2004, the Alderman was quoted in the *Chicago Sun-Times* as saying, "Have you heard of any other particular breed that has, in fact, killed or maimed someone?"[15]

There are two distressing aspects to this comment: The first is the obvious media impact, by over-reporting Pit bull attacks, on creating a public perception that only certain breeds of dogs are responsible for severe/fatal attacks. But there is a further disturbing aspect of this Alderman's comment; unlike most individuals, lawmakers have both a staff and a responsibility to research a topic thoroughly before attempting to enact life-altering legislation and making statements to the media. Proposing laws based primarily on information spoon-fed by the media is a seriously flawed approach to controlling dangerous dogs. This is evidenced by the fact that the Alderman seems totally unaware of the number of dog bite fatalities which have occurred in her own and adjacent districts in the Chicago area. In Cook

County (which encompasses Chicago), there have been 12 fatal dog attacks since 1965. Ten of these fatalities were caused by breeds of dogs other than Pit bulls.

◆ ◆ ◆

A valid and reasonable argument can be made that it is not the responsibility of the media to provide a comprehensive and accurate running log of dog bites in the United States. Editors, journalists and reporters all have both personal and professional standards and beliefs as to what is deemed newsworthy and of public interest. With an infinite number of stories about the human condition occurring each day, editors pick and choose which individual stories they believe have relevance. In a free and capitalistic society, this is perfectly acceptable and reasonable.

So it needs to be recognized that it is neither the responsibility nor the intent of the media to provide unbiased or detailed information on the number and types of dog attack injuries in the United States. One repeatedly finds in media accounts of dog attacks: inaccurate breed identifications, seriously flawed accounts of circumstances surrounding the attack and vital and relevant details concerning both human and canine conditions regularly excluded. Yet, all previous "scientific" studies on fatal dog attacks have used newspaper reports as either their sole source of reference or as an integral part of the study.

Therefore, it is vital for both the scientific community and the public to recognize that the media is under no obligation to provide balanced, comprehensive or accurate data on severe/fatal dog attacks, nor does it.

◆ ◆ ◆

The Pit bull has borne the brunt of much of the misinformation and negative handling by the media. However, all breeds of dogs and even humans suffer from this new type of journalistic approach.

One hundred, even thirty, years ago, the media provided subtle and not-so subtle tips on dog bite prevention in their telling of dog attack stories. Today, this is all but absent. It may be speculated that in today's highly competitive media climate shocking stories serve a journalistic agenda. Events that are sudden and unexpectedly violent are interesting to most people. Events that occurred as a result of "cause and effect" or events that make sense are rather boring or of less interest.

For example: "Family Pit Bull Mauls Tot to Death"
versus
"Abused Chained Dog Kills Toddler"

The first headline used two terms designed to shock: "Pit bull" and "Family." Pit bulls are now recognized as menacing and fearful animals, so placing this breed in the headlines is assured to shock and get the attention of most people. The use of the term "family" is slightly more subtle, but certainly used intentionally to re-enforce fear. A family dog killing a family member implies the most basic and shocking betrayal of trust. It implies there was a familiar bond, which the dog chose to violate. It implies the dog's behavior was unexpected, unpredictable and, therefore, shocking.

The second headline implies cause and effect, or on some level makes sense. It also removes the perception of a familiar bond, thereby removing the implication of a violation of trust. This then becomes less shocking or less attention-grabbing.

Yet, both of these headlines describe the same incident. Unsurprisingly, the first headline was the one chosen by the media.

Consider two more headlines: "Rottweilers Attack, Kill Toddler"
                                          versus
                    "Uncle's Chained Guard dog Kills Girl"

The first headline (the one chosen by the media) imports no information other than that Rottweilers had caused another fatality.

The second headline describes the same incident and provides two significant pieces of information that may prevent future dog attacks. Over 17% of children (aged 1 day to 12 years old) killed by dogs are found to have been attacked by a relative's dog. One out of every four children killed by dogs involved a dog that was kept chained. These two circumstances pose important risk factors found in canine aggression. And, of course, recognition of the function of the dog (guard dog versus companion animal) is relevant data in understanding the behaviors expected from and displayed by this dog.

Again, the media is not responsible for our edification about dog attacks; therefore, we need to acknowledge that the information presented by the media is entertainment and not a truthful account of the circumstances which contributed to cases of severe/fatal aggression.

◆ ◆ ◆

Of all the sins of the modern-day media, perhaps the most grievous has been the gross misrepresentation of the human/canine bond in the recounting of dog attacks. This is unquestionably seen most frequently in the reporting of Pit bull attacks and in the use of the term "family dog."

One of the most atrocious uses of the terminology "family dog" is found in the recent reporting of a fatal Pit bull attack in Michigan. After a 6-year-old girl was killed in an alley between two row houses, the following headlines were run in the media:

"Family's two Pit bulls kill Hamtramck girl, 6" *(Detroit Free Press, April 5, 2005)*

*"*Family Pit bulls maul girl, 6, to death as she walks to swings" *(Detroit Free Press, April 5, 2005)*

"Residents Seek Pit bull ban after Child Killed—6-year-old Attacked by Family's Pets" (ClickOnDetroit.com, April 5, 2005)
One newspaper volunteered, "The girl had known the Pit bulls since they were puppies."

This is how this dog attack was presented to the reading audience. Naturally, the public and politicians read this and found more "proof" of the unpredictable nature and temperament of the Pit bull—or another case of Pit bulls turning on their owners and/or family members.

Investigation of the incident and necropsy (animal autopsy) of these two "family pets" reveal:

- The dogs, a male and a female, had originally belonged to the mother's boyfriend, who was recently deceased.
- Both dogs were 12–18 months old and intact. The female had signs of a previous pregnancy.
- The dogs were confined in the basement of a vacant house, while the mother and girl had moved into another house.
- Upon examination both dogs were found to be underweight.
- No dog food was found throughout the entire gastrointestinal tract of either dog.
- Both dogs tested positive for brodifacoum poisoning (meaning they ingested rat poison).
- The stomach contents of both dogs were found to contain multiple foreign bodies of varied forms:
  - Male: pieces of paper and cardboard (from a box of rodenticide), plant material, small nails, and a rubber gasket.
  - Female: pieces of cardboard (from a box of rodenticide), multiple small rubber bands and black plastic fragments.

It is a gross misrepresentation to label these two dogs abandoned in the basement of a vacated house, with no food or water, with their stomachs full of rat poison, cardboard, nails, plastic and rubber bands, as "family dogs."

Any dog that has not been afforded the opportunity to socialize, interact and learn appropriate behaviors because they have been acquired for negative functions (guarding, fighting, breeding for financial gain) or maintained in semi-isolated conditions (chained, kenneled, basement/yard dogs) cannot be defined as "family dogs." These animals are "resident" dogs. Family dogs and resident dogs *cannot* be expected to exhibit similar behaviors under similar conditions.

The toddler who wandered out to the chained, intact, breeding male Pit bull in the backyard of a home in Louisiana was reported in the media to have been killed by the "family Pit bull in an unprovoked attack." One article even delicately described the heavy chain around this dog's neck as a "tether;" as the dog was reported to be "tethered in the back-yard." The circumstances this dog was maintained in are clear indicators of the degree of socialization, care and function of the dog. The level of socialization and apathy toward this dog was so low that the family never even bothered to name him. When asked the name of the dog after the attack on the child, the owner stated the animal had no name and was simply referred to as "the dog."

This is just another case of owners, in conjunction with the media, presenting an image of the Pit bull that has no basis in reality. Allowing perceptions of canine behaviors and the level of the familiar bond (family dog versus resident dog) to be determined by an owner attempting to limit personal culpability and by the media attempting to sell a story has led the public (and "experts" who rely on these accounts) to believe that certain dogs behave unpredictably and with unprovoked aggression.

Americans have always loved their dogs. So how has it come to pass that a breed of dog that was beloved and respected by Americans for over a century has become loathed, feared and abused both by individuals and society as a whole?

As stated previously, it would take a constant and persistent barrage of claims of unpre-dictability, ferocity, extraordinary abilities, powers, etc., in order to make a dog-loving country dislike a particular type of dog to the degree that the Pit bull is feared today. There can be no question that this is exactly what has transpired through the media (and more recently through outrageous claims by politicians).

- In 1987, over 800 newspaper articles were printed in which "Pit bulls" were headlined.

Over a decade later, the media is unrelenting:

- 2004, over 900 newspaper articles were printed in which "Pit bulls" were in the headline.
- In 2005, there were an incredible 1,700+ newspaper articles which headlined the words, "Pit bull."
- In 2006, the media continues to exploit the Pit bull with an unprecedented 2,800+ newspaper articles vying for their readers' attention with the words "Pit bull" in the headlines.

In a little over two decades, 1985–2006, an astounding 14,500+ newspaper articles used the words "Pit bull" in their headlines to grab the public's attention. This number does not include newspaper articles referencing Pit bulls that did not specifically use the words "Pit bull" in the headline of the story, nor does it include magazine articles, radio or television coverage of Pit bull issues.

In the first week of November 2006, for the first time in over 150 years of recorded fatal dog attacks, an unprecedented number of children (4) were killed by dogs in a single week. One of these four attacks involved Pit bulls and three were by other breeds of dogs. The circumstances surrounding all of these attacks were strikingly similar. Examination of these cases, individually and collectively, offers valuable insight into the reasons and causes for fatal dog attacks on children.

On November 7, 2006, Nancy Grace of *CNN Headline News* chose the single fatality involving Pit bulls to feature on her television show. The coverage and discussion of this fatal attack included describing Pit bulls as "killing machines" and comparing the dogs to "machine guns and Uzis." Graphic and highly disturbing stock film footage of Pit bulls fighting was played repeatedly during the show.

The other three children killed by other breeds of dogs during this week were not mentioned.

How could the average person not come to believe that Pit bulls are different than other breeds of dogs given this extraordinary, sensationalized and biased media coverage of dog attacks?

CHAPTER 14

The Real Causes
for Dog Attacks

"If an ox gore a man or a woman that they die: then the ox shall be surely stoned, and his flesh shall not be eaten but the owner shall be quit. But if the ox were wont to push with his horn in time past, and this hath been testified to his owner, and he hath not kept him in, but that he hath killed a man or a woman; the ox shall be stoned, and his owner also shall be put to death."

The Bible, Old Testament
Exodus, chapter 21, *verses 28, 29*

If this punishment seems too harsh, the penalties for owners today who allow their dogs to roam loose and attack individuals are equally too lenient, if not nonexistent. The following cases show that canine behavior cannot be examined without examining human behavior. The behavior of the dogs in these incidents was a direct result of the actions (or inactions) of their owners.

Case #1

In February of 2003, Vivian Anthony was walking down a street in Columbus, Ohio, when she was attacked by two loose roaming dogs. Her husband managed to fight the dogs off the woman, but she was critically injured. Two weeks later, as Mrs. Anthony remained on life support in the hospital, another woman was attacked by two loose roaming dogs, near the same location as the first attack. Two men beat the dogs off the woman. A newly fallen snow allowed police to track the dogs' bloody paw prints to a nearby residence. Inside the residence were three dogs, along with a newspaper clipping about the first attack.

After 53 days on life support, Vivian Anthony, the first victim, died from complications from the attack. DNA sampling of the dogs and the victims' clothing determined the same dogs were involved in the attack on both women. The owner of the dogs, a medical doctor, was charged with two counts of involuntary manslaughter, one count of reckless homicide and one count of assault.

There can be almost no doubt that the owner of these dogs knew of the first attack on Vivian Anthony and the involvement of his dogs. He lived not a half mile from where she was attacked, he had a newspaper clipping of the incident in his house and the dogs almost assuredly had to return home after the attack with blood on them. Still these dogs were permitted to run loose less than two weeks later, allowing them to attack another woman.

During the trial the owner admitted to knowing that his dogs escaped often and that they had previously been involved in attacks on two other persons. Of the three dogs owned by this doctor, two were intact males and one was a very pregnant female (she was not involved in either attack). The owner pleaded guilty to one count of involuntary manslaughter and one count of assault. He was sentenced to six months in jail and a $5000 fine.

Case #2

In 2002, a 2-year-old girl wandered too near a chained dog and was attacked and killed. This intact, male dog had worn the dirt down to a smooth bare surface in the area limited by the chain. The tree to which the dog was chained was devoid of bark as the dog paced for endless days around the tree. After the child was killed, a few neighbors commented that the dog appeared skinny and underfed. The animal control officer stated that the dog was "appropriately sized for its breed." The owner of the dog stated in the newspapers, "About the only thing I can say is I'm sorry, but I don't see how I could've stopped it from happening."

This was the story reported in the newspapers and it is incredible in the startling lack of information. Fortunately, law enforcement officials submitted the body of the dog to the state for a necropsy (animal autopsy). What was not revealed in the newspaper accounts or by the owner was that approximately one week prior to killing the little girl, the dog had killed a young cat. Now, this is not necessarily indicative of aggression towards humans, or anything else really. Dogs do kill cats. But this dog consumed the cat. Dogs don't eat cats after they kill them, unless something else is terribly wrong.

What was wrong with this animal was that it was starving to death.

The necropsy determined:

- The five-year-old, intact, male weighed only 25kg, or 55 lbs. *(This full-grown male dog should have weighed between 75–95 lbs.)*
- The dog was 10–12% dehydrated. *(Dehydration at 10% is considered severe and life-threatening.)*
- The intestinal tract contained only small particles of leaves and scant amounts of corn kernels.
- There was *no* dog food in the entire intestinal tract.

Diagnosis: Severe emaciation and malnutrition.

Yet, unbelievably, the owner was puzzled as to how he could have prevented this tragedy.

Case #3

In 2004, the mother of an eight-year-old boy allowed him to spend spring break at his father's house in Charlotte, North Carolina. One day during the week, the father was in the house with his girlfriend and the boy was playing in the backyard with the father's four dogs. Tragically, the dogs began attacking the boy. The father and girlfriend inside the house did not hear the boy's cry for help or his screams. A postman across the street did, though, and ran over in an attempt to save the boy. When he realized he could not help the child by himself, he ran to the door and banged on it for help. The father answered the door and threatened to kill the postman.

The boy died.

The police arrived and found that the father was a convicted felon, out on parole. Inside the house they found an assault weapon and drugs. The father was arrested for possession of a firearm, possession of illegal drugs and for threatening a federal employee (postal worker). He was also later charged with involuntary manslaughter in the death of his son.

A few neighbors warily stated the dogs seemed abused and said they had witnessed the owner beating them. The mother, obviously distressed and grieving for her son, started a petition to rid Charlotte of three different breeds of dogs.

What many people fail to acknowledge, even those not overcome with grief, is that a convicted felon, out on parole, would have little regard for any legislative efforts that would make ownership of a breed of dog illegal. The fact that it is was illegal to be in possession of a firearm or narcotic drugs were no deterrent to this man. It is very doubtful that he would have any regard for a law that banned a particular breed of dog.

It is not reasonable to expect normal or amiable behavior from dogs owned by a man who, rather than having intense gratitude, instead threatens to kill the man who is attempting to save the life of his son.

Addressing this as a dog breed issue will never solve the problem of canine aggression. Legislators and communities can destroy the dogs, ban breeds, mandate high insurance coverage, require fencing, or signs and any other number of measures to restrict the dog—but no amount of laws, restrictions or breed bans will save the lives of children whose parent(s) allow them to live in such high risk environments.

These are but three examples in a three-year period (2002–2004) showing behavior by owners so extreme in their negligence or criminality that they render the breed of dog a non-issue. There are many more cases like these, some as extreme, others to a lesser degree. This demonstrates that in many cases of severe/fatal aggression it is simply not possible to separate the behavior of the owners from the actions of the dogs.

If we were to take the above examples and add the three different breeds involved to statistics on fatal dog attacks, what does this accomplish? Can we seriously believe that any of the above owners were true devotees of the breed of dog which they so recklessly abused and/or mismanaged? Do we imagine that banning the breeds of dogs involved in these attacks would prevent them from acquiring another breed of dog and demonstrating equal recklessness?

As some politicians and a large portion of the media spin off in the direction of focusing on breeds, fortunately law enforcement personnel work diligently behind the scenes in an attempt to address the real circumstances which permit or encourage some dogs to act so aggressively.

Unlike some in the media and some politicians, law enforcement is keenly aware that persons involved in situations in which their dog has attacked and killed someone are liable to be less than truthful about the history, function and prior bad acts committed by their dog(s) and/or by themselves. Additionally, even if a police officer is personally inclined to believe a particular breed may be aggressive, they conduct a rational and thorough investigation, as is required by their profession. Because of this, law enforcement agencies disseminate the most accurate data and least prejudicial conclusions about the circumstances and factors behind severe/fatal canine aggression.

In recent years, some police and sheriff agencies have done extraordinary work in uncovering information and details about the owners and dogs involved in fatal attacks. Based on this information, some cases of fatal dog attacks have been deemed terrible accidents. Others were concluded to have stemmed from low level negligence or a low level of supervision of dogs/children, coupled with misfortune. Some cases were negligence bordering on criminal and other cases were clearly criminal.

The only way to come to conclusions about dog attacks being accidental or criminal is to examine the owners first, then the circumstances surrounding the attack and, lastly, the dogs. Only in this way can the origins and opportunity for canine aggression be determined.

While proponents of breed-specific legislation often seem uninterested in recognizing the distinction between dog attacks that can be attributed to canine behavior and those that can be attributed to human behavior, the criminal justice system, the police and the courts frequently recognize that were it not for the reckless disregard of some dog owners (and/or parents of the victim), these fatalities would not have occurred.

Since 1982 there have been at least 29 dog owners found guilty of murder, manslaughter or criminally negligent homicide in cases in which their dogs were involved in a fatal attack. Still other dog owners and/or parents have been found guilty of child neglect, child endangerment, child abuse and reckless injury to a child after a fatal dog attack on a child.

◆ ◆ ◆

Throughout the ages, dogs have been guardians, protectors, companions and playmates to children. Like all friendships, there may be squabbles, misunderstandings and offenses taken, but children and dogs are forgiving creatures, and both usually emerge with only the fondest of memories of their relationships together.

There are over 73 million dogs in the United States. The vast majority of these dogs interact on a daily basis with every conceivable type of child, from infants to teenagers, from gentle children to tormenting children, from handicapped children to healthy children and from family children to neighborhood children. The dogs these children live with and are exposed to include almost every recognized purebred dog along with a never-ending variety of mixed breeds. Millions upon millions of children learn about compassion, responsibility, companionship, and respect for others by living with these animals. Virtually all these children enter into adulthood all the better for their experiences with dogs.

However, about a dozen times a year, something goes terribly wrong.

Statistically, a child has a greater chance of dying from hundreds of other maladies and mishaps, both man-made and natural, than from the bite of a dog. But society is deeply shocked and offended when a child dies from an attack by a dog. For this reason we need to take a closer look at how children come to be exposed to dogs which put them at risk.

How a child becomes the victim of a fatal dog attack is dependent on either one or both of these factors: level of responsibility and risk evaluation demonstrated by the parent and/or the failure of the dog owner to evaluate risks and safeguard children from their dogs.

More often than not, children who fall prey to dogs do so as a result of negligence by either the parent(s) and/or the dog owner. Sadly, far too many children live with parents or guardians who offer them only a low level of safety. Many of the child victims of fatal dog attacks lived in an environment which allowed for a large margin of error, which in turn invited misfortune.

The following cases demonstrate that some victims of fatal dog attacks were children whose parent(s) provided them with only a low level of safety from misadventure.

In 2001, a 2-year-old boy was killed by an intact, male chained dog. It was the middle of the afternoon and the parents were seemingly unaware the child had left the house or had been killed by the dog in their yard. After an undetermined amount of time, the child was discovered dead near the stepfather's chained dog. The stepfather was unconvinced the dog had killed the child, claiming the dog's chain had been the cause of death. The dog, prior to this incident, had killed another dog. The stepfather claimed the death of that dog was also a case of "death by chain."

The evidence clearly proved the boy was killed as a result of an aggressive attack (bites) from the dog. Yet, the stepfather's refusal to acknowledge the clear evidence was only the latest in a long list of denials and irresponsible ownership practices (unaltered, chained, unsocialized dog, with previous acts of aggression ignored or excused) that directly contributed to the ultimate act of aggression displayed by this dog.

It is worthy of note that the boy's funeral needed to be delayed as the parents overslept that morning.

A fatality in 2000 involved a 2-year-old girl wandering over to one of six dogs kept on a heavy logging chain in the far corners of a yard. The owners of the dog knew it to be dangerous and had warned their own children not to go near him. When a mother and her 2-year-old girl were visiting the house, the child wandered out and was killed by the intact male dog. The owner came home and beat the offending dog to death with a sledgehammer.

All six dogs in the yard were intact, and one of the female dogs was very pregnant. Investigation revealed that the dog which had killed the child was actively used for fighting and had been matched in a fight only weeks earlier. The mother of the deceased child refused to cooperate in the investigation or assist police. She stated in so many words that she did not want to help police get her friends in trouble.

A 2001 fatality involved the tragic circumstances of a young boy who had come to St. Louis with his brother and mother in the winter of 2000. By all accounts 10-year-old Rodney was a sweet, pleasant and intelligent boy, despite his unstable home environment. Before arriving in St. Louis, Rodney and his brother had been taken twice from their mother by the Missouri Department of Family Services and placed in foster homes. Now returned to his mother, who had a history of drug abuse and an open weapons charge pending in a neighboring county, Rodney appeared to be adapting well to his new location and school.

On a Monday evening, around 5 p.m., Rodney's mother saw him leave the house with his basketball. The following morning police arrived at the mother's doorstep to inform her that her son had been killed by dogs in Ivory Perry Park on either late Monday night or early Tuesday morning. Rodney's mother was unaware that her son had not returned home the night before. She was arrested and charged with endangering the welfare of a child.

With no parental interest in keeping this child out of harm's way and no concern for his safety or whereabouts, it is not terribly surprising that this child should be the victim of some type of terrible misfortune. Sadly, dogs were the source of his tragic death. Of course, equally culpable are the unknown owners who abandoned and allowed these dogs to roam loose in the city.

One of the most frequent scenarios for dog attacks is children visiting relatives. Seventeen percent of the children killed by dogs were attacked by a relative's dog (grandparent, aunt/uncle). While cases of extreme negligence are found here, this is the one area where seemingly innocent mistakes or slight errors in judgment have resulted in tragic consequences.

The factors which appear to be at work here are:

Adults, being familiar (or having a bond) with a relative's dog, assume the dog will be equally accepting of their young children, believing their bond with the dog will automatically extend to them.

Adults visiting with children fail to take into account the territorial issues found with many dogs.

A common scenario is: A woman visits her mother. She is familiar with her mother's dog and perhaps feels comfortable with this dog which has never shown any aggression towards her or her parents. At some point the daughter becomes a mother herself. She continues to visit her parents, but now begins to bring along her child. The dog has had only

A 5-week-old infant was left unsupervised at his grandmother's home. This Labrador and Mixed breed dog fatally mauled the infant. Photo Credit: James Crosby

minimal exposure to this (grand) child and at some point the child and dog are left alone. The dog then attacks this small interloper.

The case of a child being killed by a relative's dog is perhaps the scenario in which education may make the biggest difference in the reduction of severe attacks on children. Very often these parents made only minor errors in judgment. Also, many of these parents did have lifestyles in which they provided safe environments for their children. An added awareness of the danger some dogs may present to young visiting children may help these parents avoid attacks on their own children by a relative's dog.

◆ ◆ ◆

While a significant number of fatal attacks on children may have been prevented by either responsible behavior or reasonable risk assessment by a parent and/or dog owner, some cases are truly unforeseeable events. There are a small number of cases in which parents and dog owners seemingly took all necessary precautions prior to a fatal dog attack, yet still suffered the same fate as severely negligent dog owners and/or parents.

A sad case of what could only be classified as a terrible accident occurred in April 2004 in Washington. John, an 8-year-old boy, was visiting his next door neighbor's home. John was inside the home with the teenage boys living there. At some point, John, unnoticed, went into the fenced-in backyard where the family kept two large dogs. John knew these dogs and had interacted with them before. For reasons which will never be known, the boy was attacked and killed by either one or both dogs. There is absolutely nothing about this case which suggests the dogs would have behaved this way.

The dogs had responsible and quality owners, who maintained them in a controlled and safe environment. The dogs had no other function than that of companion animals and were owned by this family for three years (since they were puppies). Even the dogs' names suggest nice family pets, Precious and Diamond. The dogs were females (although intact, there were no issues with pregnancy or puppies involved). Female dogs without puppies (or not pregnant) are exceedingly rare in cases of fatal canine aggression and are responsible for less than 2% of all fatal dog attacks.

The dogs had no history of aggression prior to the attack. They were known to be friendly with neighborhood children. Neighbors unanimously agreed the dogs' behavior was always appropriate and non-threatening. The boy had knowledge of these dogs and was aware of their friendly and non-threatening behaviors. He was old enough to make a fair and reasonable assessment of the (low) risk involved in encountering these animals.

No mistakes, no bad risk assessment, no cruelty, negligence or lack of control over the dogs—just a terrible accident involving a young boy and a tragic event for two families and two dogs.

◆ ◆ ◆

If the reason a person obtains a dog and how the dog is maintained are important signposts on the road to aggression, something as simple as a dog's name is often just as relevant to the future behaviors we expect from our dogs.

Suppose you are walking down a street and a short distance off a man is walking towards you with a large, muscular dog. The dog's leash snaps and the dog is leisurely trotting towards you. The owner yells, "Psycho, stop!"

Now envision the exact same scenario, except the owner yells, "Ladybug, stop!"

Except for those who are so petrified of dogs, or so brainwashed by the media to fear certain breeds, most people would assess the risk of each of these trotting dogs a tad differently.

It is no small coincidence that many of the dogs involved in fatal attacks have indeed been named: Crusher, Rage, Psycho, Mayhem, or a host of other names which suggest their owners wished their dogs to appear—or, worse, act—menacing.

Many dogs involved in severe and fatal attacks are found with these menacing, criminal-laced names because they had been acquired for the express purpose of intimidation. The names of these dogs coincide with their use as status symbols by urban thugs in a culture of violence, drug abuse and dog fighting.

◆ ◆ ◆

Environment and maintenance are additional critical factors (along with function and owners) which demonstrate the level of commitment and responsibility an owner has, not only to the dog but also to the community and safety of its inhabitants.

Environment is the immediate physical surroundings of the dog (chained dogs, yard dogs, loose roaming dogs, multiple dog situations, unsupervised dogs, isolated and unsocialized dogs). Maintenance is the physical condition of the dog (intact dogs, sick, abused or underweight dogs).

Chained Dogs

The potential danger of a chained dog stems from rather simple causes:

- Chained dogs can never be afforded the same level of socialization as household dogs.
- Chained dogs have a well defined and limited territory and therefore may exhibit heightened territorial issues.
- Chained dogs cannot flee a threatening situation, increasing the probability of a defensive (or fear) bite or attack (fight versus flight response).
- Chained dogs are not able to release pent up energy or frustration and this may increase aggressive or abnormal behaviors (pacing, barking, straining at chain, etc.).
- Chained dogs are exposed to extreme weather conditions, and the discomfort of heat, cold, rain, and insects. Also, chained dogs are at the mercy of tormenting children.
- Untold numbers of chained dogs are injured or die after becoming entangled in chains or ropes or are attacked by loose roaming dogs.

None of these are very complex issues. The conditions under which chained dogs are kept are in direct opposition to the conditions needed to produce a well-balanced, social dog.

An owner who keeps his dog chained does not recognize or meet the social, emotional, and even most of the physical needs of the animal. Dogs, by nature, require physical exercise, mental stimulation, social and physical interaction with other beings (dogs or human) and a sense of belonging or attachment to other "pack" members. Depriving dogs of these important behaviors and interactions with humans invites aggression.

Putting dogs in situations where they are apt to feel threatened, protective of limited territory, or experience isolation, discomfort or pain will increase incidents of aggression. This is evidenced by the fact that 25% of all fatal attacks have been inflicted by chained dogs.

Dogs that have not been provided the opportunity to develop appropriate social behaviors due to chaining cannot, after an attack on a toddler, be classified as "family dogs." Dogs maintained on chains in backyards are *not* family dogs. The term which correctly identifies the dog is "resident dog." The dog resides on the premises of the owner. The dog is

This dog fatally attacked an unsupervised 1-year-old child in 2001. Here again is another visibly emaciated dog, chained to the side of a trailer, that nobody "noticed" until after the attack. In addition to starvation, chaining, and neglect, the dog was wearing a prong collar.

not a part of the family. The distinction is important and real because it defines the relationship or bond that is so important in understanding canine perceptions and, hence, behavior.

It is exceedingly rare for a *family* dog to kill an immediate family member (despite what has been reported to the contrary). Dogs attack and severely injure or kill persons to whom they have no bonds or strong attachments.

Loose Roaming Dogs

This is, without a doubt, the longest running and most frequently found complaint about dogs in our society. One hundred years ago the newspapers were full of angry letters from citizens from New York to Chicago, complaining about loose dogs attacking livestock and harassing and seriously injuring humans. An owner who allows his dog(s) to repeatedly run loose (meaning more than once) shows an utter disregard not only for their own dogs, but also for the welfare of their neighbors' animals, and a flagrant disregard for the safety and well-being of persons in their community.

Communities which cannot or care not to enforce existing leash laws or cite owners for allowing their dogs to roam should not even consider passing additional dangerous dog legislation if they are unable to effectively and seriously penalize owners who violate this basic rule of canine responsibility.

Loose roaming dogs are simply an owner management problem. A free roaming dog is an animal acting independent of human interests. In urban and residential environments there is great potential for harm when dogs are left to their own devices. Dogs being hit by cars or causing traffic accidents, harassing and chasing other domestic animals or wildlife, as well as threatening or attacking humans, are very real and frequent occurrences when dogs are allowed to roam loose off their property and free of human direction.

The dangers here are real and obvious, yet owners continue to allow dogs to operate in this potentially dangerous way. In one year only, 2005, ten persons died because their neighbors failed to contain their dogs on their property. Of these ten fatal attacks by loose roaming dogs, eight cases involved owners allowing not only a single dog, but multiple dogs, to run loose. Not only were these dogs allowed to roam loose, but all these cases involved dogs which were intact (not spayed or neutered).

Reproductive Status of Dogs

While politicians and the media love to quote breed statistics, no statistic about the dogs involved in fatal attacks is more overwhelming than the statistical percentage of intact versus altered animals.

Over the last six years, from 2000–2005, there were 131 fatal dog attacks in the United States. Ninety-two percent of the fatal attacks were inflicted by reproductively intact (un-neutered, un-spayed) dogs. This is a significant percentage and is highly suggestive of certain conditions (reproductively viable) predisposing a dog to aggression.

However, no single statistic is a true representation of the behaviors or forces at work driving canine aggression in severe or fatal attacks. Fatal attacks are the result of an escalation of events, behaviors and circumstances which culminate in the opportunity and ability for a dog to behave aggressively. What the statistic 92% of dogs found in fatal aggression were intact does not reveal is the other contributing factors found in the environment and maintenance of these dogs.

For instance, over 70% of the intact dogs involved in fatal aggression were maintained in multiple dog residences. This is relevant. Multiple dogs in residence introduce new dynamics to canine behavior not seen in single dog households. This requires owners to be more knowledgeable about intra-species behaviors and/or aggression and the possible development of pack mentality.

Dogs which may never snarl or snap at their owners will frequently growl their displeasure at each other. Dogs in the yard, running along the fence after a boy riding a bicycle on the sidewalk, often feed off each other's excitement. Feeding time in multiple dog households can be tension-filled. There are dozens of situations in which dogs in multiple dog households can trigger each other to behave aggressively. The most obvious situation which may trigger intact male dogs to behave aggressively is the nearby presence of a female in estrus. Dozens of cases of fatal dog attacks involved intact males with females in estrus nearby. Whether this was the singular cause for aggression cannot be determined, but undoubtedly any behaviors of the male would be more intense.

This female and a similar-looking, intact male dog were running loose when they fatally attacked a man in 2005. She had recently given birth to yet another litter of puppies. Within days after the attack, the male dog died from parvovirus.

Of course, female dogs, intact and bred, may exhibit heightened aggression if there are puppies on site. Indeed, this is when female dogs are found in fatal attacks. Not surprisingly, this is one of the very few situations in which male and female dogs are found together and the female initiates the attack on a human. In almost all other witnessed cases of fatal attacks on humans, when a male and female dog were together, the male was observed to be the instigator or initiated the attack.

The point about intact dogs involved in fatalities is not just that they were intact, but that they were more likely than not to be kept in multiple dog residences, and more likely than not to be active in breeding for the financial gain of their owners. So while the singular circumstance of being intact may seem indicative of increased aggression in dogs, there are almost always other risk factors involved.

Single Dog and Multiple Dog Situations in Fatal Attacks

Single Dogs

During the past 40 years, from 1966–2005, 65% of the human fatalities from a dog attack were the result of being attacked by a single dog. However, in the vast majority of these cases there were other dogs on the premises or near the scene at the time of the attack. In the six-year span, from 2000–2005, in over 87% of the cases of fatal attacks by a single dog, there were other dogs in residence or situated near the attack.

While many of these other dogs were not able to participate due to barriers or restraints, there were a number of dogs certainly able to join the attack that simply did not. Even in cases of the alleged "dangerous" breeds, there are incidents of one dog attacking while multiple other dogs on the scene do not participate. The behaviors of these non-participating dogs are remarkable in their restraint and inhibition.

While the behavior of the one dog beginning a frenzied attack on a human must be recognized for the extraordinarily aggressive act that it is, dogs standing off and refraining from entering into a pack mentality or pack attack require equal weight in the assessment of canine (or breed) behaviors and temperament. Yet, incredibly, these behaviors (of non-attacking dogs) are never studied or given recognition in discussions of canine (or breed) temperament.

The breed of the male dog that killed a little girl in a field after she screamed when a lizard ran over her shoe has been permanently documented in the statistics as indicative of the dangerousness of this particular breed. Yet, the behavior of the female dog (of the same breed) that was also at the scene but did not participate, and was even witnessed biting the rump of the male during his attack on the little girl, has gone unrecognized. Yet, her behavior in defining breed temperament is as revealing and significant as the behavior of the attacking male.

Multiple Dogs

Over the last 40 years (1966–2005) 35% of all fatal dog attacks have involved more than one dog.

When dogs operate as a pack, their potential to do harm is obvious. Dogs will often feed off each other's excitement, thereby increasing and prolonging an aggressive episode. In multiple dog attacks, injuries and bites are apt to be more numerous and occur more rapidly. Many a victim who may have been able to survive or ward off an attack by one dog succumbed due to the force of multiple dogs.

Not all dogs in a pack situation attack with the same intensity. Some dogs will attack seemingly without inhibition, inflicting deep, penetrating wounds. Other dogs (often times the females) may participate by worrying the victim, tearing at the clothes or inflicting lesser bites. An example of this is the infamous Diane Whipple case which occurred in San Francisco in 2001. Here, two large dogs escaped from their owner's control and attacked the gym teacher in the hallway of their apartment. Bane, the male, was observed to be the aggressor, inflicting most of the severe and ultimately fatal bites. Hera, the female, was less active in the attack, primarily worrying the victim, rather than inflicting severe bites.

In multiple dog attacks that are not witnessed, it is often impossible to know the exact level of participation of each of the dogs involved. Naturally, in large packs (of four or more dogs) it is often impossible to know how many, and to what degree, each of the dogs participated. Bite impressions of the dogs' teeth, examination of stomach contents, DNA and saliva testing will often assist in identifying the major offenders, but may reveal little about the behavior of the other dogs in the pack.

A case in which the stomach contents of the dogs did reveal the obvious offenders occurred in 1990, when a 44-year-old woman was killed by dogs she maintained on her property. There were eleven dogs on the premises, which she and her husband declared to be their "pets." The house was in a dilapidated condition, with huge cracks in the walls through which the dogs could enter and exit at will. Two of the dogs appeared well-fed, while the other nine dogs were emaciated. All nine dogs were each at least 20 pounds underweight, with some of them being, as one official stated, "skin and bones."

The female owner had a history of seizures. It is believed she suffered a seizure while alone in the home and this may have triggered this large pack of starving dogs to attack her. While the two well-fed dogs were determined not to have participated in the attack, examination of the contents of the stomachs of the starving dogs revealed that seven of the nine actively participated in the attack.

Like most fatal attacks, multiple risk factors need to be present before dogs behave so aggressively. Besides these dogs operating as a large pack, starvation, poor environment, possible seizure activity in the owner and perhaps other forces were in place which allowed them to behave in the manner they did.

The Familiar Bond and The Family Dog

"If you get to thinking you're a person of some influence, try ordering somebody else's dog around."

Will Rogers

Unfortunately, this simple witticism, defining how canine behavior is dependent on the familiar bond between owner and dog, is lost on many people today. Dogs behave differently with those to whom they have formed strong attachments than they do with more unfamiliar persons. For centuries this has been understood, embraced, and heralded as the essence of dogs. Yet, today, this defining aspect of canine behavior is either grossly misrepresented or has been given no recognition in the recounting of dog attacks. The denial or ignorance of this basic tenet, which so often drives canine behavior (and aggression), has led to erroneous claims of the unpredictable nature of dogs and dog attacks.

Today, dozens of studies, quotes and percentages can be found claiming that "family dogs" are responsible for the majority of bites and attacks on children. However, even the most cursory examination of these stories about "family dogs attacking children" quickly reveals that many of these claims are a perversion of the familiar bond. Scores of examples can be given in which dogs, either seriously undersocialized, chained, used for breeding, guard dog use, and/or kept in isolated and even in extremely abusive conditions, were labeled as "family dogs."

Family Dog versus Resident Dog

Though discussed previously, it needs to be stressed that dogs maintained outside the home (on chains, in kennels or in yards) and dogs obtained for negative functions (guarding, fighting, protection, breeding for financial gain) are *not* "family dogs"—they are "resident dogs." This distinction is vital in the understanding of canine behavior and aggression. Dogs maintained as resident dogs cannot be expected to exhibit the same level of sociability as dogs afforded the opportunity to interact with humans and their families on a daily basis and in positive and more humane functions.

The fact that there is no documented case of a single, spayed/neutered Pit bull or Pit bull-type dog, maintained exclusively as a household pet, involved in a fatal attack on a human in the United States is proof that canine behavior is profoundly influenced by the function of the dog and quality of care and control practiced by owners.

It has always been mankind's great fortune that most dogs, despite the low level of care and control demonstrated by many of their owners and their acquisition for negative functions, are nevertheless wonderfully tolerant and sociable toward humans. It is for this reason that we often expect all dogs to behave amicably. However, dogs will, and do, bite; therefore, any serious study on the reasons and causes for dog attacks requires a truthful examination of each individual dog, the function for which the dog was obtained and how the dog was maintained. This is the first critical step toward understanding how a dog had the ability and opportunity to behave aggressively towards a human.

- Dogs are predators—predators chase and kill other animals.
- Aggression is a natural part of dog behavior, used to lay claim to resources, guard territory, protect offspring or ward off perceived dangers.
- Dogs are sentient beings, capable of experiencing pain, anger, fear and frustration.
- Dogs have different signs and signals they use to communicate intentions or emotions, and these are very different than the vocalizations and signals humans use to communicate intent or emotion.

Because of all these things, dogs bite. They bite other animals, they bite each other and they bite humans. Sometimes we can understand or relate to the reasons why dogs attack, other times the bite or attack seems to us to be unwarranted or vicious. As humans often have a difficult enough time understanding the intentions or aggressive behavior found in our own species, it should come as no surprise that the behavior of dogs should also at times confound and confuse us.

Few things in life come without some level of risk. Swimming pools, automobiles, household cleaning products, power tools, bicycles, stairs, and dogs all come with a certain level of potential harm. Our lives are comprised of evaluating risks on a daily basis. From how fast we drive our cars or when to cross a busy street, or cordoning off swimming pools and staircases from unsupervised children, we think about or act on the potential danger of things daily. Why then is it so difficult for so many people to understand that this applies to our dogs as well? While dogs are certainly less of a risk factor than automobiles or swimming pools, nevertheless, the same theory applies—dogs are safe when maintained in a responsible manner and when people show a reasonable level of risk assessment. Terrible, unforeseeable accidents will always occur in life, but the point is to strive to make these incidents as rare as possible.

There are presently 73 million dogs[1] in the United States and approximately two dozen human deaths per year are due to dog attacks. In approximately one half to three-quarters (12–18) of these deaths, the victims are young children. However, over 250 children under the age of five die yearly in swimming pools.[2] Comparing yearly dog bite fatalities to yearly fatalities associated with automobiles, swimming pools or lightning shows that dogs are incredibly low on the list of potential dangers.

While the risk of being killed by a dog is extremely low, serious dog bites and attacks obviously present a likelier risk. Both serious and fatal attacks can be reduced by reasonable risk assessment. Owners can reduce the risk of their dog biting someone through dozens of different methods, from educating themselves about canine behavior and enrolling in dog training classes to properly containing and supervising their dogs. Potential victims can also reduce their risk of dog attacks by learning about canine behaviors and how to respond to an aggressive-looking dog. There are literally hundreds of books written on these topics, as well as information presented on the Internet, television and even radio. For those wishing to educate themselves and lower the potential risk associated with dogs, the information is available and highly accessible.

However, just as there will always be murderers and reckless drivers, there will always be some dog owners who refuse to safeguard others from their dogs and there will always be some victims who not only failed to make an appropriate risk assessment in a situation involving dogs, but were reckless.

In 2006, an adult male climbed over a fence at 5:30 a.m. and entered into the yard of a metalworking company in California. Three large guard dogs were kept on the premises. The man was attacked and killed by the dogs.

In 1997, a man took possession of two large dogs and placed them in the fenced yard behind his trailer. In addition to obtaining the male and female for use as guard dogs, he intended to breed them "to make some money." Four days later his girlfriend arrived with her 3-year-old son. Authorities believe the mother and her boyfriend were in a drug-induced stupor when the boy wandered into the backyard where he was attacked by the dogs. An autopsy revealed the boy lay dying in the yard for at least two hours before either adult awoke and realized the child was missing.

While there is much society and individuals can do to reduce attacks, the two cases cited above demonstrate that there will always be incidents of severe or fatal dog attacks due to some people's failure to take any appropriate steps to safeguard themselves or others from their dogs. If we are truly interested in reducing the number of attacks, we need to honestly examine which behaviors are the major contributors to these events: human or canine. Unfortunately, the way canine aggression is usually examined is by simply referring to the number of deaths or bites attributed to dogs and not by an examination of the forces driving behavior.

It is inaccurate and unreliable to use the number of fatal dog attacks, and/or which breeds are involved, as "proof" of canine aggression. The reason for this is that it fails to identify exactly what it claims to be providing evidence of—namely aggression.

Consider the following deaths which are included in the Centers for Disease Control statistics on dog bite-related deaths in the United States:

- A man is bitten on the thumb by a dog. Introduced into the wound is a rapidly spreading and virulent bacteria, which results in the man's death four days later.
- A woman dies after her boyfriend physically restrains her, while repeatedly ordering his dog to attack her.
- A two-day-old infant dies after a dog picks the child up by the head and carries the infant into the room where the parents are.
- A dog attacks his long-time owner, inflicting dozens of deep, penetrating wounds, resulting in the woman's death.

These four deaths tell us only one thing—four people died as a result of dog bites. They tell us nothing about the level and type of aggression, or define what aggression is. Lumping these disparate events together misconstrues the very nature of the behavior. Is a bite to the thumb the same type of aggression as a dog inflicting dozens of penetrating and lethal bites? Is a dog that attacks due to repeated commands from his owner showing the same type of aggression as a dog that attacks a person of his own initiative? Is a dog that picks a baby up by the head and carries it into the room with the owners committing an aggressive act? You cannot provide proof of something which you have not defined. Yet these types of statistics are routinely used to "prove" the aggressiveness of certain breeds.

The answers to severe and fatal canine attacks are not to be found in statistics, or in discussing dog breeds, or in recent accounts of dog attacks found in the media. The answers to canine aggression can only be found beginning with an examination of the relationship (or lack of one) between dogs and owners.

CHAPTER 15

The Pit Bull Placebo: Conclusions on Canine Aggression

"We are alone, absolutely alone on this chance planet: and, amid all the forms of life that surround us, not one, excepting the dog, has made an alliance with us."

(Maurice Maeterlinck, 1862–1949)

Recently, in North Carolina, police responded to a report of a Pit bull and a Golden Retriever fighting. One of the dogs was found tied to a tree with his front leg broken and deep gashes to his muzzle from the bites of the other dog. There can be little doubt as to which dog was injured and how this attack came to be. We have identified the two types of dogs involved in this incident, we know their history, we've read the newspaper headlines about which dogs are involved in aggression, we've listened to politicians state that certain breeds are the source of the dog bite problem, we've even heard some "experts" and laymen alike tell us of the uniqueness of the wounds Pit bulls inflict during an attack (breaking of bones and tearing), and through all this we've come to know that there are "dangerous and aggressive" breeds and there are "friendly, non- aggressive" breeds of dogs.

Today, the human/dog bond—the most complex and profound inter-species relationship in the history of mankind—has been reduced to a simple axiom: Breed of dog = degree of dangerousness.

Throughout the centuries, dogs have elicited great pride, enduring love and extreme devotion from humans. It has never been uncommon for humans to risk their lives to save their beloved canine companions and dogs have more than returned this devotion in kind. However, as frequent as it is to find humans bestowing great affection upon their dogs, it is as frequent to find humans inflicting horrific abuse and cruelty upon our canine companions.

What reasonable or sane person could expect dogs kept in such diametrically opposed conditions (cherished versus abused) to exhibit similar behaviors? How, in a society unparalleled in its access to information, have we been bullied into believing that the condition and treatment of our canine companions has no relevance on their future behaviors? And how have we become a society so ignorant and terrified of some dogs that we have allowed a wave of panic to sweep through our communities, allowing certain dogs to be banned, muzzled, restricted and killed by the hundreds of thousands in "shelters" across the nation?

Consider how information about dog attacks has been disseminated over the last century:

One hundred years ago—Newspapers provided vivid and often detailed accounts of dog attacks. Emotional and often anthropomorphic terms were used in an attempt to understand the factors that caused the dog to attack. Dogs were described as either "vicious by nature" or "caused to be vicious." People were identified at times to be "innocent" victims, or "tormentors" who invited an attack. Dogs were understood to be complex beings reacting to human behavior. The function and condition of dogs were often included in reports, as they were understood to influence canine behavior.

Fifty years ago—Newspapers continued to report dog attacks to be a result of "cause and effect." Although dogs were no longer described in emotional terms, they were still portrayed as sentient beings that reacted to pain, discomfort, or fear. Additionally, many reports of dog attacks conveyed the understanding that aggression was a natural and expected behavior of dogs in certain circumstances. Owners and/or victims were often identified in news reports as exhibiting behaviors (intentionally or unintentionally) that caused the dog to attack.

Today—The Pit Bull Paparazzi are our source of information on dog attacks. Like their tabloid celebrity counterparts, The Pit Bull Paparazzi are ever on the alert for any incident involving their high-profile subject, pushing past or ignoring all "low entertainment" attacks, while zooming in on and hyping any incident involving the "high entertainment" Pit bull. Theories about the breed, its history and temperament, are discussed, while details concerning the circumstances of the individual dog involved are not reported. Cause and effect, or reasons for the attack, are no longer found in reports, since breed is now recognized as sufficient information to explain aggression.

Recently, some politicians have joined in the fray with their own brand of "yellow journalism," touting wild claims about canine behavior of which they know little and seem to care less. In 2005, despite the fact that only *one* of Canada's 33 documented fatal dog attacks involved any type of dog even remotely resembling a Pit bull, Ontario's Attorney General Michael Bryant began a campaign to rid the province of Pit bulls. Spouting inane and false claims about Pit bulls and aggression and refusing to consider the testimony of Ontario's own professional canine experts, the Attorney General pushed through legislation banning Pit bulls in the entire province of Ontario.

In addition to the news media and politicians, an unholy trilogy of misinformation has been formed with the Internet. The Internet has allowed for the rare incidents of severe and fatal canine aggression to be transmitted on a global scale, at times generating hundreds of sensational headlines from a single episode of aggression, grossly distorting our perceptions as to the dangerousness of dogs and the frequency of attacks. Not only are these rare cases instantly accessible, but oftentimes they become retrievable for a seemingly infinite amount of time, providing "a permanent record" of selective cases of aggression.

The information disseminated about Pit bulls and aggression by the newspapers, politicians and the Internet has led many to conclude that the solution to canine aggression is to rid society of the "breeds of dogs found in reported attacks." And, since little to no information is revealed about the other circumstances contributing to an attack, breed is now found to be the only "constant" in reports of canine aggression.

The solution or cure now touted for ridding communities of dangerous dogs is found in the guise of the Pit Bull Placebo. Like the pharmacologically inactive sugar pill dispensed to placate a patient who supposes it to be medicine, eradication of the Pit bull is heralded as the cure for severe dog attacks. However, a placebo is administered solely to appease a person's mental duress. In the present day climate of fear and misinformation about Pit bulls and dog attacks, eradication of the Pit bull is the placebo administered to ease the public's mental anxiety. This, of course, does not address the underlying cause of why dogs attack and how they have been allowed access to their victims. Nor does this address why humans feel the need to have dogs that will intimidate, attack, or fight other beings. These factors, recognized for centuries as contributing to canine aggression, are dangerously ignored when a dog attack is deemed to be a product of breed.

The distraction of blaming the breed of dog involved in attacks, while ignoring dangerous human behaviors, has created a climate of fear towards certain breeds. Paradoxically, this fear of Pit bulls allows us to maintain our sense of well-being because it permits us to believe that canine aggression can be solved without introspection.

If we truly believe that the extremely rare cases of fatal dog attacks merit extreme measures in the management of dogs—if our concern and shock is genuine—then we must be equally genuine and sincere in seeking out and addressing the real causes for these incidents. Hanging entire breeds of dogs in effigy for the actions of a miniscule percentage of their population, while ignoring the dangerous management practices of their owners, is not an effective or acceptable solution to canine aggression.

Portraying two Pit bulls abandoned in the basement of a vacant house that have desperately resorted to ingesting inedible objects and rat poison as "family dogs" is a grotesque distortion of the human/dog bond. Furthermore, claiming that the agonizing and final behaviors of these suffering animals are proof of the aggressiveness of the breed is a monstrous mischaracterization of canine behavior.

Only by acknowledging that a social hysteria has been spawned by the sensational and inaccurate reporting of dog attacks and only by extracting ourselves from the swirl of emotion, myths, rumors, and politics of dog attacks can we rationally and effectively address canine aggression in a way that may reduce these attacks.

When we put aside our preconceived notions about breed behaviors and investigate the real causes for dog attacks, we come to discover that it was actually the Golden Retriever which initiated the attack against the Pit bull in North Carolina—and it was the Pit bull who received the fractured front leg and severe bites described at the beginning of this chapter. Further investigation finds that the Golden Retriever had attacked and injured the Pit bull at the goading and urging of his teenage owner. Had we simply allowed the breed of dog to explain this attack our conclusions would have been a complete misrepresentation of the facts.

But the truth is that dog attacks are rarely investigated in such a way that reveal the real reasons why dogs attack. And so we have routinely come to draw totally inaccurate conclusions about canine behavior. These inaccurate assessments often lead to breed-specific legislation which is not only of no value in keeping communities safe, but has caused much anguish to responsible dog owners and has doomed hundreds of thousands of dogs to exile or death.

It is long past time for us to rethink our policies about dog attacks and the role humans play in this inter-species relationship. We owe it to the future safety of our children and communities. We owe it to our canine companions.

APPENDIX A

Dog Attacks Reported in Northeastern Newspapers, 1864–1899

Date	Dog Reported As	Victim	Circumstances	State	Injury Description
Dec. 1864	Bloodhound	10 yrs. - M	Attacked in field by dog	NJ	Fatal
Sept. 1866	Bloodhound	Adult - M	Baker attacked by dog	NY	Severe
May 1868	Vicious dog	1 yr. - M	Attacked after child tripped	AL	Fatal
		9 yrs. - F	Sister tried to help		Fatal
Mar. 1870	Vicious dogs	Little girl	Neighbor's loose dogs	OH	Fatal
Jun. 1870	Dog	Boy	Sent to house on errand	IA	Mangled - critical
Jan. 1871	Savage dog	Adult - F	Died 2 days after attack	MI	Fatal
Feb. 1873	Bloodhound	Adult - F	Washing clothes in yard	NY	Not expected to recover
Jun. 1873	Russ. Bloodhound	Adult - M	Police officer, loose dog	NY	Serious, throat bite
Mar. 1874	Newfoundland	Boy - M	Entered neighbor's yard	OH	Serious
Apr. 1874	Bloodhound	19 yrs. - M	Approached chained dog	NY	Lacerated throat
Jun. 1874	Newfoundland	3 yrs. - F	Went near dog being fed	NY	Possibly fatal
Mar. 1875	Large dog	4 yrs. - F	Girl entered henhouse	NY	Fatal
Jul. 1875	Dogs	16 yrs. - M	Attacked by loose dogs	IA	Severe
Nov. 1875	Ferocious dogs	Adult - F	Attacked in cow pasture	MS	Fatal
Aug. 1876	Bulldogs	Adult - F	Getting water from well	IN	Severe
Feb. 1877	Spitz	Newborn	Newborn left w/dog	NY	Fatal
Feb. 1877	Dogs	Adult - F	Walking near her home	KY	Not expected to live
Mar. 1877	English Bulldog	Little girl	Trying to feed chained dog	OH	Fatal

Mar. 1878	Mastiff	19 mo. - F	Neighbor's loose dog	NJ	Fatal
Jul. 1878	Bloodhound	9 yrs. - M	Neighbor's loose dog	NY	Bitten in face
Apr. 1879	Ferocious dog	7 yrs. - M	Neighbor's dog	KY	Fatal
May 1879	Bulldog	Adult - M	Loose roaming dog	IL	Severe
Jun. 1879	Newfoundland	Adult - M	Entered friend's yard	IL	Serious
Sept. 1879	Watchdog	Adult - F	Attacked by guard dog	IL	Severe
Sept. 1879	Noble Bloodhound	Unknown	Unknown circumstances	PA	Serious
Jun. 1880	Cuban Bloodhound	Adult - M	Drunken owner hit dog	NJ	Fatal
Jul. 1880	Bloodhound	Youth - M	Owners set dog on victim	NY	Serious
Nov. 1880	Large dog	17 yrs. - F	Getting off of wagon	NJ	Critical
Jan. 1881	Bloodhound	6 yrs. - M	Attacked while sledding	NY	Severe
May 1881	Pack of dogs	7 yrs. - M	Attacked on road	AR	Fatal
Mar. 1882	Bloodhound	13 yrs. - M	Neighbor's guard dog	NY	Severe
Mar. 1882	Bloodhound	Adult - M	Guard dog at factory	NY	Serious
Jul. 1882	Newfoundland	Child - M	Attacked while playing	PA	Fatal
Dec. 1882	Bloodhound	Adult - M	Guard dog at business	CT	Critical wounds
Apr. 1883	Dog	5 yrs. - M	Wandered to chained dog	PA	Fatal
Sept. 1883	Bulldog	Elderly - M	Neighbor's yard & dog	PA	Fatal
Nov. 1883	Newfoundland	15 yrs. - F	Entered neighbor's yard	IL	May survive
Dec. 1883	Savage dog	6 yrs. - F	Unknown circumstances	PA	Fatal
Apr. 1884	Bloodhound	Adult - F	Guard dog at hotel	NY	Expected to die
Apr. 1884	Dog	9 yrs. - M	Neighbor's dog in field	PA	Fatal
May 1884	Guard dog	Adult - M	Guard dog in stables	NY	Severe
Jun. 1884	Bulldog	Adult - M	Fighting dog at tavern	PA	Severe

Jun. 1884	Siberian Bloodhound	Adult - M	Chained dog broke loose	MA	Arm crushed
Aug. 1884	Bloodhound	Adult - M	Guard dog at soap factory	PA	Serious
Feb. 1885	Starving dogs	12 yrs. - F	Carrying meat f/butcher	PA	Severe
Jun.1885	Newfoundland	11 yrs. - M	Delivering ice cream	IL	Fatal
Jun. 1885	Large farm dog	Elderly - M	Attacked in henhouse	NY	Recovery doubtful
Jun. 1885	Strange dog	3 yrs. - M	Dog jumped fence	NY	Feared to be fatal
Sept. 1885	Ferocious dog	4 yrs. - F	Chained dog	OH	Fatal
Nov. 1885	Cuban Bloodhound	10 yrs. - F	Crossing farmer's field	MA	Severe
Dec. 1885	Newfoundland	10 yrs. - F	Closed door on dog's tail	NY	Serious
Dec. 1885	Siberian Bloodhound	Adult - M	Bitten in liquor saloon	NJ	Serious
Jan. 1886	Newfoundland	10 yrs. - M	Children sledding	NY	Serious
		14 yrs. - F	Girl pushed dog away		Serious
Nov. 1886	Collies & Newfound	6 yrs. - M	Boy tried to "harass" dog	MA	Life-threatening
May 1887	Large dog	8 yrs. - M	Neighbor's loose dog	NJ	Serious neck injury
Jul. 1887	Dog	Adult - M	Grabbed dog chasing hen	NY	Fatal
Oct. 1887	Newfoundland	25 yrs. - M	Knocked down & bitten	NJ	Severe
Oct. 1887	Shepherd dog	Child - M	Tried to pet chained dog	IN	Fatal
Feb. 1888	Newfoundland	Adult - M	Owner kicked guard dog	MO	Expected to die
Feb. 1888	Coal-mine dog	2 yrs. - M	Aunt's dog inside house	OH	Fatal
Apr. 1888	Savage dog	Adult - M	Bitten several days earlier	PA	Fatal
Apr. 1888	Pack hungry curs	Boy	Starving dogs at docks	NJ	May not recover
Apr. 1888	Bloodhound	Adult - M	Owner tried to chain dog	NJ	Arm crushed
Apr. 1888	Ferocious dog	Child	Loose dog attacked child	IA	Fatal
May 1888	Large, vicious dog	Baby	Dog took child f/carriage	NJ	Expected to be fatal

May 1888	Large hunting dog	5 yrs. - M	Went near dog w/bone	NY	Severe, disfigured
May 1888	Bullmastiff	Adult - M	Doctor delivering baby	MA	Serious
Jul. 1888	Bloodhound	Child - M	Two boys killed by dog	NY	Fatal
		Child - M	Unknown circumstances		Fatal
Jul. 1888	Bloodhd & Newfnd	Adult - F	Loose dogs in road	NJ	Dangerous wounds
Aug. 1888	Bloodhound	Adult - F	Woman attacked	MD	Severe
		14 yr. - M	Boy tried to help		Torn to bone
Oct. 1888	English Bulldogs	Adult - M	Peddler entering yard	PA	Fatal
Apr. 1889	Savage dog	Adult - M	Owner let dog kill tramp	NJ	Fatal
May 1889	Bloodhound	Adult - M	Owner set dog on man	CT	Fatal
Jun. 1889	Mastiff	6 yrs. - M	Dog chained in cellar	NJ	Severe
Jul. 1889	Siberian Bloodhound	Adult - M	Loose dog on street	NJ	Serious
Jul. 1889	Bulldogs	Adult - M	Guard dogs at stone yard	OH	Fatal
Aug. 1889	Dogs	70 yrs. - F	Attacked by loose dogs	IN	Torn to pieces
Jan. 1890	Bloodhound	Small boy	Attacked in churchyard	MD	Bitten in throat
Jan. 1890	Vicious dog	Adult - M	Farmer attacked by dog	OH	Torn to pieces
Jun. 1890	Savage dog	Adult - M	New, chained dog	PA	Severe
Aug. 1890	Savage dog	7 yrs. - F	Loose roaming dog	MA	May prove fatal
Nov. 1890	Newfoundland	Infant	Infant left alone w/dog	SD	Fatal
Mar. 1891	Bloodhound & Dog	Schoolgirl	Loose roaming dogs	PA	Fatal
Jun. 1891	Newfoundland	Young girl	Boy threw dog's bone at girl	OH	Serious
Jul. 1891	Dog	4 yrs. - F	Tried to pet chained dog	NJ	Serious
Jul. 1891	Mastiff	8 yrs. - M	Went to house for milk	NJ	Critical, torn scalp
Jul. 1891	Vicious dog	Adult - F	Mangled by loose dog	OH	Feared will die
Aug. 1891	Mastiff	Adult - M	Owner's new guard dog	NJ	Serious

Aug. 1891	Bloodhound	6 yrs. - M	Went to pet chained dog	NJ	May die, ear torn off
Sept. 1891	Mastiffs	9 yrs. - M	Dogs broke free f/pen	WV	Fatal
Dec. 1891	English Mastiff	6 yrs. - M	Loose dog on sidewalk	NJ	Severe wounds
		4 yrs. - M	Little brother went to help		Serious
Feb. 1892	Ferocious dog	Child - M	Unknown circumstances	IN	Fatal
Feb. 1892	Pack strays	Adult - M	Starving pack of dogs	KS	Fatal
		17 yrs. - F	attacked father & daughter		Fatal
May 1892	Bulldog	Adult - M	Drunken man, chained dog	IN	Serious
Jul. 1892	Ferocious dog	5 yrs. - M	Loose roaming dog	WI	Critical
Aug. 1892	Bulldogs	Adult - M	Prize-fighter's fighting dogs	NJ	Serious
Oct. 1892	Vicious dogs	14 yrs. - M	Loose dogs on road	IL	Fatal
Feb. 1893	Black Eng. Mastiff	Adult - F	Neighbor's dog in yard	KY	Fatal
Mar. 1893	St. Bernard	11 yrs. - F	Mother breeding dogs	NY	Scalp torn off
May 1893	Mastiff	12 yrs. - M	Dog chained at shop	NY	Serious
Jul. 1893	Newfoundland	6 yrs. - M	Tried to pet dog	NJ	Fear may die
Jul. 1893	Cur dog	Adult - M	Chained in bakery cellar	NY	Serious
Jul. 1893	Mastiff	Adult - M	Guard dog at livery stables	PA	Serious
Aug. 1893	Siberian Bloodhound	Adult - F	Dog with history of attacks	NY	Serious
Sept. 1893	Big brown mongrel	2 yrs. - F	Approached dog being fed	NY	Doubtful recovery
Dec. 1893	Newfoundland	14 yrs. - M	Attacked after kicking dog	OH	Fatal
Dec. 1893	Savage dog	6 yrs. - F	Loose dog on street	PA	Fatal
Jan. 1894	Vicious dog	6 yrs. - F	Unknown circumstances	IL	Fatal
Feb. 1894	Newfoundland	4 yrs. - M	Boy playing with dog	IL	Fatal
Mar. 1894	Newfoundland	Adult - M	Attacked by neighbor's dog	PA	Serious
Mar. 1894	Bulldog	3 yr. - F	Female dog w/puppies	MA	Serious

Jul. 1894	St. Bernard	Girl	Went near dog w/bone	*Unk.*	Serious
Jul. 1894	St. Bernard	6 yrs. - M	Attacked and nearly killed	MD	Precarious condition
Aug. 1894	Bloodhound	Youth - M	Guard dog at orchard	CA	May not recover
Oct. 1894	Newfoundlands	6 yrs . - M	Loose dogs on sidewalk	NY	Serious
Dec. 1894	Newfoundland	50 yrs. - M	Guard dog attacked owner	NY	Severe, hospitalized
Dec. 1894	German Boarhound	Adult - M	Tried to stop dogs fighting	CT	Serious
Feb. 1895	Newfoundland	9 yrs. - M	Child attacked by loose dog	IN	Severe
Feb. 1895	Mastiff	9 yrs. - M	Attacked & bitten	IN	Serious
Apr. 1895	Mastiff	19 yrs. - M	Guard dog at opera house	NJ	Serious
May 1895	Several dogs	Adult - M	Attacked by several dogs	NY	Likely prove fatal
Jun. 1895	Vicious dog	5 yrs. - M	Neighbor's dog	IN	Fatal
Sept. 1895	Newfoundland	4 yrs. - M	Playing near his house	PA	Serious face injury
May 1896	Ferocious dog	Elderly - F	Unknown circumstances	OH	Will probably die
May 1896	Vicious hounds	10 yrs. - M	Entered neighbor's yard	OH	Fatal results feared
Jul. 1896	Water Spaniel	3 yrs. - U	Attacked by hunter's dog	OH	Feared will die
Aug. 1896	Newfoundland	Adult - M	Unknown circumstances	OH	Serious
Sept. 1896	Guard dog	6 yrs. - M	Watchdog at tannery	NY	Fatal
Sept. 1896	St. Bernard	7 yrs. - F	Attacked girl at house party	MO	Fatal
Oct. 1896	Newfoundland	5 yrs. - M	Family pet attacked boy	OH	Serious head injury
Jul. 1897	Dog	4 yrs. - F	Child attacked by dog	PA	Severe, lost eye
Jul. 1897	Pack stray dogs	Boy	Dogs near slaughterhouse	OH	Severe
Aug. 1897	Shepherd dog	8 yrs. - F	Took bone from dog	MD	Doubtful recovery
Aug. 1897	Newfoundland	3 yrs. - F	Dog returning from "romp"	NY	Severe head injury
Oct. 1897	Newfoundland	17 yrs. - F	Dog hurt by rocking chair	NJ	Serious

Dec. 1897	Bulldog	6 yrs. - M	Feeding dog chained in barn	OH	Fatal
Dec. 1897	Bloodhound Mix	14 yrs. - F	Entered neighbor's yard	NY	Serious
Jan. 1898	Newfoundland	11 yrs. - M	Prolonged attack on child	NY	Fatal
Apr. 1898	Prized family pet	5 yrs. - M	Child playing in yard w/dog	OH	Critical head injuries
May 1898	Pet dog	15 dys. - U	Infant left alone w/dog	IL	Fatal
Sept. 1898	Savage dog	Adult - F	Entered yard to visit neighbor	CT	Fatal
Sept. 1898	Bloodhounds	Adult - F	Walking past house w/dogs	NY	Serious
Aug. 1899	St. Bernard	6 yrs. - M	Children playing with dog	NY	Bit ear off & lost eye
Sept. 1899	Great Dane	Adult - F	Feeding chained guard dog	NY	Fatal
Nov. 1899	Bloodhound Mix	5 yrs. - M	Loose dogs in alleyway	NJ	Severe

* Note *   During the next century (1900-1999), fatal attacks by Bloodhounds and Newfoundlands decreased dramatically, with only one reported fatal attack by a Bloodhound in 1910, and only two reported cases of a fatal attack by a Newfoundland, one in 1912, and one in 1988.

Dog Attacks Reported in U.S. Newspapers, 1960–1975

Date	Dog Reported As	Victim	Circumstances	State	Injury Level
Mar. 1960	St. Bern & GS	9 yrs. - M	Walking home f/school	MI	Serious
Mar. 1960	Husky-type	7 yrs. - F	Stray dog entered yard	AK	Fatal
Mar. 1960	Doberman	55 yrs. - F	Kennel owner w/ 40 dogs	NJ	Fatal
May 1960	Boxer	Adult - M	Starving dog w/puppies	OH	Serious
Jul. 1960	German Shep	4 yrs. - M	Uncle's dog eating bone	WI	Fatal
Mar. 1961	German Shep	4 yrs.. - M	Went to pet chained dog	WV	Critical
Jun. 1961	Poodle	65 yrs. - F	Owner bitten in throat, head	CA	Critical
Jul. 1961	Great Dane	12 yrs. - M	Dragged off bike by dog	PA	Serious
Dec. 1961	(3) Boxer-type	51 yrs. - F	Attacked walking her dog	MA	Severe
		55 yrs. - F	Prior attack by same dogs	MA	Serious
Apr. 1962	Black dog	2 yrs. - M	Neighbor's loose dog	WV	Severe
Sept. 1962	German Shep	4 mo. - M	Infant left alone w/new dog	PA	Serious
Oct. 1962	(2) Gr. Shep	8 yrs. - M	Boy dragged 50 feet by dogs	CA	Serious
Nov. 1962	(2) Gr. Shep	5 yrs. - M	Neighbor's loose dogs	TX	Severe
Nov. 1962	Half-shepherd	5 yrs. - M	Loose dogs in street	TX	> 50 bites
Jan. 1963	(2) Shep-type	31 yrs. - M	Guard dogs escaped f/auto	PA	Serious
		69 yrs. - M	shop attacked 2 men on street	PA	Serious
Apr. 1963	GS/Boxer X	10 yrs. - F	Neighbor's loose dog	OH	Serious
May 1963	German Shep	3 yrs. - F	Neighbor's dog in yard	PA	Severe

Jun. 1963	Siberian husky	3 yrs. - M	Chained, starving dog	CO	Fatal
Jul. 1963	German Shep	2 yrs. - F	Child alone in yard w/dog	AR	Serious
Aug. 1963	Husky	5 yrs. - F	Only had dog a few "minutes"	NV	Serious
Oct. 1963	Pointer	7 yrs. - M	Loose dog dragged boy down	WI	Severe
Oct. 1963	German Shep	2 yrs. - F	Babysitter's abused dog	PA	Fatal
Nov. 1963	(3) Mixed	10 yrs. - M	Boy on bike - loose dogs	MD	Critical
Nov. 1963	Malamute	2 mo. - M	Father's "new" guard dog	IL	Fatal
Dec. 1963	German Shep	11 yrs. - F	9 yr old girl walking dog	NJ	Serious
Mar. 1964	German Shep	23 yrs. - M	Loose roaming dogs	PA	Serious
		46 yrs. - M	attacked elderly man and		Serious
		85 yrs. - M	two men who tried to help		Severe
May 1964	Hunting dog	7 yrs. - M	Boy playing with chained dog	KS	Severe
Aug. 1964	Mixed breed	4 yrs. - M	Grandfather's dog	MO	Fatal
Aug. 1964	(5) Ger Shep	2 yrs. - F	Parent's breeding dogs	IN	Fatal
Aug. 1964	German Shep	9 yrs. - M	Loose roaming dog	PA	Severe
Oct. 1964	(3) Boxers	2 yrs. - F	Child alone in yard w/dogs	MA	Severe
Mar. 1965	(3) Boxers	4 yrs. - M	Loose dogs in alley	TX	Serious
Mar. 1965	Mongrel	22 mo. - M	Newly acquired, chained dog	CA	Fatal
Apr. 1965	Pit bull	4 yrs. - M	Wandered to chained dog	UT	Fatal
Apr. 1965	Siberian husky	4 yrs. - F	Wandered to chained dog	NY	Fatal
Jun. 1965	Collie	4 yrs. - M	Child visiting at friend's home	NJ	Severe
Jul. 1965	Labrador Ret.	4 yrs. - M	Tried to pet restrained dog	WI	Fatal
Aug. 1965	German Shep	3 yrs. - F	Attacked at motel by loose dog	VA	> 100 stitches
Sept. 1965	Bulldog	2 yrs. - M	Neighbor's chained dog	TX	Fatal
Nov. 1965	Shepherd-type	60 yrs. - F	3rd & fatal attack on owner	WI	Fatal

Nov. 1965	(3) Gr. Shep	2 yrs. - F	Child alone w/neighbor's dog	TX	Very critical
Dec. 1965	(2) Great Dane	59 yrs. - F	Loose dogs on street	LA	Severe
Jan. 1966	German Shep	7 yrs. - M	Saved smaller child from attack	FL	> 270 stitches
Mar. 1966	GS & Gr. Dane	18 mo - M	Babysitter's dogs in yard	CA	Fatal
Apr. 1966	Shepherd-type	6 yrs. - F	Walking to school - loose dog	CA	Serious
Apr. 1966	German Shep	7 yrs. - M	Visiting child attacked in house	NJ	Severe
Jun. 1966	Mongrel	2 yrs. - M	Attacked by neighbor's dog	PA	Fatal
Jun. 1966	German Shep	10 yrs. - M	Dog escaped from kennel	PA	Severe
Aug. 1966	(5) Great Dane	5 yrs. - F	Dogs escaped f/kennel	MD	Fatal
		4 yrs. - M	and attacked two children		Severe
Aug. 1966	Great Dane	2 yrs. - M	Went near dog eating	PA	Critical
Aug. 1966	Shep/Collie X	5 yrs. - F	Playing in neighbor's yard	PA	Serious
Nov. 1966	(2) Samoyed	4 yrs. - M	Loose dogs at schoolyard	AK	Fatal
Jan. 1967	(2) Malamute	6 yrs. - M	Loose dogs in alley	WI	> 100 bites
Feb. 1967	Four dogs	7 yrs. - M	Attacked by neighbor's dogs	MI	Severe
Feb. 1967	(15) Collies & Mixed breeds	72 yrs. - F	Owner attacked by her dogs	WI	Fatal
May 1967	Dog	3 yrs. - F	Wandered to chained dog	NM	Severe
Jul. 1967	Mastiff	73 yrs. - M	Owner walking dog in woods	PA	Fatal
Aug. 1967	German police	6 yrs. - F	Watchdog attacked visiting girl	SC	Serious
Aug. 1967	(2) Wolf/Lab Xs	3 yrs. - F	Attacked in babysitter's yard	AK	Fatal
Aug. 1967	Miniature Poodle	Elderly - F	Owner "mutilated" after fainting	CA	Severe
Sept. 1967	German Shep	7 yrs. - M	Chained, breeding dogs	NJ	Severe
Dec. 1967	German Shep	7 yrs. - F	Police shot dog to stop attack	PA	Very critical
Dec. 1967	(2) Sheepdog	7 yrs. - M	Riding bicycle near kennels	VA	Serious
Dec. 1967	(2) Gr. Shep &	5 yrs. - M	Two boys killed by neighbor's	VA	Fatal

	Mixed	4 yrs. - M	loose dogs & 2 stray dogs		Fatal
Dec. 1967	(3) Wolfhounds	7 yrs. - M	Dogs escaped from yard	CA	Severe
Dec. 1967	Great Dane	5 yrs. - F	Newly acquired guard dog	GA	Fatal
Feb. 1968	Shepherd-type	3 yrs. - M	Unknown circumstances	NE	80 stitches
Mar. 1968	German Shep	5 yrs. - F	Dog jumped 5 ft. fence to attack	IA	Severe
Mar. 1968	German Shep	42 yrs. - F	Tripped over sleeping dog	PA	Serious
Apr. 1968	Irish Setter	3 yrs. - F	Wandered to chained dog	PA	Serious
May 1968	Belgian Shep	3 yrs. - F	Grandmother's chained dog	CA	> 125 stitches
Jun. 1968	(2) Ger Shep	6 yrs. - M	Boy fell into guard dogs' pen	PA	Critical
Jun. 1968	German Shep	21 yrs. - M	Guard dog at auto shop	NJ	Severe
Jun. 1968	German Shep	3 yrs. - M	Children hit dog with pipe first	FL	Severe
Jul. 1968	German Shep	10 yrs. - M	Paperboy - dog chained to log	NJ	Serious
Jul. 1968	German police	3 yrs. - M	Child attacked by loose dog	NY	> 100 stitches
Oct. 1968	Doberman	5 yrs. - M	1-day-old puppies in house	PA	Serious
Mar. 1969	German Shep	1 mo. - F	Family dog jumped into crib	NY	Fatal
Apr. 1969	German Shep	4 yrs. - F	Ran past chained dog in yard	NJ	Severe
May 1969	Cocker Spaniel	3 yrs. - F	Stray dog attacked child in yard	PA	Serious
Jun. 1969	German Shep	9 yrs. - M	Attacked by relative's dog	KY	> 200 stitches
Jul. 1969	<Crazed> GS	8 yrs. - F	Loose dog on street	PA	Serious
		67 yrs. - M	Also attacked rescuer		Severe
Jul. 1969	Sentry dog	Adult - F	Recently purchased dog	NY	Severe
Jul. 1969	Dog	18 mo. - M	Child pushed dog	NY	Critical
Jul. 1969	Wolf dog	2 yrs. - F	Child left alone w/dog	AK	Fatal
Sept. 1969	Shepherd-type	5 yrs.- M	2 other dogs "saved" boy	CA	Serious
Oct. 1969	German Shep	33 yrs. - F	Shelter worker attacked in pen	PA	Serious

Oct. 1969	(Pack) Mixed	2 yrs. - F	Loose dogs entered yard	CA	Fatal
Dec. 1969	(2) Gr. Shep	59 yrs. - F	Released dogs f/pen	FL	Severe
Feb. 1970	German Shep	18 mo. - M	Child alone with dog	MO	Fatal
Feb. 1970	German Shep	3 yrs. - F	Visiting girl & new dog	PA	Critical
May 1970	German Shep	5 yrs. - M	Loose dog in street	PA	Serious
Jul. 1970	German Shep	5 yrs. - F	Child feeding dog	OH	Serious
Aug. 1970	German Shep	8 yrs. - F	Playing in yard w/dog	WI	Serious
Oct. 1970	German Shep	3 yrs. - F	Entered neighbor's home	NY	Severe
Nov. 1970	(2) Gr. Shep	4 yrs. - M	Dogs in backyard	VA	Severe
Dec. 1970	Malamute	3 mo. - M	Child left alone w/dog	WI	Fatal
Jan. 1971	Great Dane	3 yrs. - F	Child climbed 6 ft. fence	CA	Severe
Apr. 1971	Malamute	13 yrs. - F	Dog broke chain, jumped fence	PA	Severe
May 1971	Husky	4 mo. - F	Child left alone w/dog	IL	Fatal
Jul. 1971	Chow chow	18 yrs. - F	Attempting to chain dog	AR	Serious
Sept. 1971	GS/Wolf X	21 mo. - F	Child "playing" w/chained dog	CA	Fatal
Oct. 1971	Irish Setter	2 yrs. - M	Wandered to chained dog	CA	Serious
Dec. 1971	Stray dog	4 yrs. - M	Female dog protecting pups	NJ	Critical
Feb. 1972	St. Bernard	15 yrs. - M	Playing with dog at home	PA	Ear torn off
Feb. 1972	(3) Shep-type	50 yrs. - M	Attacked at farmhouse	VA	Fatal
Mar. 1972	Dog	4 yrs. - F	Female dog w/puppies	OH	> 400 stitches
Mar. 1972	St. Bernard	8 yrs. - F	Playing w/neighbor's dog	CA	Fatal
Mar. 1972	(2) Gr. Shep	3 yrs. - F	Climbed into guard dogs' pen	NY	Fatal
Apr. 1972	(3) Boxers	63 yrs. - F	Owner - dogs fighting	AZ	Fatal
May 1972	St. Bernard	12 yrs. - M	Loose dog at rest stop	IN	Fatal

Jun. 1972	Husky	4 yrs. - F	Guard dog at store	CA	Critical
Jun. 1972	German Shep	13 yrs. - M	Unknown circumstances	CA	Serious
Jun. 1972	GS & Mixed	27 yrs. - F	Neighbor's dogs	PA	Bitten to bone
Aug. 1972	Mongrel	3 yrs. - M	Loose dogs on street	PA	Serious
Aug. 1972	German Shep	2 yrs. - M	Family dog inside house	FL	Fatal
Sept. 1972	German Shep	2 yrs. - M	Wandered to chained dog	NY	Severe
Sept. 1972	Malamute	2 yrs. - M	Wandered to chained dog	PA	Fatal
Nov. 1972	Hunting dog	6 yrs. - F	Neighbor's newly adopted dog	NJ	Skull exposed
Feb. 1973	Bulldog	20 mo. - F	Fell near chained dog eating	NC	Fatal
Mar. 1973	(2) Great Danes	8 yrs. - M	Loose roaming dogs	MI	Fatal
May 1973	Irish Setter	4 yrs. - F	Wandered to chained dog	OH	> 150 stitches
May 1973	German Shep	59 yrs. - F	Attacked by chained dog	NE	Died in 3 days
Jun. 1973	(2) Great Danes	15 yrs. - F	Loose dogs on street	NE	Serious
Jun. 1973	Mixed breed	2 yrs. - M	Entangled in dog's chain	PA	Fatal
Aug. 1973	Doberman	2 yrs. - M	Approached chained dog	CA	Severe
Oct. 1973	German Shep	11 yrs. - M	Dog barged into house	WV	> 300 stitches
Nov. 1973	(2) Gr. Shep	6 yrs. - M	Loose dogs in vacant lot	NJ	Fatal
Jan. 1974	St. Bernard	4 yrs. - M	Attacked by neighbor's dog	IN	Fatal
Jan. 1974	(2) St. Bernard	9 yrs. - F	Loose dogs attacked girl	PA	Serious
Apr. 1974	St. Bernard	6 yrs. - M	Friend's dog in house	NY	Fatal
Apr. 1974	Shaggy hound	6 yrs. - F	Boy climbed into yard	TX	Severe
May 1974	Golden Ret.	6 yrs. - F	Attacked by neighbor's dog	NC	Fatal
May 1974	Irish Setter	2 yrs. - M	Child alone w/neighbor's dog	TX	Fatal
Jul. 1974	German Shep	5 yrs. - M	Threw rocks at chained dog	MD	Fatal

Jul. 1974	Malamute	3 yrs. - M	Wandered to chained dog	AK	Fatal
Sept. 1974	Dachshund	7 mo. - M	Newly acquired dog	NY	Fatal
Oct. 1974	Akita	2 yrs. - M	Neighbor's chained dog	NE	Fatal
Nov. 1974	Br. Collie & Lab	5 yrs. - M	Loose dogs entered yard	IL	Fatal
Nov. 1974	Great Dane	25 yrs. - F	Killed in house by family dog	NY	Fatal
Dec. 1974	German Shep	8 yrs. - F	Neighbor's loose dogs	PA	Ear torn off
Dec. 1974	(2) Terriers	78 yrs. - F	Attacked burying her dog	MI	Critical
Jan. 1974	Basenji	5 mo. - F	Baby left on floor w/dog	MO	Fatal
Feb. 1975	Great Dane	5 yrs. - F	Loose dogs on street	CA	Serious
Mar. 1975	Labrador & GS	6 yr. - M	Loose dogs entered yard	CO	Severe
Mar. 1975	Collie/Shep X	75 yrs. - M	Owner killed by her dog	MO	Fatal
Mar. 1975	Husky-type	4 yrs.. - M	Playing with chained dog	AK	Fatal
Apr. 1975	(3) Gr. Shep & Schnauzer	7 yrs. - M	Dogs pulled boy over fence	OK	> 400 stitches
May 1975	German Shep	2 yrs. - M	Chained dog broke loose	TX	Fatal
Jun. 1975	German Shep	3 yrs. - M	Newly acquired guard dog	OH	Serious
Jun. 1975	Small Husky-type	3 yrs. - F	Chained dog behind store	MT	Fatal
Aug. 1975	(7) Shep/Lab Xs	5 yrs. - M	Entered into neighbor's yard	NV	Fatal
Aug. 1975	Great Dane	17 yrs. - F	Neighbor's dog	OH	Fatal
Dec. 1975	German Shep	9 mo. - M	Dog burned by hot water	NY	Severe
Dec. 1975	Mixed breeds	78 yrs. - F	Owner of 40+ dogs	MI	Fatal

Note: Severe and fatal attacks by German Shepherd dogs consistently and steadily decreased over the next three decades.

Over the last decade (1997-2006) fatal attacks by German Shepherds were reduced to five deaths, with two of the five fatalities inflicted by severely abused, chained dogs.

Denver, Colorado
"Evidence" Used to Ban Pit Bulls
(Breed-Specific Legislation)

In 1989, the Denver City Council enacted an ordinance making it "unlawful to own, possess, keep, exercise control over, maintain, harbor, transport, or sell within the city any Pit bull."

A "Pit bull" was defined by Denver as "any dog that is an American Pit Bull Terrier, American Staffordshire Terrier, Staffordshire Bull Terrier, or any dog displaying the majority of physical traits of any one (1) or more of the above breeds, or any dog exhibiting those distinguishing characteristics which substantially conform to the standards established by the American Kennel Club or United Kennel Club for any of the above breeds."

In 2005, Denver's Assistant City Attorney, Kory Nelson, in defending the ban on Pit bulls in the city and the findings of the court which "found" Pit bulls to be different than other dogs, claimed that there is "only new relevant evidence that adds additional support for breed specific legislation, as the differential treatment of Pit bulls is based upon logical, rational evidence from the scientific field of ethology" (canine behavior).[1]

The "logical, rational evidence from the scientific field of ethology" that Denver introduced and their City Attorney continues to tout as "proof" of the "differentness" of Pit bulls is in reality critically flawed, limited and inaccurate data and is a combination of pseudoscience, anecdotal evidence, media generated hysteria, and unexplainable conclusions drawn from irrelevant data interpreted by those who have little to no knowledge about the "field of ethology."

In hearings defending the ban on Pit bulls, Denver presented 15 reasons or "evidence" explaining that, as a group, Pit bulls are different than other breeds of dogs. The trial court, while not believing all of Denver's 15 claims about the "dangerousness" of Pit bulls, did find "evidence" to support the following:

(Note: The court's findings are in italics)

1. Biting

"The court finds no scientific evidence proving that the biting power of pit bull dogs exceeds that of other dogs. However, the City did prove that they inflict

*more serious wounds than other breeds. They tend to attack the deep muscles, to
hold on, to shake, and to cause ripping of tissues. Pit bull attacks were compared
to shark attacks."*

The major flaw in all of the conclusions drawn by the court about the behaviors and temperament of the Pit bull is the failure to use a significant study population and the use of
seriously flawed and inaccurate data presented by the City of Denver as "evidence."

Because severe and, to a much larger degree, fatal attacks are relatively rare, and since
the focus of most epidemiological studies in the past two decades has been on breed only,
there was a scarcity of comprehensive data on the types of injuries other breeds of dogs
have inflicted and, as such, no valid comparison could be made between the types of wounds
inflicted by Pit bulls versus other breeds of dogs.

Shaking, holding and tearing are NOT breed-specific behaviors—they are canine behaviors. Injury to deep muscles and the ripping of tissue are easily and frequently accomplished
by any large dog during the process of a severe attack. The fact is, one cannot examine
autopsy reports or autopsy photographs and determine the breed of dog by the injuries
inflicted. There are hundreds of examples of grievous, tearing- type injuries inflicted by
other breeds of dogs. They were simply not entered into evidence or presented to the court.

The shark analogy has been discussed in Chapter 11, but will be addressed here as it
was presented by the City of Denver. Denver introduced a plastic surgeon from Arizona to
testify as to the specific types of injuries caused by Pit bulls. Despite the fact that this plastic surgeon had stated he had personally treated *only three non-fatal cases* of victims attacked
by "Pit bulls," he was nevertheless entered into the record as an "expert" witness. To bol-
ster his lack of personal experience with victims of Pit bull and shark attacks, this witness
then entered into the record the alleged "learned treatise" on the subject of reconstructive
surgery in Pit bull attacks printed in a *Texas Medicine Report.*[2]

The following claim was read from this study and entered into court record as evidence:

"Fourteen of the 20 recorded fatal dog attacks on people between October, 1983, and
November, 1986, were from Pit bulls or Pit bull mixes. During the one year period between
June 1986 and June 1987, 14 people were killed by dogs in the United States; ten of those
14 deaths are attributed to Pit bulls. Thus, 71 percent of the deaths during that period were
attributed to a type of dog that accounts for one percent of the dog population."

The fact is that from October 1983 to November 1986, at least 48 people were killed
by dogs in the United States (not 20). Of the 28 fatal attacks shockingly absent in this study,
24 were by breeds of dogs other than Pit bulls.[3] This degree of statistical error is so significant that it renders any conclusions based on this data invalid.

That errors of this magnitude were entered into court records to "prove" the dangerousness of Pit bulls is highly disturbing.

Equally distressing is another claim reported in this study (*Texas Medicine Report*) and
entered into evidence that "Pit bull attacks are like shark attacks." The report states: "Most

breeds do not repeatedly bite their victims; however, a pit bull attack has been compared to a shark attack and often results in multiple bites and extensive soft-tissue loss."

The study cited two sources for this claim:

"Prophylactic antibiotics in common dog bite wounds: controlled study" *(Annals of Emergency Medicine),*[4]
"The Pit Bull: friend and killer" *(Sports Illustrated).*[5]

The first cited source is a detailed medical journal report on the management of dog bite wounds. There is *no* mention or reference to Pit bulls or sharks anywhere in this study.

The second cited source is not a scientific or medical journal study, but an article written in *Sports Illustrated* magazine. The only reference to sharks versus Pit bulls is found in a comment by a field officer from a Humane Society when he stated, "A pit bull attack is like a shark attack. He keeps coming back."

It hardly needs to be said that a single comment from a single person, quoted in a *Sports Illustrated Magazine* article, does not qualify as evidence to be used in a scientific journal, nor does it qualify as evidence by which a Court can uphold a claim that Pit bull attacks are "found" to be like shark attacks.

2. Destructiveness

"The Court finds that some pit bull type dogs, due to their strength and athletic ability, can damage facilities and equipment. There is a disproportionate number of attacks by chained pit bull dogs which is indicative of their strength."

There is simply no way to explain how the Court could possibly have come to the conclusion that being attacked by a chained dog is indicative of strength. It simply is not a reasonable or valid conclusion.

The only possible explanation is that they were basing this finding on a chained dog breaking a restraint and then attacking a person (breaking a chain allegedly being indicative of strength)—see Finding #7 addressing this.

3. Fighting Ability and killing Instinct

"Importantly, there was no evidence that any AKC registered American Staffordshire Terrier or Staffordshire Bull Terrier or any UKC registered American Pit Bull Terrier was involved in any severe or fatal attack. Nevertheless, the City did prove that unregistered pit bull type dogs were responsible for a disproportionate number of severe or fatal attacks on other

dogs and human beings. Credible testimony also proved that, when a pit bull dog begins to fight, it often will not retreat."

Since the data on fatal attacks presented by the City was so significantly flawed and biased (see Finding #1), it is little wonder that Pit bull attacks appeared "disproportionate" to the Court.

As for the "often will not retreat" remark, see Finding #4.

4. Frenzy

"Many aggressive and vicious dogs can become uncontrollable when excited or challenged. No credible evidence proved that pit bull dogs were more likely to enter a frenzied state than other dogs. However, the evidence proved that once pit bull type dogs do attack, they are less likely to retreat than other dogs."

These two findings of the Court contradict each other. The Court found that Pit bulls are *not* more likely to become frenzied or uncontrollable than other breeds of dogs, but were less likely to retreat. A frenzied, uncontrollable attack by a dog is highly aberrant and abnormal behavior. The very definition of "frenzied" is "wildly uncontrollable or abnormally excessive." What the court is implying is that other breeds behave "normally" during a frenzied attack and Pit bulls behave "abnormally" during a frenzied attack.

Also, how can retreat be defined or measured in a frenzied and uncontrolled attack? At what point in time is retreat during a frenzy determined to be normal versus abnormal? One minute or five minutes after the attack? When the victim stops moving? When the dogs are subjected to other stimuli or interference? None of these components were defined or accounted for, yet the court, nevertheless, concluded that anecdotal evidence presented by the City was sufficient to find that Pit bulls "were less likely to retreat."

5. Manageability

"American Staffordshire Terriers, Staffordshire Bull Terriers, American Pit Bull Terriers, and their mixed breeds can make excellent, gentle pets. Nevertheless, credible testimony proved that proper handling, including early socialization to humans, is very important for these dogs. Even their most ardent admirers agree that these dogs are not for everyone and they require special attention and discipline. The Lockwood study reported that 13.3 percent of pit bull type dogs attacked their owners as compared with 2.2 percent of other dogs."

The study from which these claims are based (Lockwood) did not identify or define the relationship between the "owner" and the dog. Was the owner an abusive owner? Was the dog maintained on a chain 100 feet from the owner's residence? How long did the owner have the dog: 1 day, 1 month or 5 years? These are extremely important details that explain behavior and aggression, yet they were not defined, accounted for, or qualified, rendering any conclusions or statistics about aggression towards owners meaningless.

The court found that Pit bulls can make "excellent and gentle pets," yet stated it was important for Pit bulls to receive "proper handling and early socialization to humans." If Pit bulls can become excellent and gentle pets with proper handling and socialization, then how is this evidence that the breed is "different" than any other breed? This "finding" of the court about the "manageability" of Pit bulls has been recognized for centuries as the essence of all dogs—it is the very foundation on which thousands of years of dog owner-ship and management have been based. "Proper handling and early socialization to humans" is how *all* dogs come to be "excellent and gentle pets" and certainly is not a char-acteristic particular to Pit bulls.

6. Strength

"Pit bull dogs are stronger than many other dogs. The evidence showed that 42.7 percent of the pit bull type dogs attacked while restrained (Defendants' Exhibit CC and Plaintiffs' Exhibit 50)."

The court came to this totally inaccurate conclusion quoting data that in no way implied or supported this.

The statistics used to prove "strength" was a study that stated, "42.7% of Pit bull type dogs attacked while restrained."[6] The entire quote from this study reads: "Virtually all the dogs in the cases we studied were owned. A surprising number, however, were restrained at the time of the attack. In the case of pit bull bites, 61 of 143 (42.7%) involved animals that were fenced, chained, or inside prior to the incident. Twenty cases (14%) involved pit bulls that escaped by jumping fences or breaking chains immediately before the attack. Of the 135 cases involving other breeds, 36 (26.7%) involved restrained animals, but only 1 (0.7%) broke restraint to initiate the attack."

The authors of this study did not imply or suggest that this statistic was indicative of strength. The authors of this study defined "restrained" to be "animals that were fenced, chained, or inside prior to the incident." How does 42.7 percent of Pit bulls attacking some-one while fenced, chained or inside a house indicate strength?

An equally disturbing possibility is that Denver, and/or the trial court, used the wrong statistic, meaning they should have used the 14% quoted in this study of Pit bulls jumping fences or breaking chains as indicative of strength. But again, this would be an inaccurate and totally baseless conclusion since the type and strength of the "restraint" is not defined and therefore cannot be used as evidence of strength. For example, was the fence these Pit bulls jumped three feet high or five feet high? Did all of these owners use chains with the same thickness and gauge? Did the Pit bull break loose of a bicycle chain or a logging chain? None of these vital qualifiers were taken into account or measured; therefore any conclusions about the strength of any of the dogs in this study are invalid.

7. Unpredictability

"The evidence showed that most dog attacks (by all breeds) are unprovoked. However, pit bull dogs, unlike other dogs, often give no warning signals before they attack."

This is simply not true. All information about provocation and warning signals from any breed of dog is anecdotal at best and, at worst, unreliable (see chapters 11, 12, 13). A large majority of victims of dog attacks are very young children. *Young children are most frequently bitten by dogs precisely because they are unable to read and understand the warning signals that dogs so often give prior to an attack.* Also, in a highly litigious society, both victims and owners are increasingly less than truthful about their involvement or behavior preceding a dog attack, making their testimony about provocation suspicious. Additionally, any cases in which media accounts were used as evidence to support the argument that dog attacks are unprovoked are meaningless, as the media is NOT a credible or impartial source of information on the nature or behavior of dogs involved in attacks.

Notes
1. "One City's Experience, Why Pit Bulls Are More Dangerous and Breed-Specific Legislation is Justified." Nelson, Kory A., *Municipal Lawyer.* July/August 2005, Vol. 46, No. 6, p. 12–15, 29.
2. "Pit Bull Case Report Nurture Review." Viegas, Steven F., Calhoun, Jason H., Mader, Jon. *Texas Medicine.* Vol. 84; Nov. 1988. (Exhibit KK).
3. "Fatal Dog Attacks: The Stories Behind the Statistics." Delise, Karen. Anubis Publishing, Manorville, NY, 2002.
4. "Prophylactic antibiotics in common dog bite wounds: controlled study." Callaham, M. *Ann Emer Med 9 (8): 410–414, 1980.*
5. "The pit bull: friend and killer." Swift, E.M. *Sports Illustrated 67: 72–84, 1987.*
6. "Are 'Pit bulls' Different? An analysis of the Pit Bull Terrier Controversy." Lockwood, R., Rinky, K. 1987 *Anthrozoos.* Vol.1 No. 1, 1987: pg. 2–8.

Denver, Colorado: An Ineffective and Uninformed Approach to Dog Attacks

After a fatal dog attack in 1986 and a severe dog attack in 1989 in Denver, Colorado, the city/county of Denver enacted a ban against Pit bulls and any dog which may be determined to resemble a Pit bull (the type of dog involved in these two attacks). The city/county of Denver chose to blatantly ignore the dangerous and irresponsible behavior of the owners of these dogs and instead placed the blame for these attacks squarely on the back of a "breed of dog." Not addressed by their breed-specific legislation was how these dogs had access to their victims, nor was the maintenance, function, condition or history of the dogs and their owners considered relevant.

An examination of Appendices A and B demonstrates that the breeds of dogs involved in severe and fatal attacks change over the decades. A serious analysis of severe and fatal attacks reveals that while the breeds change, many of the circumstances surrounding these attacks are seen with remarkable consistency throughout the last 150 years.

The factors which contribute to canine aggression and have been found consistently in cases of fatal dog attacks over the past century are:

- Dogs obtained and maintained for negative functions—This includes dogs obtained for fighting, guarding, and protection, dogs used for intimidation or as status symbols, and dogs being bred for financial gain.
- Failure of owners to humanely care for and control their dogs—This includes owners who maintain dogs on chains or allow dogs to run loose, owners who fail to socialize, train and supervise their dogs, owners who abuse or neglect their dogs, and owners who allow or encourage their dogs to behave aggressively.
- Young unsupervised children and dogs—This includes newborns left alone with dogs, young children allowed to interact with unfamiliar dogs or children allowed to play with multiple resident dogs (pack) without adult supervision.
- Reproductive status of dog—This includes intact animals actively used for breeding, bitches guarding puppies, pregnant bitches, and intact males in the vicinity of a female dog in estrus.

In the decade from 1966–1975, fewer than 2% of all dogs involved in fatal attacks in the United States were of the breeds which today are targeted so frequently as the solution to canine aggression (Pit bull or Rottweiler). However, one or more of the critical factors listed above were evidenced in over 90% of the fatal attacks during these years.

An Examination of Fatal Dog Attacks—Colorado, 1963-2006

1963—Boulder
An unsupervised 2-year-old boy was attacked and killed by one of two chained Husky dogs in the backyard of a duplex where he lived. The owner of the dogs had gone on a three-day fishing trip and left the dogs unattended without food or water.

1977—Breckenridge
The owners of three dogs responsible for killing a 6-year old girl were charged with Criminally Negligent Homicide. The girl was walking to a friend's home when the dogs, a St. Bernard, Norwegian elkhound and German shepherd/Husky mix, attacked her, biting her repeatedly. A man caring for the dogs while one owner was out of town was also charged with Criminally Negligent Homicide as the dogs were off the property when they attacked the girl.

1985—Littleton
A five-year-old boy was killed by his babysitter's Doberman Pinscher. The intact, male dog mauled the child while he was playing with the dog.

1986—Denver
An unsupervised 3-year-old boy was attacked and killed when he wandered away from home and over to a chained, intact female Pit bull. The owner of the dog had previously been sued, charged and was on probation after another one of his dogs severely bit an 8-year-old child three years previously. Since he was unable to pay the medical bills of the previous victim, the civil suit against him was dropped. Undaunted by his inability to meet his financial and moral responsibility to the previous victim of one of his dogs, this owner proceeded to obtain additional dogs and maintain them in an environment which invited aggression (intact, chained, unsocialized, etc). One of these dogs would later be the dog responsible for the attack on the unsupervised 3-year-old child.

Instead of instituting laws to severely penalize or punish owners such as this who repeatedly obtain dogs, breed these dogs, and maintain these animals in a condition in which they have the ability and opportunity to attack children, Denver opted to ban the breed of dog.

1990—Arapahoe County

A 4-year-old boy wandered out of his house and was killed by a neighbor's loose roaming dog. The male dog was identified to be either a Chow/Malamute mix or a Malamute. The dog was maintained primarily as a chained or outside dog. The owner was charged with letting a dog run loose and harboring a vicious animal.

1994—Northglenn

A woman had borrowed a 120-lb. male Rottweiler from a friend for protection. Two days later her 5-year-old daughter was playing on a swing in the backyard when the dog "snatched her from the swing, and shook her like a rag doll." Only later was it discovered that the intact, male dog had a history of aggression and previously attacked another child in 1993.

1996—Black Forest

Two wolf hybrids attacked and killed their caretaker, a 39-year-old woman. The woman was attempting to get them back into a pen when the dogs turned on her and killed her. The wolf dogs were a male and female used for breeding and kept in outside pens. The woman was dragged over 1/10 of a mile by the animals as they continued their attack.

1998—Lakewood

A neutered, male Rott/Mastiff mix attacked and killed a 21-month old boy, as the child was crawling on the floor towards his father, seated on the couch. This fatal attack is the rare "exception to the rule" in which the parents/owners had neutered the dog, had it obedience trained and maintained the dog as a household pet. Additionally, unlike most fatal attacks, the child and dog were in the presence of supervising adults at the time of the attack.

2003—Ebert County

Three loose roaming intact Pit bulls attacked and killed a 40-year-old woman in her barn. These dogs and their owners were well known in the community due to previous aggressive episodes involving the dogs and the owners repeatedly allowing these (and other dogs) to roam the area, harassing and attacking other beings. One neighbor had previously sustained a very severe bite to her leg from dogs alleged to belong to these owners. The female owner was convicted of owning dangerous dogs resulting in a death, and received a 6-year prison sentence. The male owner of these dogs fled the jurisdiction, was a suspect in a murder case in another state and was finally apprehended in 2005.

2005—Fruita

A 7-year-old girl was attacked and killed after her mother left her in the yard alone with newly acquired male and female Malamutes. It is believed only the male attacked the girl and the child was dead when the mother re-emerged from the house a few minutes later.

An examination of fatal attacks in the state of Colorado reveals that not only are these incidents incredibly rare (10 fatal attacks in the state over a 45-year period, 1962–2006), but they involve complex human and canine behaviors.

Denver's approach to the first documented fatal attack in the state of Colorado by a Pit bull-type dog was to ban the breed. There was no examination or discussion of previous fatal attacks in Colorado or the critical role owners play in allowing their dogs to behave aggressively. Denver chose to criminalize a breed of dog rather than enact laws that would impose strict penalties to control the behavior of dangerous dog owners.

NOTES

CHAPTER 1

1. "Terrific Encounter," *Bangor Daily Whig and Courier*, January 2, 1883. pg. 2.
2. "A Dog Attacks His Master," *The Washington Post*, February 9, 1888. pg. 1.
3. "Bitten by a Mad Dog," *New York Times*, July 27, 1893. pg. 5.
4. "A Child Terribly Mangled by a Dog," *New York Times*, June 14, 1874. pg. 7.
5. *Fort Wayne Sentinel*, June 4, 1879. pg. 3.
6. *Newark Daily Advocate*, April 12, 1889. pg. 3.
7. *The Newark Advocate*, January 30, 1902. pg. 1.
8. "Bloodhounds for Apaches," *The Washington Post,* February 28, 1892. pg. 10.
9. *General Court Martial Orders No. 607*. War Department, Adjutant-General's Office, Washington, November 6, 1865. Court Martial of Henry Wirz—Charges and Specifications.
10. "Bloodhounds are Bought," *Perry Daily Chief*, February 22, 1903. pg. 2.
11. "A Lovely Father," *Olean Weekly Democrat*, January 9, 1894. pg. 4.
12. "Mangled by a Dog," *New York Times*, May 27, 1888. pg. 3.
13. "Boy Torn by Savage Hounds," *The Washington Post*, June 8, 1903. pg. 1.
14. "Saved by Dog," *The Daily Courier*, August 3, 1907. pg. 1.
15. *The Hornellsville Tribune,* April 2, 1875. pg. 2.
16. "Savagely Attacked by his Dog," *New York Times*, June 15, 1885. pg. 2.
17. *The Massillon Independent,* August 5, 1887. pg. 1.
18. "Devoured by Wild Dogs," *The Washington Post,* February 16, 1892. pg. 6.

CHAPTER 2

1. "The True Bloodhound," *Denton Journal,* June 30, 1888. pg. 4.
2. "Hunted with Bloodhounds," *The Davenport Daily Leader,* November 2, 1891. pg. 2.
3. "Molosser Dogs" (www.molosserdogs.com).
4. "A Short Account of the Destruction of the Indies (Brevisima relacion de la destruccion de las Indias)" Bartolome de las Casas, 1552.
5. *Dogs of the Conquest*. John Grier Varner and Jeannette Johnson Varner. University of Oklahoma Press, Norman. 1983.
6. "The Horrors of Slavery and England's Duty to Free the Bondsman: An Address Delivered in Taunton, England, on September 1, 1846," Frederick Douglass. *Somerset County Gazette*, September 5, 1846.
7. "A Terribly Brutal Scene: Fight Between a Professional Sport and a Siberian Bloodhound," *The Washington Post*, December 25, 1879. pg. 1.
8. "A Siberian Bloodhound Killed," *New York Times,* March 24, 1882. pg. 3.
9. "Attacked by a Bloodhound," *New York Times*, January 30, 1900. pg. 3.
10. "Peasant is Torn to Death by Savage Bloodhounds," Special cable to *The Washington Post*, November 18, 1906. pg. F5.

11. *Love and Theft: Blackface Minstrelsy and the American Working Class*. Lott, Eric. New York: Oxford University Press, 1993 (Chapter 8: "Uncle Tomitudes: Racial Melodrama and Modes of Production," p. 211–233).

12. "Life and Times of Actress EJ Phillips (1880s & 1890s): Her dramatic career, cross-country travels, family life, Golden Age of the American Theatre & Arrival of the 20th Century." Em Turner, Nickinson Kuhl and Mary Glen Kuhl Chitty (http://home.comcast.net/~m.chitty/index.html).

13. "Bloodhounds Attack Woman," *New York Times*, September 23, 1898. pg. 2.

14. "Wicked Dogs," *New York Times*: New York City, April 6, 1855. pg. 1.

15. *The Florida Historical Quarterly*: "Cuban Bloodhounds and the Seminoles," James W. Covington. Volume XXXII, No. 2, October 1954.

CHAPTER 3
1. "A Dog's Revenge," *Fort Wayne Sentinel*, November 8, 1890. pg. 1.
2. "Boy Killed by a Dog," *The Washington Post*, December 26, 1893. pg. 3.
3. "Hoboken Terrorized," *New York Times*, July 30, 1889. pg. 2.
4. "Mad Dog's Desperate Attack," *The Daily Advocate*, June 12, 1894.
5. "No Hydrophobia," *New York Times*, July 25, 1887. pg. 4.
6. "Attacked by Dog Team, Woman Dies in 2 Days," Special to the *New York Times*, April 29, 1925. pg. 3.
7. "Devil Dogs of Labrador," *The Washington Post*, September 20, 1908. pg. M4.
8. "The Dogs of Labrador," *The Chronicle*, January 29, 1903. pg. 7.
9. "Dog Pack Attack: Hunting Humans," Simon P. Avis. *The American Journal of Forensic Medicine and Pathology* 20(3): 243–246, 1999.
10. "The Dogs of Labrador," *The Chronicle*, January 29, 1903. Pg. 7.

CHAPTER 4
1. "Young Boys Attacked by a Dog," *New York Times*, December 13, 1891. pg. 2.
2. "Mutilated by a Dog," *New York Times*, May 1, 1893. pg. 8.
3. "Boy and Girl Bitten When Collie Runs Amuck," *Indianapolis Star*, May 2, 1915.
4. "Bitten by Dog," *Fitchburg Daily Sentinel*, March 29, 1910. pg. 2.
5. "Boy is Bitten 30 Times by Collie," *Oakland Tribune*, June 8, 1913.
6. "Child Bitten by a Dog," *New Oxford Item*, November 16, 1916. pg. 1.
7. "St. Bernard Dogs Termed a Menace: Swiss Doctor Says Penning-up and Cross-Breeding Have Ruined Their Tempers; Urges Their Banishment," *New York Times*, July 18, 1937. pg. N2.
8. "Bernard Dogs Reprieved After One Kills Child," *The Washington Post*, June 8, 1937.
9. "Child Attacked by a Dog," *New York Times*, June 29, 1901. pg. 2.
10. "Baby Killed by Dog," *The Washington Post*, February 4, 1909. pg. 3.
11. "Boy Bitten Twelve Times by Dog in Saving His Sister," *Syracuse Herald*, May 3, 1925.
12. "Man Attacked by Wild Dog," *New Oxford Times*, February 24, 1921. pg. 10.
13. "Dog Attacks Its Mistress," *Reno Evening Gazette*, April 10, 1931. pg. 10.
14. "Dog Meat at $125 a Pound," *Gettysburg Times*, June 21, 1918.
15. "Terribly Mangled by Dogs," *New York Times*, April 23, 1884. pg. 5.
16. "Dead, Torn by Her Dog," *The Washington Post*, March 12, 1910.
17. "Attacked by Dogs, Boy Dies," *New York Times*, August 18, 1917. pg. 5.
18. "Attacked and Slain by Hungry Dogs," *New York Times*, February 23, 1926. pg. 25.

CHAPTER 5
1. "Girl Mangled by a Pet Dog," *New York Times*, October 27, 1897. pg. 4.
2. "Attacked by Starving Dog," *Newark Daily Advocate*, February 19, 1885.
3. "Mangled by Mastiffs," *The Washington Post*, September 7, 1891. pg. 1.
4. "Torn by a Fierce Dog," *Daily Nevada State Journal*, September 26, 1905. pg. 1.
5. *Evening Observer* (from the *Boston Globe*), July 21, 1884. pg. 3.

CHAPTER 6
1. "Brave Bulldog Saves Twenty Women," *The Washington Post*, July 31, 1907. pg. 1.
2. "Settled in One Round," *The Lima Daily Times*, July 18, 1889. pg. 1.
3. "Faithful Bulldog Copper Patrols Georgetown Beat," *The Washington Post*, August 26, 1906.
4. "Woman's Battle with Dog," *New York Times*, January 19, 1905. pg. 1.
5. *The Davenport Democrat*, August 7, 1924. pg. 1.
6. *New York Times*, August 20, 1905.
7. "Killed by Dog She Beat," *The Washington Post*, February 14, 1907. pg. 1.
8. "Dog's Bite May Kill," *The Washington Post*, August 4, 1909. pg. 1.
9. "Canines," *Semi-Weekly Age*, January 20, 1888. pg. 1.
10. "Bulldog Losing Character," Special Cable to the *New York Times*, November 10, 1912. pg. C2.
11. "Bulldog Saves Life of Boy Playmate," *Oakland Tribune*, October 25, 1919.

CHAPTER 7
1. "The News of the Week," *The New Era*, October 27, 1887. pg. 1.
2. "A Dog Kills His Master," *The Wellsboro Agitator*, September 2, 1903. pg. 1.
3. "Boy Killed When Attacked by Dogs," *Bismarck Tribune*, April 13, 1928. pg. 10.
4. *The Washington Post*, July 13, 1945. pg. 5.
5. "Police Dogs," *New York Times*, July 20, 1924. pg. XX13.
6. *The Bismarck Tribune*, February 20, 1930.

CHAPTER 8
1. "Watchdogs for Chief Executives," *Daily Northwestern*, May 27, 1929.
2. "Gold Medal Voted, Dog That Killed Rattler, Saving Baby," *Syracuse Herald,* August 3, 1932.
3. "Baron, Seeing-Eye Dog, is Adopted as Family Member," *Sheboygan Press*, October 29, 1952. pg. 25.
4. "Two Dogs Attack and Kill Mistress," Special cable to the *New York Times*, June 3, 1955. pg.46
5. "Woman Owner Bitten to Death by Prize Doberman in Jersey," *New York Times,* March 20, 1960. pg. 50
6. *Carry Me Home: Birmingham, Alabama: The Climactic Battle of the Civil Rights Revolution*. Diane McWhorter. Simon & Schuster, 2001.
7. "Interview with Diane McWhorter," *Jerry Jazz Musician,* July 25, 2002 (www.jerryjazzmuscian.com).

CHAPTER 9
1. "Increase in Dog Bites Linked to Ghetto Growth," *Evening Bulletin*, June 26, 1974.
2. "Dog Bites: Surgeon's Warning," *Evening Bulletin*, May 14, 1978.

CHAPTER 10
1. "Pit Bulls: Months of Hysteria Lead to a Distorted Response," *Detroit Free Press*, August 10, 1987.
2. "Father Held in Tot's Death after Telling Pit Bull Story," *San Jose Mercury News.* June 19, 1987.
3. "A Boy and his Dog in Hell," Sager M. *Rolling Stone*, July 2, 1987. pg. 39–40, 62–65.
4. "Beware of This Dog," Swift, E.M. *Sports Illustrated*, July 27, 1987. pg. 72–84
5. "Time Bomb on Legs," *Time,* July 27, 1987.
6. "An Instinct for the Kill," *People Weekly*, July 7, 1987.
7. "Dog Attack Leaves 5-year-old girl with 120 stitches," *The Boston Globe*, August 19, 1989.
8. "Dog Bite-Related Fatalities From 1979 Through 1988." Sacks JJ, Sattin RW, Bono SE., *JAMA* 1989; 262: 1489–1492.
9. "A community approach to dog bite prevention." AVMA Task Force on Canine Aggression and Human-Canine Interactions. *JAVMA.*, 200.1 218: 1732–1749.
10. "Breeds of Dogs Involved in Fatal Human Attacks in the United States between 1979–1998." Sacks JJ, Sinclair L, Gilchrist J, Golab G, Lockwood R., *JAVMA* Vol. 217, No. 6, September 15, 2000.

CHAPTER 11
1. Ontario Superior Court of Justice Affidavit of Dr. I. Lehr Brisbin, Jr., Senior Research Scientist, University of Georgia.
2. "Mauling by Pit Bull Terriers: Case Report." Baack, B.R., Kucan, J.O., Demarest, G., Smoot, E.C. *Journal of Trauma*, Vol. 29, No. 4. 517–520, 1989.
3. "Dog bites in children: Epidemiology, microbiology, and penicillin prophylactic therapy." Boenning, D.A., Fleisher, G.R., Campos, J.M. *Am. J. Emerg. Med.*, 1: 17–21, 1983.
4. "Dangerous Encounters: Bite Force." Dr. Brady Barr. *National Geographic*. August 18, 2005.
5. Dr. I. Lehr Brisbin, Jr., Senior Research Scientist, University of Georgia.
6. "New York Police Remove 400-pound Tiger from Housing Project," *New York Daily News*, October 4, 2003.
7. "Keep the Pit Bull Ban—and Put Some Bite in It," *The Washington Post*, October 2, 2005.
8. *The Jaws of Death.* Xavier Maniguet. Crescent Books, Avenel, New Jersey, 1996 (Chapter 3: An Extraordinary Machine, pg. 45–47).
9. ReefQuest Centre for Shark Research, R. Aidan Martin, Director (www.elasmo-research.org).
10. "Alderman Wants to Ban City's Pit Bulls," *Chicago Sun-Times*, December 1, 2005.
11. *The Hornellsville Tribune*, April 2, 1875. pg. 2.
12. Of the two victims reported to have been killed by Pit bulls: Autopsy results listed one victim's death as caused by cardiac arrhythmia (unrelated to dog bites), the other cause of death was from blunt force trauma (the result of an assault by a human during a robbery

attempt). The victim reported to have been killed by a Rottweiler: Autopsy determined the manner of death to be "natural" with the cause of death as "atherosclerosis, cardiac disease and chronic liver disease." National Canine Research Council (www.nationalcanineresearchcouncil.com).

13. "Breeds of dogs involved in fatal human attacks in the United States between 1979 and 1998." Sacks, JJ., Sinclair, L., Gilchrist, J., Golab, G., Lockwood, R., *JAMVA*, Vol 217, No. 6. September 2000.
14. The National Child Abuse and Neglect Data System (NCANDS), 2002.
15. "A Nation's Shame: Fatal Child Abuse and Neglect in the United States." U.S. Advisory Board on Child Abuse and Neglect. U.S. Department of Health and Human Services, Washington D.C.
16. *Daily News*, September 20, 2004.
17. *Toledo Blade*, January 12, 2003.
18. Legislative Assembly of Ontario, 38th Legislative, 1st Session. Bill 132, Second Reading, November 15, 2004.

CHAPTER 12

1. "Mobile Man Convicted of Dog-fighting, wife acquitted," *Tuscaloosa News*, March 19, 2005.
2. The Anti-Cruelty Society, Chicago, Illinois (www.anticruelty.org).
3. "Dog Fighting Detailed Discussion," Hanna Gibson. Animal Legal and Historical Center. Michigan State University College of Law, 2005 (www.animallaw.info).

CHAPTER 13

1. "Patient Dog Bitten 6 Times by Boy, 2," *Evening Bulletin*, April 21, 1971.
2. "Boy, 11, Braves Pet Dog's Bites to Free Him from Steel Trap," *Evening Bulletin*, December 29, 1948.
3. "Hot Popcorn Hits Family Dog, Children Bitten," *Evening Bulletin*, May 1, 1972.
4. "Policeman Steps on Police Dog, Is Bitten on Leg," *Evening Bulletin*, February 23, 1968.
5. "Dog Kills Owner in Trying Rescue," *Syracuse Herald Journal*, March 23, 1950.
6. *Red Zone: The Behind-the-Scenes Story of the San Francisco Dog Mauling*. Aphrodite Jones. HarperCollins, N.Y., 2003.
7. *Death of an Angel: The Inside Story of How Justice Prevailed in the San Francisco Dog-mauling Case*, Joseph Harrington. Quantum Entertainment, June 2002.
8. *Morris Daily Herald*, November 8, 2005.
9. "Elderly Man Narrowly Escapes Pit Bull Attack," KGO-TV (ABC 7 News), June 23, 2005.
10. "Pit Bull Traps Boy, 4, on Car Roof," *Courier Journal*, November 22, 2005.
11. "Two Teenagers Escape Serious Injury After Pit Bull Attack near Hanover," *The Citadel*, November 14, 2005.
12. WorldNow and WTVO, Channel 17 News: April 14, 2003, April 15, 2003, April 29, 2003.
13. "Pit Bull Angers Resident," *Herald News,* January 8, 2005.
14. *The Reporter*, December 20, 2005.
15. "Fed-up Alderman Wants to Rid City of Pit Bulls," *Chicago Sun-Times*, January 15, 2004.

CHAPTER 14
1. *APPMA Advisor*, Quarterly Newsletter, National Pet Owners Survey. American Pet Products Manufacturers Association. May 2005/Issue 6.
2. "CPSC Warns about Pool Hazards, Reports 250 Deaths on Young Children Annually." U.S. Consumer Product Safety Commission, Washington, D.C., May 25, 2004. Release #04–142.

Index

About the Author

Karen Delise is a licensed Veterinary Technician with a degree in Veterinary Science Technology.

She has worked for the Suffolk County Sheriff's Office, Long Island Game Farm, the New York State Marine Mammal Rescue Program, the East End Emergency Animal Hospital and was a volunteer for the Bide-A-Wee Pet Therapy Program which brings pets to nursing homes to visit with patients.

Her book is based upon 15 years of research and interviews with hundreds of Animal Control Officers, Law Enforcement Officials, Medical Examiners, Public Health Officials Epidemiologists, Shelter Workers, Detectives and journalists.

She is the author of *Fatal Dog Attacks: The Stories Behind the Statistics*, and is the founder and lead researcher for The National Canine Research Council.

www.nationalcanineresearchcouncil.com